Political Money

POLITICAL

★$★$★$★$★$★

A Strategy for
Campaign Financing
in America

David W. Adamany
George E. Agree

MONEY

THE JOHNS HOPKINS UNIVERSITY PRESS
Baltimore and London

Manufactured in the United States of America

The Johns Hopkins University Press
Baltimore, Maryland 21218

The Johns Hopkins University Press Ltd., London

Library of Congress Catalog Card Number 75-11351
ISBN 0-8018-1718-8

Library of Congress Cataloging in Publication Data

Adamany, David W
 Political money.

 Includes bibliographies and index.
 1. Elections—United States—Campaign funds.
I. Agree, George E., joint author. II. Title.
JK1991.A64   329′.025′0973   75-11351
ISBN 0-8018-1718-8

Dedicated by David Adamany to his teachers, Leon Epstein and David Fellman.

Dedicated by George Agree to Stephen R. Currier, to whose life there are many still unmarked monuments and whose encouragement of the original voucher idea was important in the genesis of this work.

We had never met when we became involved in this study. The encouragement of the Twentieth Century Fund brought us together to examine public financing of political campaigns. What we had in common was a belief that the existing method of financing campaigns was inconsistent with democratic ideals and that public financing of some kind was a necessary response.

These convictions stemmed from our political experience and our studies of campaign financing. Both of us had been active in campaign management and financing. Both of us had testified at congressional hearings in favor of public subsidies for campaigns. David Adamany had taught and written widely on political financing for many years. George Agree had worked with Senator Lee Metcalf on his 1966 proposal to provide vouchers on the Treasury that taxpayers could give to presidential candidates of their choice.

If we agreed on the principle of public financing, we were far apart on the method. David Adamany was primarily concerned that enough money be provided in all campaigns for all offices to stimulate vigorous competition in every race, and consequently he leaned toward some system of flat grants to candidates whose parties obtained a minimum qualifying vote. George Agree's focus was on voluntarism, a guarantee that citizens

PREFACE

would participate in allocating public money and that public grants would reflect their current preferences. His advocacy of the voucher system reflected these principles.

As we studied each other's approach, cataloging and analyzing the goals of political finance policy in a democracy, we realized that our differences were rooted in fundamental dilemmas. Many important policy objectives appeared to be in conflict with one another. And study of American regulatory legislation, European financing experiments, and congressional proposals led only to the conclusion that none effectively addressed the issue of political financing in the complicated context of American democracy. We finally concluded that any satisfactory arrangement must weigh various goals against one another, recognizing the importance of each. The recommendations of this study do just that: they recognize the principle of voluntarism by making public financing contingent on citizen participation through vouchers, and they recognize the need for adequately funded, competitive politics by using those vouchers to trigger flat and proportionate grants of generous amounts.

Time and again, we were compelled to re-examine these principles and recommendations. While this book was in progress, Congress passed the Federal Election Campaign Act of 1971, imposing limits on media spending and providing full disclosure; the Revenue Act of 1971, authorizing a tax check-off for campaigns and tax incentives for small contributions; the Debt Ceiling Act of 1973, altering the check-off plan; and the sweeping Federal Election Campaign Act of 1974, setting expenditure and contribution limits, creating a Federal Election Commission, and authorizing a form of public financing of presidential campaigns. More than forty states also changed their campaign finance laws, adopting many forms of limitations, enforcement methods, and public financing.

At each turn, new ideas were thrust into the public arena. Many were meritorious; some would seriously unbalance political processes in the United States or were of doubtful constitutionality. All these initiatives challenged us, and we have shamelessly included their lessons in our analysis and recommendations. In the end, however, no state or federal legislation accommodated either the dual principles that must underlie any sound reform or the array of other policy objectives that seem desirable. We hope our recommendations will help to reconcile these dilemmas and inspire additional constructive debate on how the United States should finance its political campaigns.

Our interest in this project was originally encouraged by Richard W. Richardson, to whom we are grateful. Kay Klipstine, the project research associate, played an indispensable role in the analysis of present and proposed policies. She developed the public opinion poll that tested voter attitudes about campaign financing, analyzed media advertising expenditures before and after they were regulated by the Campaign Communications Reform Act, studied congressional voting patterns on political finance bills, and searched out a mountain of books, articles, congressional documents, and fugitive papers on campaign money. Most important, she was a strenuous critic of much of what we advanced and wrote.

Herbert E. Alexander also contributed greatly to this study. He suggested revisions that sharpened and strengthened the manuscript and, as director of the Citizens' Research Foundation, was immensely helpful in supplying research materials and campaign finance studies.

Several congressional offices took pains to provide congressional documents and to obtain data from executive departments. Special assistance was generously provided by Senator Gaylord Nelson and Representatives Les Aspin, Robert Kastenmeier, and William Steiger.

Many state officials went far out of their way to supply information about state tax incentives and state public financing plans. Especially helpful were Martin Huff and Ivan Ervin of California, C. H. Mack of Oregon, Gerald D. Bair of Iowa, Louis Goldstein of Maryland, Robert Raymar of New Jersey, Ernest H. Johnson of Maine, Arthur Roemer of Minnesota, Howard Vralsted of Montana, John Norberg of Rhode Island, and Elvin Todd of Utah. Larry McCoy of the Office of Federal Elections was unfailingly kind in supplying information about the Federal Election Campaign Act of 1971 and data on presidential campaign receipts and expenditures.

Fred Wertheimer and Ken Guido of Common Cause were unstinting in providing information about congressional campaign financing, disclosure litigation, and legislative initiatives. Similarly, Susan King and Neal Gregory of the Center for Public Financing of Elections were a gold mine of current editorial comment, current poll data, congressional strategy and roll calls, and other useful commentary on the unfolding battle for national campaign finance legislation.

Overseas, government officials, party leaders, and members of the press and the academic world were consistently helpful and uncommonly generous in taking time for interviews, in data gathering, in providing confidential records, and in offering their hospitality. It would be taxing to the reader to list them all and unthinkable not to mention any, so to all their countrymen not named here, we tender thanks through Ernesto Mieres Calimano, General Supervisor of Elections, and Hector M. Hernandez, special assistant to Governor Ferre, in Puerto Rico; Werner Blischke, parliamentarian of the Bundestag, and Dietmar Knopp in Germany; Professor Harry Forsell of the University of Umea and C. E. Nordling, director of the Royal Commission on Party Finance, in Sweden; Professor Pertti Pesonen of the University of Helsinki, Finland; and Professor Henry Valen of the Institutt for Samfunnsforskning in Oslo, Norway.

Finally, Mrs. Lloyd Renneberg can claim credit for converting doodles and scribbles into a clean, readable manuscript.

We absolve all who assisted us from errors of fact or conception in the manuscript, but the Americans among them, like all other Americans, must share with us the responsibility for a political finance system that undermines the ideals and hampers the performance of American democracy. We hope that what we have done, with their assistance, will mark a step toward a new system of political financing in which all Americans can proudly share.

Madison, Wisconsin   David W. Adamany
North Tarrytown, New York   George E. Agree
March, 1975

CONTENTS

Political Money

Political power is so attractive that men have incessantly bought, stolen, coerced, and killed for it. Within modern democracies, killing, coercing, stealing, and many forms of buying have been outlawed as means to political power.

Today the ability of democratic societies to accommodate growing populations, external threats, ecological menace, economic crises, social and cultural change, and a host of other issues is in serious question. The future of democracy depends on how well its practitioners learn to adapt their processes to new and more difficult circumstances.

Democracy is a system of government whose purpose is to implement the will of the people. But it is not only that. It would be most difficult, for instance, to prove that the actions of the Nazi government on any given date in 1938 were less in accordance with the will of the German people than the actions of the government of the Bundesrepublic on the same date in 1973, thirty-five years later. Yet the Bundesrepublic is eminently democratic and the Nazi regime was not.

Democracy is also a system for discovering what the will of the people may be and for ensuring that government cannot act without frequent and regular reference to and control by that will. Intuitive or empathetic leaders, no

 1

DEMOCRACY
AND
DOLLARS

matter how inspired or how carefully attuned to public opinion, cannot by themselves make democratic decisions. Decisions can be democratic only if in the decision-making process the participation of the people is critical and controlling.

In large political units, maintaining such participation is a problem—one that has been solved, for the most part, through the institution of elections. But E. E. Schattschneider has aptly said that in elections citizens are "a sovereign whose vocabulary is limited to two words, 'yes' and 'no'."[1] Accordingly, the worth of a democratic system depends on putting questions to the people and on the import and relevance of those questions. Democracy therefore requires electoral contests, in which the means are available to place alternatives before the people.

In a town meeting democracy, the question of political finance has little significance. Issues are defined in common, and the voters and candidates know and have equal access to each other. The wealth or lack of it at a speaker's disposal may influence the degree of respect he is accorded, but it can hardly influence whether he is heard or affect his ability to say what he wants to say.

In a modern mass society, in which democracy must be representative rather than direct, the question of political finance can be of decisive importance.

MONEY AND DEMOCRACY

In the United States as in other democratic countries, political activity has traditionally been financed through private, voluntary contributions to parties and candidates. Since all citizens have an equal right to political participation, traditional democratic theory assumes that all interests and points of view will receive financial support and expression in proportion to the numbers of their adherents. In fact, however, since all persons do not have equal financial means, the views and interests of the wealthy are expressed far out of proportion to their numbers.

Financial means, of course, are just one of the inequalities in a democracy. Other political resources are also spread unevenly among individuals and classes. Specific traits—an imposing stature, attractive face, commanding voice, personal charisma, high energy level or intellect—aid one candidate or one citizen activist as against others. And some political resources other than money are closely linked to the social and economic system. Education helps one to understand issues and master the skills of politics. Leisure time gives one opportunities to engage in political activity. Prestige and community standing help one to be listened to attentively. Of course, incentives to political interest or activity are unequal. Money may affect even the cloudy realm of personal motivation. Those with family traditions of political activism, with a sense of personal effectiveness, with high needs for and expectations of ego satisfaction may be more likely than others to engage in political activity.

But at the outset inequalities of money are probably greater than inequalities in time, energy, education, and personal traits. Other political resources—though admittedly more widespread among the well-off—are also frequently found among other social and economic groups and, more important, can be more readily developed by activists within those strata.

Those with money are more likely than those without it to participate in politics. The wealthy have continuing interests to defend, an understanding of the continuity of those interests, a quicker appreciation of the immediate and long-term advantages of political participation, and a social milieu that favors political activism. In other sectors of the society, political awareness and activism tend to be spurred by visible and exciting events, whereas the participation of the moneyed is linked to ongoing institutions and social structures.

Money, unlike other political resources, is liquid. Dollars are easily moved from across the nation into, say, Alabama to assure that a senior senator, chairman of a powerful committee affecting national financial interests, will retain his seat in the world's greatest deliberative body and, therefore, the influential chairmanship that would otherwise go to the second-ranking majority party senator, perhaps a liberal midwestern maverick. The citizen outside Alabama who can give only his time, energy, or skills cannot easily use them to affect the Alabama senatorial election. But dollars are legal tender anywhere in the United States.

Money moves silently as well as easily. Cash leaves no tracks. Checks can be laundered—passed through intermediates, individuals or committees. Transfer payments among committees can obscure the original source of funds, whereas the citizen who serves on a political committee, canvasses his neighbors, posts a sign on his car or lawn, attends a caucus, or in other ways uses his time, energy, and skills can hardly conceal his attempt to influence politics. The public can evaluate who he is, what he wants, and what his support implies about his candidate or party.

Finally, money can buy most non-economic political resources. It can pay canvassers, or skilled campaign managers, or publicists, or researchers. It cannot endow a candidate with intelligence, but it can buy him a brain trust. It cannot change his voice or face, but it can hire a make-up man, a voice coach, and a clever film editor. Those with money can buy virtually any of the resources that other citizens give directly.

The inequality of wealth among citizens would by itself jeopardize democracy. But in a modern industrial society, financially powerful business, labor, and other organizations which have no standing as part of the electorate and to which no one has ever dreamed of extending the franchise have acquired, by deploying money, a kind of corporate citizenship. Much political giving today is not really private but institutional in character.

Historically, the influence of money has been held in check by the press, public interest groups, social movements, and other non-economic forces in society. But time and again the final check has been the authority of voters and the vigor of opposition politicians to hold office-holders accountable in elections.

In recent years, traditional voter loyalties, class identification, and political organizations have withered. Split-ticket balloting and highly unpredictable election outcomes reveal that voters are increasingly without electoral moorings. Long-accepted political leaders and institutions no longer influence voters. A better educated, highly mobile, and increasingly middle-class electorate receives its campaign information not from neighborhood precinct workers but from the communications media.

In politics, a long-static pattern of organizations and institutions has been displaced by technology. Technology is for sale, at prices that stagger old-line politicians. Public opinion polls, broadcast media time, film producers and editors, computers and their attending armies of technicians, and advance men to organize the carnivals that gull newsgatherers are expensive.

Campaign costs have not only made politicians more vulnerable to pressures from those who have money, they have also made the wealthy more vulnerable to extortion by the politicians. Whether they want to or not, those who are regulated by or otherwise economically dependent on government—as is virtually every business and profession in a modern post-industrial society—often feel that they must contribute to politics when solicited. Asked why he had authorized the illegal contribution of company funds to meet the solicitation of presidential money managers, the chairman of the board of one of the nation's largest corporations replied, "A large part of the money raised from the business community for political purposes is given in fear of what would happen if it were not given."[2]

THE REFORM IMPULSE

Some campaign finance reforms had been enacted before that congeries of activities clustered under the unhappy label Watergate came to light. In 1966 Congress passed a one-dollar tax check-off to finance presidential campaigns, although the next year the plan was set aside as opponents of public financing were joined by those who feared the political consequences of the act's specific provisions. After losing a bill to limit spending on broadcasts to a presidential veto in 1970, Congress enacted the Federal Election Campaign Act of 1971, which combined full disclosure of campaign finances with expenditure limits for communications media, including radio and television advertising. Congress also amended the Revenue Act of 1971 to provide tax deductions and credits for campaign contributions and to revive the tax check-off to finance presidential campaigns. In the face of a presidential veto threat, however, public financing of presidential campaigns was set aside, except that the check-off option would appear on the tax form in 1973.

Watergate added impetus to those reform movements. Its impact can be measured by public opinion polls. Less than a decade ago, Americans rejected public financing of presidential campaigns by a lopsided 71 to 11 percent. By the fall of 1973 the public mood had dramatically reversed itself: 65 percent favored tax support for both presidential and congressional campaigns, only 24 percent opposed it. A year later public support had increased to 67 percent.[3]

Congress has been the scene of unprecedented reform agitation. The Senate, in 1973, gave a sweeping eighty-two to eight approval to a revised Federal Election Campaign Act, which provided comprehensive spending limits, tight contribution ceilings, additional disclosure requirements, and an independent enforcement commission. An amendment to the act providing public financing of general election campaigns was defeated fifty-three to thirty-eight. In the House of Representatives, the recalcitrant chairman of the Administration Committee, Wayne Hays, blocked action on campaign finance reform bills. But reform demands mounted among House members as more than 150 representatives joined Morris Udall and John Anderson as cosponsors of a bill providing matching public grants for contributions of fifty dollars or less.

The House did, however, concur in a Senate amendment to the Debt Ceiling Act of 1973 requiring that the tax check-off option be printed on the face of the universally used tax forms 1040 and 1040A rather than being hidden on the obscure separate tax schedule provided by the Nixon administration in 1973.

The next year reform pressures became irresistible. Despite President Nixon's threat to veto any public financing of campaigns, the Senate on April 11, 1974, passed a measure providing full public financing of presidential and congressional general election campaigns, partial public financing of presidential and congressional primary campaigns through a matching grant system, a negative tax check-off to pay these costs, comprehensive limits on campaign spending, tight contribution limits, a ban on cash contributions over $100, and an independent Federal Election Commission to enforce the law. Other provisions allowed media debates between major-party candidates by repealing the equal time rule, standardized the closing time of the polls to prevent early vote returns in one region of the country from affecting voting elsewhere, prohibited foreign contributions to campaigns, and established election day as a national holiday.

On August 8 a laggard House passed a substantially weaker measure. It authorized full public financing of presidential general election campaigns and partial public financing of primaries through matching grants; both were to be paid for through the tax check-off. It added public financing of national conventions. But public financing of congressional campaigns was turned down 228 to 187. Expenditure limits were imposed for all primaries and general elections for federal offices, and a tight lid was clamped on contributions. An independent enforcement commission was created, but its powers were weaker than in the Senate version.

In October, 1974, a compromise measure emerged from a long-deadlocked conference committee and was swiftly passed by both houses.[4] Proponents of public financing won full support of presidential general election campaigns and partial support of primaries through a matching grant system, with costs to be paid through the tax check-off. The House conferees succeeded, however, in killing any public financing of congressional races. National conventions are publicly financed, expenditure limits are set for all primary and general election campaigns for federal offices, and low contribution limits are set. An independent Federal Election Commission with some civil enforcement powers is established; its members are appointed both by the President and by congressional leaders. Despite his long record of opposition to public financing of campaigns, President Ford on October 15 signed the measure "with reservations," remarking that "the unpleasant truth is that big money influence has come to play an unseeming role in our electoral process. This bill will help to right that wrong."

THE FUTURE OF REFORM

The conventional wisdom has it that incumbents will never support public financing of campaigns; office-holders, who can raise money with relative ease, would be unlikely to throw away their advantage by financing their opponents. Congress apparently affirms this wisdom by its willingness to authorize public financing of presidential but not congressional campaigns.

There are forces at work that suggest, however, that the 1974 reform bill is only a beginning. Congressional action has been stimulated by outside forces—changing public opinion, a vigilant media, the 1971 act's exposure of many campaign financing practices, and the agitation of public interest groups such as Common Clause and the Center for Public Financing of Elections. The internal dynamics of Congress also foreshadow new initiatives on election reform, as the sweeping Senate bill in 1974 demonstrated. The self-interest of congressmen—now hopelessly outdistanced even in their incumbency by the financial gluttony of campaigns—is important.

But officials, like all of us, are motivated by altruism as well as self-interest. Their civic instincts often triumph over base and selfish calculations and may ultimately lead them to bold reform steps when public opinion is permissive, when the need is apparent, and when the intellectual means are at hand. But they must also realize that they are not the masters but the captives of the present system. Their integrity and judgment are menaced—and too often compromised—by the need to raise money and the means now available for doing it.

Even fund raisers are deeply troubled by the present system. At a recent Senate hearing, members of the Senate and Joseph Cole, finance chairman of the Democratic National Committee, spoke frankly about financing campaigns:

Mr. Cole: And I would comment on one other point, and that is the large contribution, a subject with which I have considerable experience. I tell you that this is the most unattractive and difficult thing about running for public office today. When I watch a presidential candidate demean himself and drive himself to rush to spend a minute or two for a potential large contributor instead of tending to his business or tending to the issues of the campaign, the priority that is given to win favor with these large contributors is very disheartening to observe. . . .

Senator Pastore: It is personal pride and self-respect. I, myself, have always been embarrassed and humiliated and had butterflies when I had to do these things. You almost feel like a beggar. If you are independent, it isn't a matter of whether or not you will become beholden, it is a matter of whether or not you are putting your self-respect on the line. . . .

Senator Moss: If the Senator will yield, I feel the same thing. I have had my campaign men say, "Now, look, Senator, if you will just pick up the phone and say a few words to Joe, we can go over and pick up some money." I say, "To heck with it; I have got nothing to say to him."[5]

Senator Hugh Scott, pleading with the Senate to support his public financing amendment to the Federal Election Campaign Act of 1973, put it bluntly:

> No member of this body could be honest with himself if he did not admit that in running for reelection, he had found it necessary to accept contributions, often large contributions, certainly large contributions, from those contributors who were willing to support his cause. I would have said [who] believed in his cause, but I do not know. I only know they supported him, but those contributions have inevitably raised a sense of obligation. Deny it how we will, the sense of obligation persists, and all of us have been involved in the exercise. I have used it myself. . . . I have to ask myself, what is the obligation involved. I wonder, when someone comes back later and asks me to do something—hopefully they ask me to do something I can do—would he embarrass me by asking me to do something that I should not do.[6]

Few politicians in modern presidential politics have been as under-financed as Hubert Humphrey, in both 1960 and 1968. He has added his voice to the others in the Senate calling for public financing of elections:

> I have been in a number of campaigns, and I enjoy the campaigns. . . . But the most demeaning, disenchanting part of politics is related to campaign finance. . . . Most of us, when we campaign, are on the telephone, calling up our friends, calling up committees, meeting with people, often times begging for help. Searching for campaign money is a disgusting, degrading, demeaning experience. It is about time we cleaned it up.[7]

THE PROBLEMS OF REFORM

The first problem of reform is to enable a nation with a private property economy and, consequently, a massive inequality of individual and institutional means to preserve opportunities for all its citizens to participate equally or nearly equally in financing politics. One possible solution is to limit the size of contributions to an amount that everyone, or nearly everyone, can afford. This approach, on its own and if enforced, would produce a genuine equality of opportunity; but it might also impoverish parties and candidates, stifling the competition necessary in a democracy.

An effective adversary process in elections requires that at least two candidates have sufficient campaign funds to establish their personal identities and qualifications, to advance their programs and ideologies, to criticize the records and positions of their opponents, and to link themselves to a party or to other candidates holding the same views. Constituencies where public opinion is fragmented rather than polarized may require more than two candidates. Without adversary campaigns elections are as irrelevant to democracy as the balloting in authoritarian nations with one-party systems.

These conditions may seem simple—even simple-minded. Yet the posture of too many reformers and large segments of the public is that we must curb the amount of money spent in campaigns. Instead, we must ask, "Do we spend enough money in American campaigns?" In 1968, campaigns to nominate and elect 524,000 public officials cost about $300 million; in the same year, a single soap company, Proctor and Gamble, spent $275 million on advertising. Democratic elections, one hopes, are far more important to Americans than detergents.

In 1972, national, state, and local governments spent almost $350 billion, about 40 percent of our national income. The $425 million Americans spent on campaigns to elect the men and women who manage these expenditures is piddling by comparison. And despite our unusually large number of elective offices, Americans spend proportionately less on politics than do the people of most other democracies. Swedes, for instance, spend four times as much per capita, even though the government carries the financial burden of registering voters and supports the parties with free radio and television time.

Hence, the second problem of political finance reform is to structure a system that will provide enough money for vigorous, competitive campaigns for public office.

A recurring pattern in the United States is the great disparity in campaign expenditures between opposing candidates for the same office. Although the personalities of the candidates, their stands on issues, their party affiliations, the public relations and prestige advantages of incumbency, the strength of local party organizations, and other considerations all may affect the outcome of an election, a candidate who is at a financial disadvantage may be unable to get a fair hearing for his case. The public's interest here is not, of course, the candidate's opportunity to promote his own career, but their opportunity to hear from candidates in a balanced way. Only if the hearers get enough information from two or several candidates can they intelligently exercise their control over government at the polls.

Disparities in the timing of campaign funds, as well as the amounts, have become critical in a technological age. Polling, purchase of radio and television time, preparation of sophisticated spots, assembling and computerization of mailing lists, telephone banks, and the highly professional staffs needed to make them all work, are increasingly expensive and also require constantly earlier investment.

All candidates are not, however, entitled to equality in campaign financing. Some are frivolous, representing no substantial viewpoint in the nation. Others may speak for older interest groups or parties, once powerful but now in decline (like the Whigs after the emergence of the Republican party in the 1850s). On the other hand, newly emerging groups with no track record in elections may express the discontents of many Americans. Robert La Follette in 1924 and George Wallace in 1968 were spokesmen for large movements, but they could not demonstrate by any past history that they or their ideas would claim widespread loyalty. The third problem of political finance is to ensure that each candidate is entitled to a fair share of the financial resources through a formula flexible enough to acknowledge newly emerging as well as established movements without rewarding frivolous candidacies or propping up decaying political organizations.

The fourth problem of reform is to free candidates and elected officials from undesirable or disproportionate pressure and influence from contributors and to free citizens from pressure by politicians to give financial support to candidates or parties.

Many who give money to politics expect something in return. They may merely expect candidates to keep their pledges on foreign and domestic affairs or to conduct government in an honest and economical manner. But some contributors have more selfish motives. Contractors may contribute generously in order to protect their business arrangements with government. The underworld may contribute to buy protection for illicit activities. Regulated industries may contribute to obtain more favorable rulings from regulatory agencies. The spectacle of milk cooperatives giving hundreds of thousands of dollars to the Nixon campaign in 1972 and almost immediately benefiting from an increase in dairy price supports has struck even the most naive observers as suspicious.

The subtle, yet plain, pressures by contributors on politicians have been candidly described by Senator Joseph Biden of Delaware, pleading for public financing of campaigns:

> During my campaign for the United States Senate in 1972, I paid a visit to certain leaders of a labor union whose members worked in the aircraft industry, and who intended to contribute $5,000 to the campaigns of various Senate candidates. It was an honest and open procedure, and payment was by check. They asked what my chances of winning were, and I explained for perhaps the hundredth time of the campaign why I thought I would win. I want to emphasize that no one asked me to promise my vote on

any particular issue, but they did ask, "Well, Joe, had you been in the ninety-second Congress, how would you have voted on the SST? And while you are at it, how would you have voted on bailing out Lockheed?" A candidate does not have to be very sophisticated to know the correct answers to such questions posited by labor leaders.

Later in the campaign, when I began to show strength in the polls and it looked as though I might win, thirteen multi-millionaire Republicans from my state invited me to cocktails. The spokesman for the group said, "Well, Joe, let us get right to it. You are a young man, and it looks as if you may win this damn thing, and it appears that we underestimated you. Now, Joe, we would like to ask you a few questions. We know that everybody running for public office feels compelled to talk about tax reform, and we know that you have been talking tax reform, particularly capital gains and gains for millionaires by consequence of unearned income." Then one man leaned over, patted me on the knee in a fatherly fashion, and said—as if to say it just among us—"Joe, you really don't mean what you say about capital gains, do you?" Again, I knew what [sic] the right answer to that question was $20,000 in contributions.

I did not give the "correct" answers in either instance, and accordingly, I received no money. But it is no secret that, in similar situations, other candidates have not hesitated to answer "correctly."[8]

Conversely, politicians may invoke the powers of government in demanding financial support. The Finance Committee for the Reelection of the President set quotas for companies and for wealthy individuals based on the volume of government business or personal net worth. Extortion, or practices that differ only in being more genteel, are the Janus face of undue influence by contributors.

These practices require no explicit promise or threat. Merely giving large sums influences government. It advances some views ahead of others in the electoral arena. It makes officeholders attentive to the views of those who provide their campaign funds. It furnishes access to decision makers at critical moments. It subtly invites preference in government contracts, appointments, and other activities for those who have been helpful in financing elections. On its other face, money can be extracted from citizens without threats. Every request from an elected official who influences legislation or regulatory activity is an implicit demand. The contributor fears the consequences of failing to respond. He fears that his competitors may gain an advantage if they are more generous than he. Private contributions in these circumstances defile democratic ideals.

Where explicit understandings accompany either solicitation or giving, the issue is not pressure or influence but corruption in its legal sense. Preventing corruption is thus the fifth problem of reform.

Political financing raises issues quite apart from the campaigns of candidates. It bears on the ability of American parties to perform the functions—quite separate from election campaigns—that are expected of them in our society.

The notorious weakness of American parties has recently been the subject of much anguished analysis and discussion. It is a source of much of the incoherence and lack of focus of American politics.[9] Yet it is rooted in our constitutional structure and national temper. State legislators, governors, representatives, senators, and the president have separate governmental powers, staggered terms of office, and independent electoral constituencies. This fragmentation discourages party cohesion and virtually destroys discipline on politics or policy. The well-known ethnic heterogeneity, regional diversity, and non-ideological bent of the American people further decentralize our parties. We lack the communal or class cohesion that has provided the emotional glue for parties in other western democracies. Our electoral institutions and our traditions have maintained a two-party system, but each party has been a wide-ranging coalition of many different groups and interests.

In recent years the importance of ethnic and religious diversity in American politics has declined. Higher educational levels, nationally uniform mass media, and high mobility among regions have increased the cultural homogeneity of Americans. The decline of ethnic, religious, and cultural factors in politics has been accompanied by a deepening of ideological differences between the two main parties.[10] Minority elements have attempted to prod both major parties toward even greater purity on certain issues, at the cost of old-time coalitional strategies. The Goldwater coup of 1964 and the McGovern takeover of 1972 were manifestations of the impulse toward ideological coherence in parties.

But the pressure for ideological coherence has not made the parties any more organizationally centralized. Indeed, issue-oriented partisans find organizational loyalty too confining, and they share the historic American disdain for the mechanics of political parties that is expressed in the epithets "machine" and "bossism." In the long run, issue-oriented politics might conceivably inspire an organizational revival in parties, and these traditional political structures might then emerge as important fund raisers. But every sign in recent years indicates that party organizations have grown weaker and no longer play a leading role in financing campaigns.

What these decentralized parties contribute to American democracy may be difficult for the layman to define, since so much of the political activity he sees is performed by candidates. The Democratic National Committee, for example, spends only about $1 million annually. Yet Democratic presidential campaigning in the 1968 general election cost over $11 million and in the 1972 general election over $37 million.

But parties do play a significant role during and between elections. Basic to the democratic process is the recruitment and certification of candidates, and the presence of parties tends to assure that opposition candidates will be recruited even in traditionally one-party districts. The spectacle of a group of dogged party leaders paying visit after visit in an effort to find someone to run for an open office is familiar in most of the United States and is indispensable to our electoral process.

Parties also enlist the activists who man the polls and do the many other chores necessary to make the political system function. Although the centrally led, well-oiled political machines of yore have all but disappeared, modern parties still provide candidates with manpower, talent, and money for their campaigns and provide elected officials with personnel to staff the government.

Parties engage in still another form of recruitment that is basic to the democratic process but that in most other countries is done by government. They "recruit" the electorate: they register voters and get them to the polls. The ratios of voter registration and voter turnout to the potential American electorate suggest that party resources, and perhaps party efforts, have not been adequate to the task. Certainly the parties have received assistance from labor unions and such civic groups as the League of Women Voters, but parties do most of the work of getting eligibles to register and to vote. Their labors have a direct relation to the subject of political finance. For if the government were responsible for registration, as it is in most other democracies, the financial relief to the parties would substantially improve their ability to perform other functions.

Possibly the most grievous single shortcoming of the parties, the rectification of which would most require a massive infusion of funds, has been their failure to sustain an opposition presence at the grassroots level in inter-election periods. Without shadow governments of the kind found in parliamentary systems, Americans must rely on the opposition party organization to serve as watchdog over incumbents and to maintain a drumfire of criticism against them. But our financially starved parties have been so lax in this pursuit that the role of opposition is very often taken over by interest groups and news media, whose attention is highly selective and frequently inadequate for effective review of those in power.

Despite or perhaps because of these problems, the need to fund parties goes largely unrecognized. Candidates are the usual focus of citizen contributions. The financial weakness of the parties troubles only their functionaries and a few academic students of the system. Moreover, officeholders and the public look suspiciously on parties. In the present decentralized state of American politics, candidates and officials view parties as competitors for political resources. The public's distrust of parties is so well known that candidates spend hours dreaming up scenarios that will allow them to run against "the party bosses."

Nonetheless, parties do play an important role in American politics. "No America without democracy, no democracy without politics, no politics without parties," runs the opening passage of one of our best-known books about the nation's party system.[11] And if we address the problem of financing candidates but ignore the funding woes of parties, we upset delicate balances between the party organization and the party's officeholders. These relationships should not be tampered with lightly in a nation whose politics may be moving toward more ideologically coherent and possibly even more organizationally centralized parties. If parties are indispensable to democracy (and even the most hostile among us can scarcely imagine our politics without them) and if delicate balances between officeholders and party organizations mark our evolving political system, then whether and how to finance political parties is the sixth problem facing advocates of reform.

A seventh objective of reform is to enhance public confidence in the electoral system. On one level, a relatively equal opportunity for citizens to participate in political finance should cause more people to feel that they are effective in politics and that the system responds to them. Enough money for campaigns and a fair opportunity for candidates to be heard should mute much of the present sentiment that only the rich or those supported by the rich can run for office. Steps to curb pressure, influence, and corruption through campaign contributions should diminish popular belief that the governmental tune can be called only by wealthy piper payers. Probably support of political parties will do the least to nourish public confidence in our politics, but enough money, fairly apportioned money, and clean money for parties as well as candidates should at least neutralize the image of corruption and wrongdoing in our political arrangements.

But campaign finance reform has deeper implications for public confidence in government. The failure or ineptitude of government in meeting public wants is a far greater cause of citizen disaffection than the financing of political campaigns. Officials elected without effective opposition, because challengers cannot find financing, are unlikely to be responsive to popular needs. And officials who are attentive to interest groups, because they provide campaign money, are unlikely to govern in ways that satisfy the needs or win the confidence of the vast majority of Americans. The goal of political finance reform is ultimately to win public confidence by creating a more responsive and effective electoral and governmental system.

The successful resolution of all these issues raises an eighth problem: the cost of maintaining a democratic electoral system. Obviously, an absolute dollar figure is only a starting point. Other perspectives are also relevant. How much does politics cost in relation to our ability to pay, that is, to our national wealth—or perhaps more specifically, to our national personal income, since that is the source of campaign funds? How much does it cost compared to political finance expenditures in other democratic nations? How strong is the claim of a democratic electoral system on resources that might otherwise go for food, housing, education, health care, defense, recreation, and a host of other personal and governmental budget items?

The American people are already paying direct costs of election administration that may be reasonably estimated at almost $250 million in each election year.[12] The cost of all nomination and election contests was about $300 million in 1968 and probably $425 million in 1972.[13] Reform may cost double or triple that amount.

But reform may also reduce the indirect costs imposed by the present system. If the present system benefits those who want something from government, then the rest of us must pay for that something. For example, if $600,000 spent on politics by maritime unions helps influence Congress to maintain a $500 million subsidy for a shrinking national merchant marine, the present system increases the taxpayers' burden by that amount.

Other "indirect" costs may arise from campaign financing practices and legislative loopholes. The Internal Revenue Service has assessed no gift tax against campaign contributors who give sums of $3,000 or less to many different committees supporting the same candidate. The loss of gift tax on a total contribution of $100,000, or $2 million, or more must be made up by other taxpayers. When contributors give appreciated stock to a campaign, reporting the gift at its purchase price while the campaign sells it at the current market price, and neither the giver nor the political committee pays a capital gains tax, the loss of that tax revenue must be made up by other taxpayers.

Finally, political finance policy should be as straightforward as possible in its results and its administrative arrangements. Nothing in our politics arouses such suspicion as campaign funds. Nowhere is there so much conviction that laws are broken, regulations bent, and ethics trammeled. Long years of wholly ineffectual laws and freebooting finance practices have confirmed the public's suspicion. Any new policy must, therefore, be simple enough to gain public understanding, at least for its basic rules and perhaps even for its specific operations.

Citizens of each party must be able to see clearly when their own champions are in violation of the regulations and to realize that the whistle is not being blown by a partisan referee. And if a political finance policy requires public participation and support and if it entails expenditures of tax money, citizens must be able to assess it easily. Their assessment will bear heavily both on their own willingness to participate and on their reaction to the community's collective participation through the tax system.

THE RAW MATERIALS FOR REFORM

It is not difficult to find raw materials from which to construct a political finance policy. Traditional regulatory approaches reduce the disproportionate influence of private fortunes. Public financing makes up the difference.

Expenditure limitations may curb spending disparities by leveling down excessive campaign outlays, but they may do so at the price of limiting political activity and perhaps of crimping constitutional freedoms of expression and association. Contribution ceilings may reduce the dangers of pressure, influence, extortion, and corruption. Full disclosure can assist enforcement, heighten public understanding, and ease evaluation of policy. These reforms would not, however, channel enough money into politics to sustain vigorous campaigns, assure fair opportunities for candidates, or assist political parties. Ultimately only some kind of public financing shows any promise of providing enough fairly distributed and untainted money for politics.

But if the principles are easy, the practical arrangements are not. Should spending limits be set? At what level? And is there any effective means of enforcing them? How can meaningful contribution ceilings be established, and at what level? Can disclosure of campaign financing be enforced, and can the information disclosed be adequately communicated to the public for its judgment? How can public funds be channeled to campaigns fairly without wasting it on frivolous and self-serving candidates, and how much public money is needed for campaigns? What is the appropriate means for financing political parties to support their significant activities and to maintain delicate balances within the political system? Do these measures run afoul of constitutional guarantees, by using public money to support the private goals of candidates and parties, by distributing money unequally to them, or by trenching on the freedoms of speech, press, and association?

These issues have been the main intellectual barriers to reform. But like the political opposition, they are not insurmountable. On every side there is evidence that the political climate, public opinion, and the leadership mood are right for sweeping reform, including public financing. The means, we believe, are not yet at hand. It is to these intellectual issues, then, that we address this book.

In 1972, total campaign spending in all primary and general elections for all national, state, and local offices reached an all-time high. Since 1952, total outlays as well as expenditures for each eligible elector and for each vote cast have increased steadily. Total spending has tripled, and we spend substantially more than twice as much per voter for elections now as twenty years ago (see Table 2-1).

The costs of presidential contests have increased more rapidly than those of campaigns for most other offices. In 1952, presidential general election spending by national political committees amounted to $11.6 million, nineteen cents per vote cast. In 1956, the figure was $12.9 million, twenty cents per vote cast.[1] From 1912 till then, and perhaps from even earlier (with some variations in particular presidential years), the going rate for presidential campaigns was nineteen cents per vote.[2]

But in 1960 the lid blew off. National Republican, Democratic, and labor spending soared to $20.7 million,[3] then to $38.9 million in 1964,[4] and again to $38.9 million in 1968, when still $7.2 million more was spent on behalf of George Wallace's third party presidential bid.[5] Expenditures broke loose from the traditional mooring of nineteen cents per vote during these years,

2

THE
COST
OF
POLITICS

TABLE 2-1   The American Campaign Price Tag, 1952–1972

Year	Total Spending All Elections	Spending/ Vote Cast	Spending/ Eligible Voter
1952	$140 million	$2.27	$1.40
1956	155 million	2.50	1.52
1960	175 million	2.57	1.60
1964	200 million	2.83	1.75
1968	300 million	4.10	2.49
1972	425 million	5.66	3.04

SOURCE: The 1952 and 1956 estimates were made by Alexander Heard, *The Costs of Democracy* (Chapel Hill: University of North Carolina Press, 1960), pp. 7–8. The 1960, 1964, and 1968 figures are drawn from the quadrennial reports of Herbert E. Alexander summarized in his *Financing the 1968 Election* (Lexington, Mass.: Heath Lexington Books, 1971), p. 7. The 1972 estimates are the authors', based on reports by the Office of Federal Elections and the projections of Herbert E. Alexander.

going to twenty-nine cents in 1960, thirty-five cents in 1964, and a fantastic sixty cents in 1968.[6]

The campaign financing extravaganza did not end with the election of Richard Nixon. Even George Wallace's absence from the ballot as a third party candidate in 1972 did not slow the inflation in American politics. The second Nixon-Agnew campaign spent more than $56 million, at least $47 million of it in the general election. The McGovern-Shriver ticket accounted for an additional $49 million, of which $11 million was spent during the pre-convention sweepstakes. With other national level committees, general election campaign costs reached at least $100 million, a staggering $1.31 per vote cast.[7]

Total presidential campaign costs have always been much more elusive than general election outlays, because until recently legal reporting requirements and news coverage in the pre-convention period were nominal. One commentator has set 1964 primary and general election expenditures by all presidential candidates at $60 million and 1968 spending at $100 million.[8] The 1972 total will surely rise above $115 million—a striking increase, because in 1972 there was neither a serious Republican nomination contest (in 1968, various GOP aspirants spent $20 million) nor a wealthy candidate who, like Robert Kennedy or Nelson Rockefeller in 1968, could bring substantial personal and family resources to the fray.

The costs of congressional campaigns have also increased. In 1970, the reported total primary and general election costs of all campaigns for the House and Senate came to an estimated $71.6 million.[9] In 1972, a Common Cause survey of congressional campaign spending reported under the sweeping Federal Election Campaign Act of 1971 turned up total House and Senate outlays of $77.2

million.[10] Because the act did not go into effect until April 7, 1972, some congressional spending was excluded from the filed reports, and the full amount was probably several million dollars above the Common Cause figure. Even the $6 million increase in reported expenditures has heightened significance because it occurred during a presidential election year. Candidates for lesser offices usually are unable to raise as ample war chests in presidential election years as in off years when their solicitations need not compete with the power and glamour of the presidency .

More telling than the total picture of congressional campaign expenditures are rising costs in specific races. In 1964, Governor Gaylord Nelson of Wisconsin spent just under $200,000 to win a seat in the United States Senate; six years later his expenditures topped $450,000 in an easy re-election contest. In 1968, Kentucky Democrat Katherine Peden spent $76,300 in her unsuccessful race for the United States Senate; in 1972, Walter Huddleston, running for the same office on the same ticket in the same state, spent $658,600 to win. Ms. Peden's opponent, Republican Senator Marlow Cook, spent $101,600 to win in 1968, and former governor Louie Nunn spent $603,600 to lose in 1972. In California, in 1964, Democrat Pierre Salinger spent $415,900 to go down to defeat in his senatorial campaign; in 1970, Democrat John Tunney spent $1,338,200 to win. In 1964, Republican senatorial candidate George Murphy spent $910,000 to vanquish Salinger; six years later, he spent $1,946,400 to suffer defeat at Tunney's hands. In Massachusetts, in 1966, Republican Edward Brooke spent $291,900 to win his Senate seat; by 1972, his expenditures had risen to $368,000. (But his war chest also held an additional $304,300, which he found he did not have to spend to trounce a weak and weakly financed Democratic opponent.)[11]

In the mid-1950s, Alexander Heard estimated that a typical statewide campaign in New York would cost $1 million; in 1970, Nelson Rockefeller spent $9 million to win a fourth term as governor. Heard also estimated that statewide campaigning in Oregon would cost $100,000 to $150,000. But Common Cause reports that, in 1972, Senator Mark Hatfield spent $299,600 to win re-election against former Senator Wayne Morse, whose campaign cost $251,900. Heard's mid-1950s estimate for statewide campaigning in Montana ranged from $40,000 to $60,000; in 1972 Democratic Senator Lee Metcalf spent $136,000 on his successful re-election bid, and his Republican challenger, Henry Hibbard, spent $286,700.[12]

Campaign funds in races for the House of Representatives have received little attention over the years. The fragments of information available show the same cost increases for lower house races as for the Senate and the presidency. In 1968, Democratic House candidates in Connecticut averaged expenditures of $53,300 and Republican aspirants $53,600. Four years later the Democratic average had climbed to $74,400 and the Republican average to $86,800. In neighboring Massachusetts, Democratic congressional contestants in 1968 spent an average of $12,300, and GOP contenders spent $23,300. In 1972, they spent $74,200 and $60,100, respectively. In Oregon, between 1968 and 1972 the Democratic average rose from $17,500 to only $20,600, and the Republican average went from $39,800 to $45,800. In Wisconsin, between 1968 and 1972, the Democratic average rose from $17,900 to $31,000 and the Republican average from $29,600 to $33,900.[13]

A study of campaign expenditures for the offices of president, senator, representative, governor, and state legislator in seven states and the United States indicates that in the late 1960s spending increased between 10 percent and 90 percent *annually* in various locales but that the average yearly increase was 33 percent. According to these findings, politicians must "calculate that, from one biennial election to the next, they must raise half again as much as their most recent election effort."[14] In fact, politicians usually base their calculations on the largest campaign outlays rather than on the averages. In this perspective, the task of fund raising frequently appears hopeless to well-qualified candidates who wish to advance a program or to challenge the record of an incumbent.

WHY COSTS RISE

Most citizens believe that the staggering increases in campaign costs are a sinister consequence of the self-serving greed of ruthless politicians. But careful students of political finance find other factors at work, many wholly beyond the control of politicians and some within their control but not dishonorable.[15]

Part of the cost increase results from the increasing number of people who are eligible to vote. Campaigners must increase their spending as the electorate expands; sending a first class letter to every elector would have cost more in 1972, with 136 million eligibles, than in 1968, with 120 million eligibles (even if postage costs had remained constant, which they did not). Media costs vary with the size of the audience. Demands for bumper stickers, brochures, and other essential campaign materials also depend on the size of the constituency. The growth of the electorate in recent years is due in part to the baby boom of the 1940s and 1950s. In addition, the Voting Rights Act of 1965 brought additional millions of blacks into the electorate and the Twenty-Sixth Amendment enfranchised millions of eighteen-, nineteen-, and twenty-year-olds.

The cost increase is also due to general inflation. The Consumer Price Index was 5 percent higher in 1964 than in 1960, 18 percent higher in 1968, and 41 percent higher in 1972. And such goods and services as the salaries of skilled and experienced staff workers, postage stamps, mass media advertising, and air fares have gone up faster than the 3.5 percent average annual increase in the Consumer Price Index. Prices increased still more rapidly between 1968 and 1972 than in prior years, and this trend continues as we hurtle toward the 1976 elections. Just doing the same thing, at much higher prices, accounts for a substantial share of the increase in campaign spending.

Changes in technology also are responsible for higher costs. The advent of radio and then of television sent costs soaring. And the use of special production teams and skilled film makers has drastically increased preparation costs for television. In Wisconsin, media production costs for a gubernatorial candidacy went from $6,000 in 1962 to $65,000 in 1970. Estimates for the same office in 1974 range from $100,000 to $200,000. Public opinion polling is another increasingly expensive campaign practice. In presidential races polling outlays run to hundreds of thousands of dollars. Even in a Senate race in a medium-sized state, a three-phase polling operation in the year prior to election day will cost a minimum of $25,000. In the old days, of course, politicians relied on inexpensive but unscientific straw polls at supermarkets or in schools.

"Personalized" letters to voters are the newest style in campaigning. The preparation of these letters requires the installation of elaborate phone banks, manned by paid operators, months before the election. Information solicited about and from voters is then transferred, at high cost, to computer cards or tapes. The computer then summons up names of certain categories of voters—Roman Catholics, union workers, conservatives—and types a letter geared to the category and personally addressed to each voter. Postage adds to the price of this electronic version of the personal contact vote solicitation that was once the work of now virtually extinct precinct captains.

Before voters object to the cost of these technologies, they should remember that in the United States politics must compete with a host of other diversions for the attention of an electorate accustomed to sophisticated, amusing, or subtle media advertising, news, and programming. The decline of party organizations has eliminated the reliable system of precinct workers who both took the public pulse and tried to regulate it. Politicians resort to polls and personalized letters in an effort to fill the vacuum. The old-time mass rallies—hundreds of thousands in Cadillac Square to kick off the Democratic presidential campaign—are virtually gone. Americans sit stubbornly at home before their television sets, and the politicians must woo them electronically.

The geographical size of constituencies adds further costs. Nationwide campaigning by jet plane—especially since Hawaii and Alaska have become states—is far more expensive than the front porch campaigns or even the systematic city-by-city whistle stops of an earlier day. The one-man one-vote rules laid down by the Supreme Court have shifted House representation to cities and suburbs, leaving fewer representatives to cover sparsely settled regions. Maintaining headquarters and staff in many parts of a large geographical district adds to high costs.

The decline of traditional party organizations has also increased campaign costs. The reliable, year-in year-out ward organization got voters registered, tallied their pre-election preferences, and took them to the polls. Now candidates must painstakingly and expensively build citizen organizations for each new campaign, or they must pay workers to get these tasks done. Often several candidate organizations and political committees (such as union political action groups) work the same areas, at greater expense and with less effectiveness than Frank Skeffington's precinct minions.

Competition, too, sends costs soaring. Candidates and their friends, as well as interest groups, big contributors, and party leaders, have always spent more money in districts and circumstances where the race is likely to be close than in opposition-dominated districts where the purpose of running a candidate is primarily to aid the ticket and give heart to the party faithful.

But competition has spread in the past twenty-five years. Republicans have broken open the once solidly Democratic South; outlays in Senate and House races in the region have accordingly shot upward. Democrats, in turn, have become equal competitors in the Midwest and Plains, staunchly Republican since the Civil War, and, more recently, in the once impenetrable white collar suburbs. The decay of the Roosevelt New Deal coalition has also made presidential contests much more competitive.

"Reform" of nominating procedures also raises the cost to a candidate. When nominations were made by party caucuses or conventions, he had to appeal to only a relatively small number of persons. Speeches at party meetings, hospitality at delegate receptions, and front porch or parlor visits sufficed. But the convention system has been abandoned in most states, and the selection of national convention delegates occurs more and more frequently in primaries. Candidates must therefore wage not one but two full-scale appeals to the electorate: first for nomination in the primary and second for office in the general election. If the trend toward going to the public in nominating procedures continues, expenses for primary campaigns will continue to grow.

The availability of money is, of course, crucial to the level of expenditures. In recent years a substantial number of personally wealthy individuals financed by their own resources, families, business associates, and friends have competed for high office. Such candidates spend freely and virtually force their opponents to do likewise. Much of the cost of the 1968 presidential nomination campaign resulted from the efforts of the other candidates to keep up with the Kennedys and Rockefellers. Money is also available because a larger, better educated, and better informed electorate includes more givers. While 12 percent of the eligible electorate contributed to campaigns in both 1960 and 1972, the electorate had increased 30 million during those years and the number of contributors rose with it from roughly 13.1 million to 16.8 million.

Finally, the large number of offices contested in the United States multiplies the overall campaign bill. No other nation has our Jacksonian, long-ballot tradition; and we pay a price for selecting 524,000 local, state, and national officials at the polls.

DISPARITIES IN SPENDING

Campaign spending is not only high but also unequally distributed. First, more money is spent for executive offices than for legislative races. In the 1972 presidential race, the primary and general election campaigns cost an estimated $115 million. In the same year, primary and general election outlays to elect one-third of the Senate were approximately $30 million and to elect the entire House were about $46 million.[16] One obvious effect of this disparity is to help make the issues and personalities in presidential contests more familiar than in congressional races. The difference in campaign spending may enhance the prestige of the presidency at the expense of the prestige of Congress.

Money also flows to competitive rather than non-competitive races. The Common Cause Study shows that total expenditures by both major-party general election candidates averaged only $46,200 in districts where the winner received more than 70 percent of the vote, $58,300 where he received 65 to 70 percent, $85,400 where he received 60 to 65 percent, $128,200 where he received 55 to 60 percent, and $208,500 where he received less than 55 percent. This distribution of money makes good sense from the perspective of a political party strategist; money is directed to those races where it can mean the difference between winning and losing. Special interests give token contributions to friendly candidates in safe districts and go all out financially to aid their supporters in marginal districts.

But from the perspective of democratic accountability, the starvation of campaigns in safe districts is nonsense. A vicious cycle develops in which a candidate wins an election, becomes stronger because of incumbency and the political composition of his district, and finally becomes almost invulnerable because few of the usual sources of campaign funds are willing to gamble on his long-shot opponent. These secure officeholders do not feel accountable to voters in elections. Electoral competition is the most important means of holding an officeholder responsible for his actions, but in safe districts challengers cannot raise enough money to expose the incumbent's conduct and record for public scrutiny or to advance alternative qualifications and programs.

The third significant disparity in campaign spending is between incumbents and challengers. Fred Wertheimer, legislative director of Common Cause, observed: "The money flows to incumbents because it is an incumbent who has the power. . . . The result is that in Congress today we have neither a Democratic or Republican party. Rather, we have an Incumbency party which operates a monopoly."[17]

If the rhetoric is overdrawn, the financial edge of incumbents is nonetheless accurately stated. Incumbent United States senators outspent their opponents in 1972 by an average of $495,400 to $244,100. Democratic incumbents had an average $381,100 to $312,400 edge over GOP challengers, while Republican senators outspent Democratic challengers $559,700 to $205,700.[18]

A similar pattern prevailed in House races. Incumbents outspent challengers by an average of $50,900 to $32,100. Democratic incumbents had an edge of $50,000 to $33,560 over Republican challengers, and Republican representatives outspent Democratic hopefuls by an average of $51,900 to $30,300. Races with no incumbents were financial toss-ups in both houses; in Senate races Democrats averaged $496,300 and Republicans $465,300, and in House contests Democrats averaged $89,400 and Republicans $88,400.

The financial edge held by officeholders does not, of course, include the other campaign advantages of incumbency: high name recognition among voters, good will won through services to constituents, familiarity with institutional and media leaders throughout the district, a paid staff and free office space, the franking privilege, and others. In using these perquisites, "the line between the congressman's function as a representative of his district and his function as a campaigner for re-election is not easy to draw."[19] Conducting government business inherently has political effects back home. One commentator has said the perquisites of office are worth a minimum of $16,000 in each election for activities connected more to campaigning than to representing. "This rough and probably very low estimate includes $6,000 for congressional staff time used for campaigns, $2,400 for government offices and facilities used, $7,200 for campaign material mailed under the frank, and $2,500 that incumbents can forgo and challengers need for minimal name exposure on billboards to offset the recognition that inheres in an incumbent by virtue of his position."[20] The latter estimate seems especially low, for many challengers spend virtually all their funds simply trying to build name identification among voters.

Beyond these inherent incumbency advantages, an officeholder can raise far more cash than his opponent to publicize his record, to promote his program, to state his qualifications, and to support a campaign organization. Like the financial disparity in one-party districts, the unequal dollar resources of incumbents and challengers reduces accountability by diminishing the intensity of opposition campaigning and increasing the incumbent's ability to overwhelm whatever assaults are made on his official conduct and record.

CAMPAIGN SPENDING IN PERSPECTIVE

Although both the total national campaign bill and expenditures by candidates for specific offices have risen sharply in recent years, even our 1972 commitment of $3.04 for each eligible elector or $5.66 for each voter is not necessarily too high a price to pay for the essential campaigning that gives citizens the opportunity to determine who will govern. If campaign costs were shared equally, the ordinary citizen would scarcely feel the burden. The $5.66 per vote cast represents wages for only one and one-half hours of work for the average American production worker; the $3.04 expenditure per eligible voter represents only forty-eight minutes of wages. Citizens in many other democracies have been willing to pay a substantially higher price for politics.[21]

A national campaign bill of $425 million represents .037 percent of the 1972 Gross National Product, only a trivial increase over the .034 percent of GNP that campaign costs represented in 1968. All campaign expenditures in the United States come from Personal Income; but only .045 percent of total national Personal Income was committed to campaign costs in 1972, and the 1968 campaign bill absorbed virtually the same proportion of Personal Income—.044 percent.

Even the increase in campaign spending is modest when seen in perspective. In the United States, between 1952 and 1972, national Personal Income, from which we must pay the politics bill, rose at a more rapid rate (267 percent) than the increase in campaign spending (204 percent). Even the unprecedented 42 percent increase in campaign spending between 1968 and 1972 was not sharply disproportionate to a 36 percent increase in Personal Income. Equal sharing of campaign costs in 1972 would absorb a somewhat larger proportion of an average production worker's wages than in 1952— one hour and thirty minutes' wages rather than one hour and six minutes' wages. On the other hand, the percentage increase in total national, state, and local government expenditures has been more rapid than the percentage increase in campaign spending, which is, in a literal sense, one cost of managing the level and the allocation of public service expenditures.

Although the dollar costs of politics stagger the individual citizen, from a national perspective campaign expenditures are quite modest. They are an insignificant portion of national Personal Income, only a few dollars per eligible voter, and less than two hours' wages for an average worker. Nor are campaign costs rising inordinately. Personal Income and government spending have both increased more rapidly. Most important, we pay only a small sum for competitive campaigns that pose choices of officials, clarify the programs of candidates, and expose the records and qualifications of those seeking to govern. After food, clothing, shelter, and perhaps religious affiliation, what greater necessity is there for citizens in a democracy than the political process by which they select officials and programs? Three or five dollars in an election year seems a small price indeed for self-government.

In perspective, the problem is not that campaign spending is too high. On the contrary, the present system of private financing may supply too little money to support vigorous campaigning for all offices in all constituencies across the nation. It also creates a dangerous mal-distribution of campaign funds: higher spending for executive offices than for the co-equal legislative houses, greater outlays in competitive districts than in non-competitive races where officials should also be held accountable, and more money by far for incumbents than for challengers. Historically it has also directed more money to conservative candidates and parties that speak for established groups and institutions than for those challenging the standing order of things. The modest cost of politics suggests that Americans can easily afford to spend more to finance vigorous campaigning and to correct these imbalances. The issue of campaign spending does not turn on its high level but on how much more to spend, where to get it, and how to channel it.

Never in the history of American campaigns were so many appeals made for financial support as in 1972. On the eve of their convention the Democrats staged a telethon. Senator McGovern mailed appeals to millions of Americans. Democrats for Nixon followed television spots with fund solicitations. The Republican National Committee redoubled its already successful fund-raising letter campaign. The disclosure requirements of the 1971 Federal Election Campaign Act and the watchfulness of leading news media kept Americans aware of the high cost of politics and the predominant role played by big money in campaigns.

In 1972, 34 percent of the adult population of the United States were asked, either in person or by mail, to contribute to a political party or candidate. In 1968, only 20 percent had received such solicitations, and in 1960 and 1964 only 15 percent. In 1972, 12.4 percent of eligible voters made a contribution to some campaign for office; in 1968, 7.6 percent had reported making such contributions. But 1968 was an atypical year because 12 percent, virtually the same proportion as in 1972, said they contributed in both 1960 and 1964. Expanded solicitations and greater attention to money in politics have not broadened participation in campaign finance. In the non-

3

FILLING
THE
CAMPAIGN
COFFERS

presidential years 1962 and 1966, respectively, 9 percent and 8 percent of the electorate contributed to campaigns. The level of financial participation in political campaigns has shown surprisingly little change from presidential to non-presidential years. And in all years, as well as over time, it remains quite low.[1]

Why do most Americans fail to contribute to political campaigns? Twenty percent of those polled in 1972 said that too much money was already being spent in campaigns. Another 14 percent believed that their small contribution wouldn't make any difference. Seven percent had misgivings about the way politicians would spend their money. Only 4 percent took the cynical view that the outcome of elections did not make any difference. The remaining respondents either reported having given at some time in their lives (26 percent) or gave other, widely scattered reasons for not contributing.[2] Social scientists suggest that some Americans refrain from participating in political affairs generally, including campaign financing, because they do not understand politics and because they do not believe they can influence the course of events.

THE ACTIVE MINORITY
That only a few Americans actively participate in politics has become a commonplace of modern political science. Some observers maintain that this domination of politics by "activists" is desirable because activists are interested in politics, are informed about it, and are committed to the rules of the democratic game. On the other hand, E. E. Schattschneider has warned that the activist "chorus sings with a strong upper class accent."[3] The upper class predominates even more strongly among those who fill the collection plate than in politics generally. Table 3-1 shows that those with four or more years of college education are five times more likely to contribute to political campaigns than those with only grade school education. Participation is about ten times as great among the well-off as among the poor. Candidates may find it necessary to adopt issues acceptable to the upper classes if they hope to finance their campaigns. The upper-class bias in campaign giving may also reward candidates whose style or manner conforms to class expectations. Lower-class citizens may be discouraged from political participation and indeed from confidence in government by their correct perception that the financing constituency of politics has an upper-class bias. Even resistance to financing reform may be class-based if givers calculate that their political influence will be diminished by changes in the way we fund campaigns.

Surveys reveal that strong partisans tend to give more readily than independents. Those who only weakly identify with a party or who

TABLE 3-1   Income and Educational Class Bias Among Campaign
Contributors

Income Group	Percentage Contributing		Education	Percentage Contributing	
	1968	1972		1968	1972
$ 0–$ 4,999	3.0	3.7	0– 8 Grade	4.8	5.4
5,000– 9,999	7.3	11.5	9–12 Grade	5.5	9.6
10,000– 14,999	8.4	11.7	Some College	10.0	17.8
15,000– 19,999	14.3	19.8	College: 4 years or more	18.6	28.4
20,000 or more	24.1	32.0			
All	7.6	12.4	All	7.6	12.4

SOURCES: The 1968 figures are retabulations of a University of Michigan
Survey Research Center poll. The 1972 tabulations are based on the Twentieth
Century Fund Survey.

are wholly unaffiliated are also most likely to vote a split ticket and
to shift from support of one party's candidates to the other's in succeeding elections. But if candidates must appeal to strong partisans
for a disproportionate share of campaign funds, they are likely to take
stands on issues that please that constituency rather than the whole
electorate. The candidate must win the constituency that provides
campaign resources—money, manpower, skills, endorsements, and the
like—before he can appeal to the non-activist constituency.

Political finance studies show as well that candidates touching on
deeply emotional issues also draw substantial financial support.
George Wallace, for instance, reported that of $6.7 million raised
from February to October, 1968, more than 85 percent was in contributions of less than $100, from as many as 750,000 contributors.
Eugene McCarthy's drive for the 1968 Democratic presidential nomination likewise received some 150,000 small contributions—along
with a handful of very big gifts.[4] Republican committees in 1964
received 650,000 small contributions, and while some of these were
earmarked for the party's sustaining fund, most were to support the
Goldwater candidacy. In the pre-convention period, Goldwater had
been supported by more than 300,000 small contributions.[5] The
McGovern campaign in 1972 claimed 600,000 small contributors,
and preliminary reports suggest that only $13 million of the $49
million contributed to McGovern's campaign fund was in gifts
larger than $100.[6]

What these campaigns had in common was an emotional issue
that for many people also tied into larger ideological commitments.
Candidates addressing issues that intensely concern even relatively
small groups of people may be rewarded by many small and even
some large contributions. Some have mistakenly characterized the

financing of candidates like Goldwater, McCarthy, Wallace, and McGovern as "broad-based" or "grassroots." But 600,000 contributors is only 0.4 percent of the eligible electorate and only 4 percent of the 1972 contributors. In a money-starved political process, with few other sources of money, this small and unrepresentative corps of contributors makes an enormous financial impact.

Moderate candidates, however, cannot even summon this many contributors. Most of their constituents are not sufficiently aroused to take the unusual step of contributing to campaigns. Politics simply is not important enough to them. Moderates must therefore raise their campaign funds from traditional partisan or interest sources. Like the ideological contributors, these traditional money constituencies are different from the electorate as a whole, and a candidate's appeals to them may involve commitments somewhat different from those he might make if his only constituency were the voters.

THE BIG GIVERS

The outpouring of small gifts in the Goldwater, McCarthy, Wallace, and McGovern campaigns is exceptional in American politics. More often, campaign treasuries are filled by a relatively small number of large contributions. Harry Truman's "give 'em hell" grassroots campaign, for instance, received 69 percent of its campaign funds in sums of $500 or more. In Dewey's 1948 campaign, such large gifts represented 74 percent of the total campaign funds. Even as predictable a loser as Adlai Stevenson in 1956 relied mainly on large gifts from moneyed individuals and interests rather than small ones from hardcore Democratic loyalists at the grassroots.[7]

In recent years, both the biggest givers and the ideological small giver constituencies have simultaneously come to dominate American political campaigns. From 1952 to 1960, givers of $10,000 or more numbered about 100 in each presidential year, with gifts totaling from $1.6 million to $2.3 million. In 1964 the number of these givers went up slightly, to 130, but their total financial contribution was still only $2.2 million. The 1968 campaign was a watershed; the number of $10,000-plus givers jumped to 424 and their total contributions were in excess of $12.2 million.[8]

American politics in 1972 witnessed a sharp acceleration of the big giver trend. Not only did the Nixon campaign war chest almost double the previous high—$63.2 million, compared with $34.9 million for Nixon's nomination and general election efforts in 1968—but it also was the most heavily dependent on very large gifts of any in modern American history. Comparatively little money was raised in small gifts. The Office of Federal Elections reported that $37.6 million was raised in contributions of more than $100 after the 1971

TABLE 3-2　Percentage of General Election Funds of National-Level Party Committees Raised in Sums of $500 or More

Party	1952	1956	1960	1964	1968
Democrats	63	44	59	69	61
Republicans	68	74	58	28	47

SOURCE: Herbert E. Alexander, *Financing the 1968 Election* (Lexington, Mass.: Heath Lexington Books, 1971), p. 163.

act went into effect. Estimates put total receipts during that period at $43.3 million. More telling is the role of very large contributors in the Nixon campaign.[9] Records of the Finance Committee for the Re-election of the President, released as part of an out-of-court settlement of a Common Cause lawsuit, revealed a total of $19.9 million raised before the 1971 act went into effect on April 7, 1972; eighty-seven contributors of $50,000 or more contributed $12.4 million of that sum. Of the $43.3 million raised after April 7, $4.4 million was given by thirty-seven contributors of $50,000 or more. These large givers contributed $16.8 million, or 27.9 percent of all Nixon-Agnew campaign funds.

The McGovern campaign highlights the other side of modern giving. Only $13 million, or 30.2 percent of approximately $43 million raised after April 7, 1972, was in contributions of $100 or more; 86.8 percent of funds received by the Nixon campaign was in contributions of $100 or more. Thirteen givers of more than $50,000 gave $2.4 million to the McGovern campaign—only 4.9 percent of post–April 7 contributions.[10] (McGovern's campaign before April 7 is not fully accounted for, but the total sums were small—about $5 million—and mainly in very small contributions raised by mail solicitations.) McGovern received most of his money in small gifts from issue advocates who were not representative of the majority sentiment in the nation or in the party about either McGovern's platform or his personal qualifications.

The big-giver pattern also prevails in congressional campaigning. The Common Cause Study tallied $69.6 million in receipts reported under the 1971 act. Individual contributions accounted for $41.3 million (59.3 percent), while committee gifts, loans, and cash on hand on April 7 totaled $28.3 million (40.7 percent). More than 50 percent of individual contributions were over $100, and almost 30 percent were over $500 (see Table 3-3). Thirty-five donors of $20,000 or more gave $1.4 million in 1972 congressional races. These givers included leaders in publishing, insurance, data processing, manufacturing, and sports. The largest amounts, however, came from persons

TABLE 3-3   Individual Contributions to Congressional Campaigns

Amount of Contribution	Total Amount (Millions)	Per-cent	Senate Amount (Millions)	Per-cent	House Amount (Millions)	Per-cent
$100 or less	$19.6	47.5	$6.6	40.5	$13.0	52.0
$101–$499	9.5	23.0	4.4	27.0	5.1	20.4
$500 or more	12.2	29.4	5.3	32.5	6.9	27.6
Total	$41.3	99.9	$16.3	100.0	$25.0	100.0

SOURCE: Common Cause Study (see Chap. 2, n. 10).

linked to oil companies: they supplied $251,000 to congressional hopefuls.[11]

THE SELF-FINANCING CANDIDATE

The steady rise in campaign costs and the increasing difficulty of raising funds give men of means an increasing advantage in politics. Party workers, interest group leaders, and others are likely to recognize a wealthy candidate as a serious aspirant and therefore to give him weighty consideration in their own strategic planning. They will often endorse or support him because they want to be with a winner early or because they calculate that he will not seek as great a financial commitment from them as a less affluent candidate will.[12] Representative Bertram Podell of New York put it plainly:

> When I ran for Congress the first question asked me was whether I could finance my own campaign. If I had said, "No, I cannot," I would not have been a candidate. When you mention candidates for public office, you are only mentioning men of affluence.[13]

Not only does wealth give a candidate built-in advantages in waging his own campaign, it often has an intimidating effect on others. Potential opponents of modest means may be scared out of the race or they may divert their ambitions to other offices, fearing that they will be unable to compete against the money of a wealthy candidate.

In recent years the list of wealthy candidates has lengthened appreciably. It includes, among others, three Rockefellers, three Kennedys, Howard Metzenbaum, Milton Shapp, Pierre S. du Pont IV, and H. J. Heinz III. The Federal Election Campaign Act of 1971 limits contributions by candidates and their families to $50,000 in presidential races, $35,000 in Senate contests, and $25,000 in House campaigns. At least sixteen congressional candidates made gifts of $20,000 or more to their own campaigns in 1972.[14]

The 1971 act anomalously restricted a candidate from using his own money to campaign but allowed him to receive unlimited gifts from other individuals or from interest groups. The 1974 Federal Election Campaign Act reverses that oddity: it retains the 1971 limits for candidate spending but restricts contributions by individuals to $1,000 and by organizations to $5,000, once again restoring the rich candidate's edge over the hopeful who must solicit gifts from others. No matter how drafted, it is unlikely that statutory prohibitions will in any case completely eliminate the advantage of wealthy office seekers. The rich can usually win financial support from well-heeled friends and relatives.

Campaign finance scandals have ironically reduced opposition to the very rich candidate, lending plausibility to his assertion that because he is rich enough to bear his own campaign costs he need not become the captive of special interests. This increasing receptiveness to the personally financed candidate indirectly reimposes the means test for public office that has been discredited in American politics since the Jacksonian revolution of the 1830s.

INTEREST GROUP GIVING

Special interest contributions are as old as the Republic. New England merchants generously supported the Federalists in the first campaigns under the Constitution. During Franklin Delano Roosevelt's campaigns the modern pattern of interest group contributing evolved, and it has persisted.[15] Manufacturers, bankers, stockbrokers, and other financial interests have generally preferred the Republicans. Union labor has generally preferred the Democrats. Other groups, especially those directly reliant on government business or regulation, have been switch hitters, playing to whichever side seemed most likely to advance their interests and to both sides if necessary.

Oil companies, construction firms, truckers, and brewers are among the latter groups.[16] Organized crime, too, makes contributions and switches.[17] In recent years, doctors have played a large role in politics, lobbying actively on national health insurance, Medicare, and other advances of government into financing or regulating medicine.[18] Usually they have supported Republicans.

Tracing special interest money with accuracy is impossible. Some money passes under the table, especially where an interest is held in low esteem by the community or where a specific *quid pro quo* is at stake. The decentralization of American institutions also obscures the magnitude of special interest money. In 1968, for instance, the American Medical Political Action Committee reported $682,000 in expenditures at the national level, but three to four times that amount was spent by various state affiliates and was not reported nationally.[19] The proliferation of political committees permits special interest groups to contribute money to various party committees, which then transfer money to the candidates earmarked by the special interests. The candidates may be informed of the sources of large contributions; but because this money is mingled with many other contributions in the party treasury, the public cannot know which party candidates received the special interest funds.

Corporation executives use corporate facilities and staff to solicit large contributions; candidates travel in corporation aircraft; and corporate managers take company time for political activities. All these forms of support are unreported as campaign contributions. Finally, contributions made by individuals, such as corporation officers and directors, often cannot be linked to the special interests they represent. The 1971 act has for the first time prompted widespread disclosures of these gifts by requiring identification of contributors' principal occupations and business places.

Reported contributions by leaders of thirteen business and professional organizations—including the American Bar Association, American Medical Association, American Petroleum Institute, and American Iron and Steel Institute—totaled $751,900 in 1956, $493,500 in 1960, $468,200 in 1964, and in excess of $1.3 million in 1968.[20] Republicans received 98 percent of this money in 1956 and 88 percent in 1968. Only in 1964, when Goldwater was the Republican candidate, did business and professional interests contribute heavily to the national Democratic campaign.

Members of the Business Council, an elite group of those who own, finance, or manage the country's major enterprises, followed a similar pattern. Their gifts of $500 or more totaled $272,000 in 1956, $276,000 in 1960, $223,000 in 1964, and $364,000 in 1968. Between 40 and 60 percent of the members gave during those campaigns, compared with only 7 to 12 percent of all Americans. In 1972 Business Council contributions reflected the national trend toward larger gifts from an increased number of big givers. Total contributions rose to $1,169,000, and more than 80 percent of Business Council members gave. Their contributions went overwhelmingly to the Republicans in 1956 (99 percent), 1960 (87 percent), 1968 (77 percent), and 1972 (87 percent); but in 1964 they abandoned Goldwater in favor of Johnson and gave 61 percent of their dollars to the Democrats.[21]

In 1968, officers and directors of the twenty-five largest contractors with the Pentagon, the National Aeronautics and Space Administration, and the Atomic Energy Commission, together with the twenty-five largest corporations on *Fortune* magazine's list of the 500 largest industrial firms, gave $1.5 million in sums of $500 or more. In 1972, their gifts soared to $3.2 million. Like other businessmen, these company officials strongly preferred the Republicans. Eighty-three percent of these funds went to the GOP in 1968 and 86 percent in 1972.[22]

Two studies by Representative Les Aspin of Wisconsin have shown the magnitude of special interest giving to the Committee for the Re-election of the President. Contributions by officials of the hundred largest Department of Defense contractors totaled $5.4 million; all but fourteen companies made some contributions. Gulf Oil accounted for more than $1 million; sixteen firms provided more than $100,000 apiece; eleven more fell in the $50,000-to-$99,000 category. Almost two-thirds of the total, $3.2 million, was contributed before April 7, 1972, when the 1971 act took effect, and would have remained unknown if not for disclosures forced by a Common Cause lawsuit. Campaign contributions by 413 directors, senior officials, and stockholders of 178 leading oil companies totaled almost $5 million, according to Aspin. Again, Gulf Oil's $1,176,500 led the list. Ten other companies gave more than $100,000 apiece.[23]

Direct organizational giving in 1972 by nationally registered special interest groups and political party committees was $14 million to congressional candidates and $2.2 million to presidential hopefuls.[24] Additional organization contributions were apparently made by local and state groups that did not report in Washington. General election candidates for Congress reported receiving $3.1 million more from groups than nationally registered organizations reported giving.

Congressional candidates received total organizational contributions of $13.5 million in the general election, with $8.5 million coming from interest groups and $5 million from party committees. Of the party committee money, however, more than $1.3 million also came from special interest groups. Special interests therefore accounted, directly and indirectly, for $9.8 million in congressional gifts. All organizational contributions were 19.5 percent of the $69.7 million raised by congressional candidates running in the 1972 general election, while direct interest group gifts were 14 percent of that total.

Table 3-4 reports total contributions by leading interest groups to congressional candidates and party congressional campaign committees. The most prominent business committees were the Business-Industry Political Action Committee (BIPAC) with direct gifts to candidates and committees of $410,600, the banking industry with $119,900, and the construction industry with $218,200. The American Medical Association's AMPAC gave about $800,000. Three leading

TABLE 3-4   Direct Interest Group Contributions to Congressional Campaigns and Political Party Congressional Campaign Committees

Interest Group	Candidate Contributions	Party Contributions	Total
Business	$1,708,000	$ 490,000	$2,198,000
Agriculture	662,000	568,000	1,248,000
Health	947,000	32,000	979,000
Labor	3,633,000	197,000	3,830,000

SOURCE: Common Cause Study (see Chap. 2, n. 10).

dairy groups (ADEPT, SPACE, and TAPE) together contributed just under $600,000.

Business, agriculture, and health groups overwhelmingly favored Republicans with their campaign gifts, while labor groups heavily supported Democrats. Business gave Republicans $1.2 million and Democrats $500,000; agriculture groups provided $460,000 to Republicans and $201,000 to Democrats; health organizations supplied $755,000 to Republicans and $192,000 to Democrats. Labor's gifts to Democrats totaled $3.5 million, while Republicans received only $178,000 from unions.

Incumbents had a long lead in special interest contributions. Business favored incumbents with 66 percent of its funds, agriculture with 57 percent, health groups with 52 percent, and labor with 53 percent. Challengers rarely received significant help, underlining the advantage that incumbents have both in raising money and in scaring money away from their opponents. Interest group funds that were not given to incumbents mainly found their way into districts that had no incumbent seeking re-election. Business targeted 22 percent of its funds to these districts (compared with 12 percent to challengers); agriculture 30 percent (and only 13 percent to challengers); and health groups 31 percent (with 14 percent to challengers). Labor broke the pattern, giving 27 percent to challengers and 20 percent in districts with no incumbents.

An additional word must be said about labor's political financing.[25] Like business, health, professional, and agriculture groups, unions are a major source of campaign contributions. Unlike the others, their spending for in-house programs of political education, training, and activation may be greater than their direct campaign contributions. With at least 20 million union members and perhaps three times that number in union families, the labor movement is the only major source of campaign funds that also has a mass voting base. Massive internal spending for politics is therefore a wise strategy. Much of this money is drawn from dues payments and is never reported in campaign finance reports. Further, the in-house political action programs of hundreds of state and regional union groups and of thousands of local unions may not directly influence federal elections and therefore are not reported in Washington.

One characterization of labor's efforts in 1968, when it bent every resource to aid its long-time ally Hubert Humphrey, is drawn from COPE's own assessment and is reported by Theodore H. White:

> Registration, by labor's own efforts, of 4.6 million voters; the printing and distribution of 55 million pamphlets and leaflets out of Washington, 60 million more from local unions; telephone banks in 638 localities, using 8,055 telephones, manned by 24,611 union men and women and their families; some 72,225 house-to-house canvassers; and, on Election Day, 94,457 volunteers serving as car-poolers, materials-distributors, baby-sitters, poll-watchers, telephoners.[26]

Labor's total dollar effort is also staggering. In 1956, seventeen national labor committees reported total spending of $2.2 million. By 1964, thirty-one committees spent $3.7 million. The herculean labor effort of 1968 featured thirty-seven committees making total disbursements of $7.1 million.[27] A preliminary analysis of thirty-five labor committees spending more than $25,000 and registered with the comptroller general in 1972 revealed union expenditures of $14.8 million.[28] As much as two-thirds of these outlays were for in-house political activities, and only small amounts were contributed to presidential candidates because the AFL-CIO did not endorse a nominee in 1972. Millions of dollars were also presumably spent at the state and local levels by labor unions and their political committees for activities not covered by federal reporting requirements.

Direct labor contributions to Democratic presidential candidates have traditionally been a major source of support. Humphrey received $541,000 (almost 10 percent of his funds) in direct contributions from national labor committees in 1968, about one-third of it during the pre-convention period.[29] Other labor money from local and state union political committees also reached the Humphrey campaign, but no accounting can be made because of loopholes in disclosure provisions of the old Corrupt Practices Act. Although the AFL-CIO did not endorse a presidential candidate in 1972, the United Auto Workers endorsed George McGovern and the Teamsters endorsed President Nixon. Seventeen labor committees that have been closely studied contributed $966,000 to the McGovern campaign; UAW sources supplied two-thirds of this amount, and other substantial contributions came from the Machinists and the Communications Workers. The Nixon-Agnew campaign received $141,000 from these seventeen labor committees, primarily from the Seafarers International Union and the Laborers International Union.[30]

GIVING AND GETTING

- In 1970, representatives of the American Milk Producers, Inc., wrote President Nixon that they had contributed $135,000 to Republican congressional candidates and that they were interested in channeling $2 million to his campaign. In the same letter they protested Nixon's slowness in approving import quotas on ice cream and other dairy products. Within two weeks the quotas were approved.[31]
- In 1971, the President announced price supports for milk of $4.66 per hundredweight. Twelve days later the government support was raised to $4.93. In the meantime, campaign contributions from dairy political action groups had begun flowing to the Committee for the Re-election of the President, and dairy leaders had met with the President to talk about both price supports and campaign support. This support totaled at least $420,000 for 1971.[32]
- Former Commerce Secretary Maurice Stans and other Nixon campaign fund raisers set a quota of 1 percent of a wealthy man's net worth or 1 percent of a company's gross annual sales as "expected" contributions to the Nixon re-election effort. Often these quotas were scaled down to a standard $100,000. At least eleven major American companies have been found guilty of illegal corporate contributions—American Airlines, Minnesota Mining and Manufacturing, Goodyear Tire and Rubber, Braniff Airways, Gulf Oil, Ashland Petroleum Banon, Phillips Petroleum, Carnation, Diamond International, Northrop Corporation, and Lehigh Valley Cooperative Farmers. Columnist Jack Anderson has reported that, presumably as a reward for generosity, Ashland won governmental approval for an oil agreement with Iran that will produce billions of dollars in sales for the company. And American Airlines won White House support to name a Civil Aeronautics Board commissioner favorable to the company's merger and expansion plans.[33]
- In 1970, opposing the recommendation of his own Cabinet task force, President Nixon refused to abolish oil import quotas. The effect of this refusal was to make prices for oil consumers higher by about $5 billion annually. Oil men had lobbied heavily against abolishing the import quotas. Certain oil executives had contributed at least $500,000 to the 1968 Nixon-Agnew campaign chest, and Representative Aspin's figures indicate they gave nearly $5 million in 1972.[34]
- In 1972, the American Medical Association's Political Action

Committee contributed $76,000 to twenty-three House members and $20,000 to fifteen senators who had sponsored Medicredit, the AMA's alternative to national health insurance. It also supported nine members of the House Interstate and Foreign Commerce Committee, which handles all major health legislation except health insurance. Both Democrats and Republicans received AMA dollars. Special interest groups contribute to key committee members and bill sponsors regardless of political party affiliation.[35]

- Senator Vance Hartke's presidential primary campaign received $10,000 from the Brotherhood of Railway, Airline and Steamship Clerks, $7,800 from the United Transportation Union, and $1,000 from the Seafarers Union. Hartke, whose presidential ambitions were never taken seriously, is chairman of the Commerce Subcommittee on Surface Transportation.[36]
- Senator John Sparkman of Alabama, then chairman of the Senate Banking, Housing and Urban Affairs Committee, received $16,100 from the Banking Profession Political Action Committee. Their support was stimulated partly from fear that if Sparkman was defeated, Senator William Proxmire, frequently at odds with the bankers, would become committee chairman.[37]
- Calvin Kevens, head of a Florida construction company, who was convicted in a mail fraud trial also involving former Teamsters Union president James Hoffa, contributed $30,000 to the 1972 Nixon campaign. In January, 1972, Kevens had been pardoned early from a federal prison.[38]
- In 1972, maritime unions contributed at least $622,000 to presidential and congressional campaigns. For years these unions have been contributing heavily to campaigns and lobbying Congress, successfully, to continue subsidies to the nation's uncompetitive and dwindling merchant marine.[39]
- Dairy cooperatives contributed more than $50,000 to Representative Wilbur Mills' quixotic 1972 bid for the Democratic presidential nomination. Mills was chairman of the House Ways and Means Committee, which writes tax legislation important to dairymen as well as to most other special interest groups.[40]
- As Governor of Maryland and perhaps as Vice President, Spiro Agnew received "political contributions" from government contractors amounting to between 3 and 5 percent of the value of the contracts awarded them. Agnew apparently kept 50 percent of the contributions and turned the other half over to political cronies.[41]
- Reports from Philadelphia indicate that 5 percent of the value of a public works contract must be contributed to political party committees; in New Orleans a 10 percent "finders fee" for public works contracts goes to politicians.[42]

- In New Jersey, sixty-eight officials have been indicted and forty-six convicted in a three-and one-half-year period for extorting kickbacks, allegedly for campaign funding, mainly from engineering firms. The convicted include a former Democratic congressman, a Democratic mayor of Newark, and a Democratic state secretary of state as well as a former Republican state secretary of state and other officials of the Republican state administration. Alleging that, across the country, public officials frequently require kickbacks from architects and engineers, the executive director of the American Institute of Architects has said: "It stinks: the whole business of financing campaigns stinks. The architect is put into a box he can't get out of. He's a cow to be milked."[43]

- In Illinois, a stock brokerage firm contributed $20,000 to a fund-raising dinner to pay off the campaign debts of Governor Daniel Walker; a partner in the firm bought an additional $6,000 in tickets. In the same month, the firm was retained as adviser to the state on a $100 million bond issue, with a fee estimated at $75,000 to $100,000.[44]

- Nine Nixon appointees as ambassadors or heads of foreign missions each contributed more than $20,000 to the President's 1972 re-election campaign; their gifts totaled $1.1 million. Of thirty-four non-career heads of foreign missions appointed by President Nixon during his first term, fifteen had contributed a total of $252,000 to his 1968 campaign. Dr. Ruth Farkas, who gave more than $200,000 to the Nixon campaign after the 1972 election, was nominated as ambassador to Luxembourg in February, 1973. Her nomination was held up by the Senate until the Comptroller General confirmed her assertion that she had pledged $300,000 before the election and had simply waited until afterwards to obtain a better price for the securities she and her husband used to pay the pledge.[45]

- In Chicago and Cook County, in Indiana, in Pennsylvania, in New York, and in other cities, counties, and states, public employees are regularly "maced"—that is, they must contribute a percentage of their salaries to the political party in power as campaign contributions.[46]

These real or apparent abuses do not, of course, exhaust the list of contributor or candidate motives. Many contribute because they support a candidate's record or platform, because of party loyalty, because of personal friendship with a candidate or fund raiser, or because of their sense of civic duty.[47] Some give money for wholly nonpolitical reasons—to please a friend or business associate who solicits them. Despite the decent motives of many, and probably most, contributors, the private financing system in the United States embodies powerful elements of undue influence, unequal access, extortion, and class bias.

Few Americans contribute to politics, and those who do are disproportionately from upper socio-economic classes. A handful of Americans are truly big givers, making contributions ranging from $10,000 to more than $2 million. Established interest groups—business, health, agriculture, and labor—loom large in financing candidates, and some spend additional money for direct political action. Occasionally an ideological candidate, especially for the presidency, wins an outpouring of small contributions by appealing to a narrow segment of the population which is highly polarized on deeply felt issues.

The pattern of giving distorts American elections: candidates win access to the electorate only if they can mobilize money from the upper classes, established interest groups, big givers, or ideological zealots. Other alternatives have difficulty getting heard. And the voters' choice is thereby limited. The pattern of giving also threatens the governmental process: the contributions of big givers and interest groups award them access to officeholders, so they can better plead their causes. In some cases, contributions directly corrupt government by purchasing decisions. In others, governmental power is brought to bear, directly or implicitly, to squeeze contributions from those subject to governmental regulation or retaliation.

The private financing system does not supply enough money for politics, and the funds it does provide distort both elections and decision making. The equality of citizens on election day is diluted by their inequality in campaign financing. The electorate shares its control of officials with the financial constituency. Campaign financing policy should assure sufficient money for vigorous campaigns in a way that allows all citizens a roughly equal opportunity to participate in financing as well as voting and that eliminates the disproportionate influence of outright corruption that marks existing contributing practices.

The Progressives ushered in the first sweeping campaign finance regulations in the United States. Watergate touched off a second wave of reforms. Like many Progressive programs, such as utility and railroad rate regulation, limitation was the central principle of political finance legislation, with full disclosure playing an important supporting role. The third general thrust toward reform, public subsidies, died aborning in the Progressive era. Although Theodore Roosevelt called for public funding in 1907, the idea was not adopted either at the national level or in those innovative states that served as laboratories for Progressive programs.

By the 1950s, reformers were disillusioned with limitations, particularly those on campaign spending. Full disclosure became the main hope for reform before Watergate, and public financing was mentioned with greater and greater frequency. The spark of Watergate ignited a conflagration that again heated public enthusiasm for limitations, kept bright the faith in disclosure, and swept the national government and eight states to public financing of campaigns.

Many still argue that the traditional reform principles of limitation and disclosure will make campaign financing consistent with democratic principles; public financing is therefore unneces-

LIMITATIONS
AND
LOOPHOLES

sary. We find nothing in the history, practice, or theory of limitations and disclosure, which we consider here and in the next two chapters, to support that view. These conventional approaches are essential components of any successful reform, but neither alone nor together can they democratize campaign financing.

The number and variety of limitations imposed on campaign money are a testament to the political ingenuity and imagination of the Progressives. So sweeping were their experiments that even the rush of new legislation following Watergate embodied few new ideas. All these regulatory packages, old and new, are variations on four general approaches: (1) limiting the amount any individual can give to a candidate or political committee, (2) limiting the institutional sources of campaign gifts, (3) limiting the uses of campaign funds, and (4) limiting the amounts spent.

CURBING BIG GIVERS

The Progressives attempted to curb undue contributor influence over officials by limiting the amount that any person could give to any candidate. Secondarily, contribution limits would curb the special campaign advantages of rich candidates or those backed by wealthy interests. Here the concern is not undue influence, for the candidates hold views consistent with those of the wealthy, but rather the unfair access to voters gained by small groups of wealthy citizens sponsoring a compatible candidate. These arguments prompted many states to enact contribution limits; and the Hatch Act of 1939 set a ceiling of $5,000 on campaign gifts to federal office candidates.

By 1971, however, interest in contribution limits had waned. Only seven states restricted the size of gifts.[1] And in 1972, Congress repealed the Hatch Act's individual contribution limits (except for candidates) in the Federal Election Campaign Act. Despite the endorsement of such limits by the President's Commission on Campaign Costs in 1962, reformers and legislators had become discouraged because contribution ceilings had proved largely unworkable. The majority of members of the Twentieth Century Fund Task Force on Financing Congressional Campaigns reflected the general despair. "Several members of the Task Force favor a limit on the amount an individual, including the candidate himself, may contribute to a campaign," the Task Force observed. "However, we were unable to prescribe an effective device for enforcing such a recommendation," and "we were reluctant to recommend anything that we did not think could be enforced."[2]

Similarly, in testimony before the Senate Commerce Committee on the Federal Election Campaign Act of 1971, Deputy Attorney General Richard Kleindienst portrayed contribution limits as "ineffective, unrealistic, and incapable of enforcement." He, like most modern reformers, emphasized that if there were full disclosure, large or special interest giving "becomes an issue among all the others on which the voter makes his judgment, and limitations are established at the ballot box."[3] Presumably politicians anticipate these public reactions and impose limits on their own conduct to avoid retaliation at the polls.

Loopholes and Evasion. Most laws were drafted to limit an individual's gift to each candidate and committee. By multiplying support committees, a candidate could receive contributions from the same individual up to the legal limit for each committee. To avoid the $5,000 contribution limit, the Humphrey-Muskie managers created more than ninety-five different committees in 1968.[4] (In addition, this procedure allowed givers to break up their large total contributions into sums of $3,000 to many different committees, thus avoiding the federal gift tax on amounts over $3,000.)

Evasions are also possible at the giving end. Many members of a large, wealthy family can each give up to the legal limit to the same candidate or committee. In 1968, thirty-two Du Ponts gave $107,000, twenty-two Mellons contributed $299,000, twenty-one Rockefellers supplied $1.8 million, eleven Pews accounted for $214,000, and so forth.[5] A large number of wealthy persons associated with the same profession, business, or interest can channel individual contributions within the legal spending limit to the same candidate or committee. If the checks are all delivered by the same messenger at the same time, the interested nature of the total contribution is not lost on the candidate and his staff.

The decentralization of American parties also erodes contribution limits. Once a contributor has made his maximum lawful contribution to a candidate, he can give the legal maximum to each of a series of political party committees, earmarking the funds for his favored candidate. This technique also "launders" political gifts by concealing the identity of givers. Increasingly, legislation prohibits such laundering. To avoid the law contributors simply make their checks to a party committee and give it to the candidate. His delivery of the money to the party committee implicitly signals party leaders that the money is intended for his campaign. This practice is especially hard to detect, since officeholders often have a role in party fund raising that does not involve earmarking.

Another circumvention uses the federal system, by channeling money through political committees in other states. A contributor gives money to an out-of-state political committee, which in turn contributes it to the donor's designated candidate in his home state.

Technically the contribution is from the out-of-state committee. These transactions were especially difficult to trace in the pre-Watergate period, when contributions could be passed through political committees in one of the dozen jurisdictions that did not require reporting of receipts. Most have now closed this loophole.

Finally, contribution limits can be evaded if the donor spends money directly to support a candidate after he has given the maximum gift allowed by law. Because past contribution limits have been loosely drawn, this avoidance has not been often practiced. General Motors heir Stewart Mott spent about $100,000 on newspaper advertising urging Nelson Rockefeller to become a presidential candidate in 1968.[6] Although Mott's direct spending was not aimed at bypassing contribution limits, others could follow his direct spending format for that purpose.

Wealthy Candidates: A Special Problem. The usual objection that big contributors might unduly influence officeholders does not apply to the wealthy candidate financing his own campaign. Apprehension turns instead on the rich candidate's unequal access to voters simply because he is wealthy. Without even a modest following among voters, he can pay for a vigorous campaign. And, of course, when a wealthy candidate also is allied with a particular interest group, his fortune serves both to advance his personal ambitions and to give unusual campaign advantages to that special interest.

Will Rogers once remarked that the United States Senate was the best that money could buy.[7] His comment reflected the Senate's historical reputation as a rich man's club. Temporarily, during the New Deal era, wealthy candidates became less prominent in America. But the post-war years have been marked by a resurgence of self-financing aspirants. One commentator has estimated that Nelson Rockefeller's 1964 and 1968 presidential nomination bids involved $10 million of family money and that another $10 to $12 million supported his four successful New York gubernatorial campaigns. In Rockefeller's 1970 gubernatorial race, family funds accounted for $4.1 million of total outlays of $6.8 million. His brother Winthrop invested at least $5 million in his 1966, 1968, and 1970 Arkansas gubernatorial races and in rebuilding that state's Republican party.[8]

Others do not even approach the Rockefeller standard, but their outlays are nonetheless dazzling to mere citizens. The Kennedy clan has always been more tightfisted and close-mouthed about their campaign financing, but one estimate put Joseph Kennedy's personal outlays for John Kennedy's presidential campaign, beginning in 1958, at a minimum of $1.5 million.[9] Kennedy money was also used indirectly to help John's campaign: family members set up a corporation to rent an airplane that was leased inexpensively to the campaign, Kennedy family retainers were set to work as campaign staffers, and Kennedy influence was used to raise money from others.

In his search for the Pennsylvania governorship, Milton Shapp spent $3.8 million in 1966 and $2.7 million in 1970, most of it from personal funds.[10] Congressman Richard Ottinger spent $2 million to win the 1970 Democratic senatorial nomination in New York and a still larger amount to lose the general election; virtually all his financing came from his family, which had founded U.S. Plywood. Norton Simon's nomination quest cost him almost as much, $1.9 million, in California's 1970 Republican senatorial primary, which he lost. And Howard Metzenbaum laid out more than $800,000 of his own money to beat former astronaut John Glenn in Ohio's United States Senate primary in 1970 and to be beaten in turn by Robert Taft, Jr., in the general election.[11]

These high-spending campaigns by wealthy candidates in the late 1960s and in 1970 aparently had an impact on Congress. The Federal Election Campaign Act of 1971 emerged from Congress with only one limit on giving: a candidate or his family could not contribute to his own campaign more than $50,000 in each nomination and election contest for president and vice president, $35,000 for the Senate, and $25,000 for the House. A candidate's family was defined broadly by the act to include his spouse, child, parent, grandparent, sibling, and their spouses. Family members might, by passing money through political parties or independent committees, find themselves in violation of the act's ban on making contributions in the name of another person, and the candidate might find himself in violation of the companion provision against knowingly accepting contributions made by one person in the name of another.

These limits on family giving had a heavy incumbency bias, which made them acceptable to members of Congress. In ordinary circumstances, the sitting member carefully retains the support of major contributors and special interests in his district. If he doesn't become lazy, he steadily cements his relations with the party organization, mass membership groups, and major media outlets. He carefully wins the friendship of all those who can offer significant resources in a primary contest. Within the limits imposed by opposition party activity, he woos those who might supply money, manpower, and talent in the general election.

The one formidable challenge he cannot easily forestall is from the ambitious, self-financed, "instant" candidate who attempts to offset the incumbent's advantages with an expensive and skillful campaign that ignores traditional support bases and employs broadcast media advertising, public opinion polls, and computerized mass mailings.

The act created the anomalous situation in which a candidate could lawfully be supported by hundred-thousand-dollar gifts from the specially interested but not by his own personal wealth. Thus Mr. Nixon's support from the Clement Stones, Bebe Rebozos, Walter Annenbergs, and others was sanctioned by law; but Nelson Rockefeller's support from his own family was outlawed. If Congress had set out to develop the worst of all possible schemes to restrict individual contributions, it could not have done better than the 1971 act.

Contribution Limits after Watergate. The orgy of big giving in the 1972 presidential race renewed interest in contribution limits. By August, 1974, the number of states imposing ceilings on campaign gifts had risen from seven to seventeen. Most hold donations to gubernatorial campaigns under $5,000, and New Jersey sets the lowest limit, $600, which is matchable under that state's public financing plan. Congress also reinstated contribution limits for federal office candidates in the Federal Election Campaign Act of 1974. The new law:

- Limits an individual's annual contribution to a candidate for federal office to $1,000 in each election. Primaries, run-offs, and general elections are considered separate elections, except that the pre-nomination period in presidential campaigns is considered a single election. Gifts made in a non-election year to support a candidate are counted as gifts in the year of the election.
- Limits an individual's total aggregate annual political contributions to candidates for federal offices to $25,000.
- Prohibits a person's aggregate direct spending to support a candidate from exceeding $1,000 in any year.
- Limits contributions by any political committee to any candidate to $5,000 in each election.
- Reduces a candidate's contributions to his own campaign to an aggregate of $50,000 for president, $35,000 for senator, and $25,000 for representative in all elections rather than in each election separately; excludes family members' contributions of their own funds from this limit, to cure constitutional problems raised by limits on participation due solely to consanguinity; and imposes the $1,000 individual contribution limit on family members.
- Provides that any earmarked or indirect gifts are counted against the contribution limits established by law.
- Bans all contributions by foreign nationals.
- Bans cash contributions to any candidate that exceed $100 in the aggregate.
- Requires that all expenditures, except petty cash outlays not exceeding $100, be made by check.

These contribution limits are the most comprehensive in American history and are substantially lower than most of those adopted previously. Prohibiting significant cash contributions and expenditures helps enforce the limits. The ban on contributions by foreign nationals and the provision regulating indirect and earmarked gifts guard against laundering. And the $1,000 limit on expenditures beyond the contribution limit prevents avoidance of contribution ceilings by direct campaign spending.

The $1,000 individual limit is severe by any standard, allowing a husband and wife who contribute the maximum in both the primary and general elections to give a total of only $4,000 to a candidate. The $25,000 maximum for each individual's aggregate contributions prevents big givers from amassing influence by contributing in many different campaigns or channeling massive sums to a single candidate through various intermediary committees.

These two provisions apply, however, only to contributions to candidates for federal offices. Unlimited contributions can still be made to national, state, and local party committees, which can spend money for activities indirectly assisting a candidate such as registering voters, getting out the vote, building party organizations, and preparing research materials. To be fully effective, the law should also impose the $1,000 limit on gifts to committees and apply the $25,000 aggregate limit to contributions to political groups as well as candidates.

The $5,000 limit on committee gifts is also very low by past standards. The limit does not, however, prevent multiple committee giving; hence the district, state, and national committees of the same interest group can each give up to $5,000. Congress did not take a widely recommended step to block undue influence through multiple committee giving: limit the percentage of a candidate's funds (or of his expenditure limit) that could be received in committee gifts. It did, however, try to prevent the calculated multiplication of committees for this purpose during campaigns. The $5,000 committee limit is available only to groups registered for more than six months, receiving contributions from more than fifty persons, and making gifts to five or more candidates for federal offices. Other groups are subject to the $1,000 individual contribution limit. These precautions disturb some who say they will also prevent $5,000 gifts by groups formed late in a campaign either in response to newly emerging controversies or in late recognition of a candidate's posture on a significant problem.

Finally, there is some concern that the new, low individual and committee limits reverse the anomaly of ceilings on candidate contributions that existed under the 1971 act. Even with their somewhat reduced contribution limits, candidates are now permitted to give vastly more to their own campaigns than are other individuals and political committees. The rich candidate again has an advantage in being able to provide his own start-up fund while the candidate of modest means must find many backers to do so. Indeed, the $25,000 that a House candidate can contribute to his own canvass is almost 36 percent of his $70,000 spending limit in each primary or general election and 18 percent of his total expenditure ceiling in the two.

RESTRICTING THE SOURCES

Lawmakers have more readily limited the sources of money than the size of gifts. Certain elements in society, they fear, are very strongly motivated to influence or to corrupt government and must therefore be kept out of campaigns. Conversely, some restrictions on sources of funds protect those vulnerable to extortion by politicians. Restrictions also help maintain confidence in the integrity of government by assuring a suspicious public that prominent special interests are not a significant source of campaign gifts.

Thus, thirty states and the federal government have enacted a variety of restrictions on campaign giving by identifiable interests. They ban direct contributions by corporations, sometimes singling out such particular business interests as banks, utilities, or railroads. In Florida, holders of horse and dog racing permits and holders of licenses to sell alcoholic beverages are prohibited from contributing, apparently in an attempt to thwart trafficking in these governmental franchises. Eight states and the national government prohibit contributions from union dues money.[12]

The federal law has long contained a provision prohibiting any person or firm negotiating or holding a contract with the government from making contributions. The 1974 law makes clear, however, that this does not prevent gifts by voluntary political fund groups associated with such contractors. Contributions by or solicitation of government employees have been regulated to prevent forced giving. A recent limitation on political "contributions" is the 1971 act's ban on the use of War on Poverty funds for any registration drive or campaign activity.

One other restriction on contributions involves unpaid debts incurred by campaigners. In recent years a number of campaigns, including the 1968 primary effort of Robert Kennedy and the presidential campaign of Hubert Humphrey, have run up large credit accounts that they were unable to pay. Businessmen can carry these as collectable accounts for a reasonable duration. But eventually they must either settle them at a reduced rate or label them uncollectable and write them off on taxes. In either case, the firm has in effect made an indirect contribution to a political campaign. The dollar difference between what is finally collected plus what is recovered through tax write-offs and the value of the goods and services rendered accrues as a gift to the candidate or party.

A special facet of the problem involves regulated industries, which often are afraid to deny or cut off credit because the severed creditor may, after all, soon be naming the regulators. The Federal Election Campaign Act of 1971 required the Civil Aeronautics Board, the Federal Communications Commission, and the Interstate Commerce Commission to promulgate regulations prescribing the conditions under which credit will be extended to candidates by regulated industries. These agencies have now done so, relieving the pressure on those industries.

Provisions limiting corporation gifts have had only limited effect. Individual contributions are often substituted for institutional gifts, but the result is the same. When corporate officers and directors contribute substantially to politics, everyone believes that the corporation's interests are being advanced. Corporation officers and directors are a major source of funding in the United States. For example, studies of federal elections and of politics in Wisconsin, Michigan, and Connecticut have shown very heavy support for the Republican Party from banking, financial, utility, and heavy manufacturing interests. The Nixon-Agnew ticket benefited in 1972 from unprecedented gifts by officers and directors of oil companies and government contractors.

In recent years, an increase has been noticed in the number of political action groups associated with corporations and trade associations. These groups accentuate the fact that the campaign gifts are from identifiable economic interests and are not merely the random contributions of individuals. Typically a corporation political action group solicits voluntary contributions from officers and management employees and later disburses these funds to candidates or party committees. Sometimes solicitations are made on the corporation's premises and the books are handled by its accountants. Trade or professional associations operate in much the same way, but their funds are raised from a broader base of members.

The development of corporate and trade association political groups parallels the earlier development of labor unions' voluntary political action committees. Unions have operated political education committees for years. Acting through affiliated committees in individual locals and through the dues-supported political apparatus of the union, these committees have collected contributions from large numbers of union members to support candidates for federal office and for state office in those states that ban contributions of dues money. In most states, labor stretches its influence by using its dues money to support state and local candidates and diverting its voluntary money to aid federal candidates who cannot receive funds directly from the union treasury. Occasionally, individual union leaders make substantial contributions, but usually labor gifts are institutional transfers because individual union members and most union officers simply do not have sufficient personal resources to make a substantial individual impact.

In addition to the voluntary committee device for avoiding statutory limits on giving, both business and labor make substantial in-kind contributions (the use of facilities, gifts of postage stamps, transportation in corporation aircraft, and other comparable support) and engage in sweeping programs of "political education." Under most state and federal laws in-kind support is a political contribution unless it involves voluntary personal services. But the line between voluntary and paid services is obscure. Many union staffers devote considerable on-duty time to politics; corporation officers use company offices and time to solicit political gifts; employees are permitted to engage in political activity during working hours. While an argument can be made that this encourages good citizenship, it still is a contribution of corporation and union funds to campaigns.

Corporations and unions vigorously pursue activities labeled political education, but many of these activities have distinct partisan or campaign effects. For example, union campaigns to register voters and get out the vote tend, because of the known political leanings of union members and their families, to benefit Democratic candidates. Similarly, selective publicizing of legislative voting records aids Democrats because of the congruence between that party's views and those of most union members on economic issues. Some corporations and many unions define political education as the training of personnel in legislative and campaign activities, but those who receive training are usually identified with the active leadership of the firm or union and therefore will aid particular candidates or causes that the institutional leadership favors.

Many union and corporation political activities, previously conducted in a cloudy area under the law, were finally overtly permitted by the Federal Election Campaign Act of 1971. Excluded from the regulated categories of contributions and expenditures were fund raising for segregated voluntary campaign funds, non-partisan registration and get-out-the-vote drives, and communications with stockholders or union members "on any subject." The families of union members and stockholders were also included in these permissible institutional activities.

The array of legislative attempts to curb contributions from various sources raises serious questions quite apart from the demonstrated unworkability of most of these laws. Foremost among them is what role private institutions should play in the electoral process. European democracies accept the legitimacy of political activities on the part of private institutions, since they are directly affected by government policy. Unions and corporations contribute money to parties and candidates from their treasuries, engage in direct advertising about public issues, and participate in the whole range of political activities.

The American view, on the other hand, is based on fear that these private institutions, which possess massive resources, will dominate government policy making. Further, Americans tend to feel that the leaders of economic institutions do not speak for their members or shareholders on political matters. But even if institutional leaders could correctly be described as representing most members, there would still be a concern for the political preferences of minority elements. This concern is heightened where membership is not voluntary, as in the case of the union shop.[13]

Americans also recognize that our political parties are not structured to check the influence that can be won by campaign contributors. European parties are highly ideological, making it difficult for an incompatible interest group to gain much clout by making campaign contributions. One cannot imagine, for instance, that industry could gain a major foothold with the German Social Democrats by contributing to the party treasury. American parties, by contrast, are coalitional, welcoming every group in society. Although it cannot dominate the Democratic party, business can easily work its way into the decision-making process. Republicans, as the Teamsters have shown, are not exclusively a business-oriented party.

The danger of direct institutional gifts is heightened by the American separation-of-powers arrangement. Not only can interests seek influence separately in the Congress and the presidency; they can search out key pressure points in Congress, such as powerful committees or committee chairmanships, and pour their energies and money into elections for those seats. A central governmental leadership that imposes party discipline, takes a national perspective, and makes close calculations about national policy and national electoral response can better balance many different interests and political factors and thus check against undue institutional influence in politics. Such a leadership exists in some European democracies but not in ours.

There seems, then, a sound basis for limiting the role in campaign finance of such private institutions as unions and corporations. Not only do they threaten to overwhelm private citizens in politics, but they also may be quite unrepresentative of their own members. And the impact of their massive resources is heightened by the decentralization and pragmatism of American government and parties. The problem has been, first, to define those institutions that must be limited. Banning corporate contributions in twenty-seven states while curbing union giving in only four, as has been done, does not solve the problem; and banning associational activity by corporation executives or union members simply because of contractual relationships with the government is not a solution. Since the government's role in a modern industrial democracy is large and growing, more and more citizens will have their political activities curtailed because of some economic relationship to government at just the time when the scope of government heightens both its impact on citizens and their need to participate in elections and policy making.

Regulatory legislation has failed to reflect a deliberate balance between the need to limit institutional giving and the merit of protecting individual participation in politics. As long as individuals are closely linked to institutions, especially in leadership roles, and as long as they give large sums of money that potentially influence governmental policy, this balance will be difficult to strike. What is needed is a policy that at once bans institutional giving yet does not bar voluntary associations of individuals even if these are formed along economic lines.

LIMITING THE USES OF MONEY

While curbs on the size and sources of gifts regulate the relationship between contributors and politicians, limits on spending regulate the relationship between politicians and voters. "Segmental" limits aim at specific kinds of expenditures, either to curb total spending by restricting certain high-cost activities or to ban campaign techniques regarded as immoral or improper. Some segmental limits mandate what campaign activities money may be spent for and by implication exclude other outlays.

At the simplest level, segmental limits ban the bribery of voters. Some states also restrict the value of campaign novelties and entertainments given to electors. These rules are designed to prevent monetary motives from replacing free voter evaluation of candidates and issues.

Because motives are difficult to define, some states prohibit candidates from making payments to those who might be induced to exercise their unusual influence in elections. Hence Wisconsin bans salaries or payments by candidates to newspaper editors and radio station owners. These restrictions can be circumvented, however, when candidates purchase advertising at outrageous rates with the implicit understanding that editorial endorsements and favorable news coverage will follow. A few states have prohibited election day expenses or salaries for campaign workers, fearing that candidates will give money to local power brokers who can deliver certain vote blocs. Precinct committeemen and leaders of closely knit racial or ethnic populations have often been the target of this legislation.

As recently as 1974, sixteen states had provisions prescribing the purposes for which money could be spent.[14] These legitimate campaign expenses typically included headquarters and hall rental, postage and other mailing expenses, campaign literature, posters and banners, advertising in print and broadcast media, wages and expenses of campaign personnel, buttons and matchbooks and other novelty items, and whatever else was familiar to the legislators who drafted the law. One commentator has pointed out that Oklahoma approved expenses for transporting ill, poor, or infirm voters to the polls and notes that by implication "the transportation of healthy, vigorous voters is apparently illegal!"[15]

There can be little question that the ban on bribing voters is proper and on some occasions useful. But other regulations and enumerations of spending are ill conceived. First, it is doubtful what the public interest is in specifying which among otherwise legal activities may be supported by campaign funds. The quality of campaigning is difficult to guarantee by the choice of campaign methods.

Second, the prescription of approved campaign methods very quickly becomes antique. Campaign technology changes as fast as other communications. Many unrevised state laws ignore a wide range of modern campaign methods: television, public opinion polls, and computerized mail appeals. Third, it is difficult to write statutory limits specifically enough. Does a sanction of "postage" and "brochures" include a computerized letter which, while mass-produced, is given the appearance of personalization? Fourth, enforcement of such laws is difficult. The public is not likely to support prosecution for campaign activities that are legal when engaged in for nonpolitical purposes.

Finally, the regulation of some expenditures usually displaces money to other campaign activities. The most significant modern experiment with segmental campaign spending limits was the Campaign Communications Reform Act of 1971. It restricted spending for communications media and especially for radio and television advertising. The act's purposes were twofold: to limit overall campaign spending, and to curb the saturation radio and television advertising blitz that had become common in the late 1960s and in 1970. The act failed on both counts, and it was repealed by the 1974 law. Its lesson about the usefulness of segmental spending limits is so significant, however, that we analyze its operation and effects fully elsewhere (see Chapter 5 below).

Schemes either prescribing or proscribing specific campaign expenditures—except the bribery of voters, election officials, and others involved in administering elections—are not likely to be useful or workable.

LIMITING TOTAL EXPENDITURES

The favorite Progressive reform was limiting total campaign spending. As recently as 1965, thirty states and the national government still had limits on total expenditures. The Federal Corrupt Practices Act of 1925 imposed ceilings on general election expenditures by candidates for federal office: $3 million for interstate political committees; $5,000, or three cents multiplied by the number of votes cast in the last election but not to exceed $25,000, for Senate candidates; $2,500, or three cents multiplied by the number of votes cast in the last general election but not to exceed $5,000, for House candidates. State laws invoked one of four limitation formulas: an actual cash limit; a limit based on some percentage of the salary of the office at stake; a limit based on a fixed amount for each vote cast in the last election; a limit based on a fixed amount for each registered voter.[16]

The Decline of Spending Limits. The post-war trend, until Watergate, was away from spending limits. Studies by the Committee for Economic Development, the Twentieth Century Fund Task Force on Financing Congressional Campaigns, the President's Commission on Campaign Costs, and the National Municipal League explicitly rejected expenditure ceilings.[17] A leading scholar of political finance said that "the case in favor of imposing limits on spending is simplistic, not realistic."[18] From 1965 to 1971, at least eight states and the national government repealed laws limiting total campaign expenditures while only one state enacted such limits. The number of states with spending ceilings had fallen to twenty-three in 1971.[19] The usual replacement for spending controls was full disclosure of receipts and expenditures, a reform we consider fully in Chapter 6.

Disenchantment with spending limits arose from bad experiences and from serious questions about their wisdom. Most spending limits had virtually no effect. First, they were without exception too low to reflect the realities of modern campaigning. The Federal Corrupt Practices Act set a $3 million limit for interstate committees, but as long ago as 1920 Republicans reported spending $4.4 million for their presidential candidate.[20] When presidential campaign costs had risen to almost $11 million for the Democrats and $25 million for the Republicans in 1968, the $3 million limit was still on the books.

Spending limits on gubernatorial campaigns were scoffed at in states like Arizona ($2,500), Ohio ($5,000), and Wisconsin ($10,000).

Second, spending ceilings were often fixed by erroneous criteria. Some states set them as a percentage of the salary for the contested office. But this practice views campaigning as a strictly personal enterprise, related only to the candidate's economic interest in winning office. It ignores other motivations for a political career and, most important, it overlooks the public's interest in vigorous campaigning that presents alternatives to voters. Third, limits on campaign spending rarely acknowledge inflation, larger electorates, heightened competition, developing campaign technologies, and other changing factors that affect political costs. Even if set originally at realistic levels, spending limits very soon become obsolete.

Finally, spending limits were rarely enforced. Sometimes laws were so badly drafted that evasion was easy. Expenditure ceilings applied to candidates but not to supporting committees, for instance. Few laws specified how expenditure limits would apply to outlays by party committees on behalf of an entire slate of candidates. Similarly, would expenses by unions, business political action committees, and similar groups to inform members of candidate records or recommendations be covered by statutory spending limits? Even where limits were clearly transgressed, the law was generally viewed as so unreasonable that enforcement officials did not act. The Twentieth Century Fund Task Force on Financing Congressional Campaigns reflected the general sentiment when it concluded that expenditure ceilings "are unenforceable and while some members of the Task Force would prefer legal limits we believe that no workable set of limits can be devised."[21]

Spending Limits after Watergate. The outpouring of money in the second Nixon-Agnew campaign, the stigma on campaign money that followed Watergate, and rising expenditures in state races triggered new support for spending limits. By the fall of 1974 the number of states with expenditure ceilings had risen to thirty-four, from twenty-three in 1971.[22] States with limits already on their statute books also acted, making spending ceilings more realistic and enforceable.

Less than three years after it repealed the spending limits of the Corrupt Practices Act, Congress reinstated such limits in the Federal Election Campaign Act of 1974. These provisions were the most sweeping in American history. The new legislation:

- Sets spending limits for candidates in presidential general elections at $20 million and in presidential primaries at $10 million. In primaries, a candidate may not spend more in any state than twice as much as a primary candidate for senator.

- Limits outlays by candidates for senator in primaries to the greater of eight cents times the voting age population or $100,000, and in general elections to the greater of twelve cents times the voting age population or $150,000. House candidates in states with only a single representative are governed by the same limits.
- Fixes ceilings on spending by other House candidates of $70,000 separately in each primary and general election.
- Allows additional expenditures by candidates of up to 20 percent of their spending limits to pay the costs of fund solicitation.
- Authorizes a national political party committee to spend up to two cents times the voting age population to support its presidential candidate, national or state political party committees to spend up to the greater of two cents times the voting age population or $20,000 to support their senatorial candidates and their candidates for the House in states with a single representative, and both national and state party committees to spend up to $10,000 to support each other House candidate.
- Allows spending limits to increase by the same percentage as increases in the Consumer Price Index.
- Prohibits expenditures by any person on behalf of a candidate in excess of $1,000.
- Requires all expenditures, except for petty cash outlays not exceeding $100, to be made by check.

These spending limits appear low in presidential general elections. The $20 million base, the $4 million (20 percent) allowance for fund raising, and the national party limit of two cents per eligible voter (approximately $2.9 million) total $26.9 million, contrasted with 1972 spending by George McGovern of about $38 million and by Richard Nixon of $47 million. If presidential candidates receive $20 million in check-off funds, as the 1974 act provides, the $4 million fund-raising allowance will of course not be needed or spent. Presidential primary limits appear ample by past standards. House spending limits including the allowance for fund raising expenses and party disbursements, amount to about the existing mean in marginal districts, and the Senate ceilings are well above average current spending levels. Spending ceilings in congressional races take into account changes in the size of the electorate, but no similar adjustment is provided in presidential expenditure limits. All campaigns are adjusted by the cost-of-living escalator, which should help ward off early obsolescence. But other factors known to bear on campaign spending are not accounted for in the 1974 act, as they have not been in other laws and probably cannot be.

Several plausible objections have been registered against the new federal regulations even before their first trial. The authorization for supplementary spending by national and state party committees plainly discriminates against independent candidates. It may also discriminate against party candidates in states where minor parties nominate a major party candidate as their standard bearer. In New York, for instance, the Democratic national and state committees each can spend two cents per eligible voter to support their United States Senate candidate, and the Liberal party can spend another two cents per eligible voter for the same candidate if they have also nominated him on their line. In some states the formation of new parties is so easy that artificial parties might be created to allow an additional spending allowance on behalf of major party candidates.

The $1,000 limit on direct outlays by persons does not include an aggregate ceiling on their total spending. Hence an individual could spend $1,000 directly in each Senate and House race across the country. It appears to be only a drafting error that an aggregate limit on total direct expenditures similar to the $25,000 limit on aggregate contributions was not imposed.

All spending limits in the 1974 act apply only to candidate support. This permits party committees, for instance, to make unlimited outlays for registering voters, getting out the vote, organizing, and so forth. Candidate committees have traditionally spent money for many of these activities, but the trend will now be to shift these functions to party committees to allow the candidate to use his full quota for direct appeals to voters. Further, when candidates have reached their spending limits, they will encourage givers to channel money to party committees for activities such as getting out the vote that will indirectly aid the campaign. This practice will increase because of the lack of limit on a contributor's gift to party committees.

Finally, the act ignores the treacherous question inherent in all spending limits: what outlays are counted as part of the expenditure ceiling? Does spending to criticize or oppose a candidate count against his opponent's expenditure limit? And if he has several opponents, against which one's limit? Further, does others' spending that mentions a candidate but does not endorse him count as part of his spending limit? And is such independent spending now banned if it exceeds $1,000? Finally, does the limit curb spending simply for discussion of an issue without mention of any candidate when the candidates' stands on that issue are well known or where they are campaigning on it?

These problems are by no means far-fetched. Negative spending was so troublesome under the Campaign Communications Reform Act that the Comptroller General issued a regulation excluding it from the law's media spending limits.[23] A non-endorsing comment spawned a major lawsuit when the American Civil Liberties Union was blocked under the act from purchasing advertising in the *New York Times* censuring President Nixon's support of anti-school busing legislation and listing an "honor roll" of congressmen who opposed his recommendation.[24] And issue advertising which does not mention a candidate has been undertaken from time to time by "right to life" (anti-abortion) groups and the National Rifle Association.

A Second Look at Spending Limits. Proponents of expenditure ceilings usually justify them by insisting that costs must be held down so the ordinary citizen can run for office, that candidates must be prevented from buying elections by vastly outspending their opponents, that excess and wasteful outlays should be stopped, that the influence gained by high-spending rich candidates and wealthy interests must be curbed, and that candidates must be freed from the inordinate money-raising pressures usually accompanying unrestrained campaign spending. There are strong objections both to the underlying assumptions of these arguments and to the efficacy of spending limits as a means toward these goals.

There is little public interest in assuring every citizen the opportunity to compete equally for public office. To accomplish this, spending limits would have to be so low that competitive campaigning which articulated alternatives to voters would be impossible. The goal is not "every man a candidate," but rather each significant viewpoint represented by a candidate with sufficient means to present his program to voters.

Similarly, it is difficult to understand the objection to "wasteful" or "excess" spending. A situation is conceivable in which enough is spent to make information easily available to every voter and to encourage every citizen to participate by registering and voting. This is not a real world condition even in the most costly contemporary campaigns. In a less than perfect world, each new campaign dollar presumably marginally supplements efforts to inform and activate voters. Finally, of course, advocates of spending limits cannot specify a point at which campaign spending becomes excessive or wasteful. Constituency variables dictate different spending needs in different districts; the widely varying significance, complexity, and intensity of issues in different races justifies different levels of spending; and the effectiveness of campaign techniques is so uncertain that no level of spending can be prescribed as appropriate for reaching voters.

Spending disparities between candidates, unusual campaign advantages for rich or richly supported candidates, and fund-raising pressures on office seekers are better addressed by public financing and by contribution limits than by spending ceilings. Expenditure limits do not ameliorate disparities in funding where one candidate cannot raise enough money to bring himself close to the ceiling while his opponent can. Disparities are better addressed by supplying enough public funds for candidates to wage vigorous campaigns. Tight contribution limits might then allow additional citizen participation, but neither side is likely to substantially outdistance the other in such fund raising. The usual cause of disparities is not the number of contributions each candidate wins, but the size. If all private contributions are small, the disparities in funding—public and private —will be small. Further, campaign spending probably brings diminishing returns as it reaches higher and higher levels, so that the significance of modest private financing disparities on top of generous public grants is reduced.

Public financing and tight contribution limits are also preferred responses to the campaign advantages of rich candidates and wealthy interests and to the fund-raising pressures on candidates. Rich candidates and interests can be curbed if their contributions are limited to modest amounts. Public financing relieves most of the fund-raising pressure on candidates by providing them an adequate campaign treasury. If additional funds are needed, the pressure on contenders is not to woo big givers but rather to appeal broadly for the small donations permitted by low contribution limits.

The arguments for limits are not, of course, wholly without merit. In some circumstances they will produce the results claimed. But those objectives can usually be achieved more effectively by public financing and low contribution limits. These alternative means appear even more attractive in the face of powerful arguments against spending limits. They are virtually impossible to enforce. No one has yet suggested how negative spending, non-endorsing comments, or issue discussions can be handled within an expenditure limit scheme. If they are excluded from limits, money will simply be displaced from candidate support to these kinds of campaigning. And it may be less desirable to force people into negative appeals than to allow them openly to spend money to endorse their favored candidate.

To prevent the multiplication of committees spending up to the legal limit, some kind of centralized treasurer or principal campaign committee device, such as that enacted in the 1974 act, must be adopted. But this means that citizens can participate only through the campaign treasurer, who will regulate what is said. This leads easily to a campaign in which the views of contributing citizens are censored so that no issues are raised that do not conform to the candidate's strategy. Even if the treasurer is required by law to accept all contributions and spend them for purposes earmarked by the givers, some citizens cannot get heard. When earmarked money has been received and spent up to the statutory expenditure ceiling, other citizens' gifts must be turned back.

Implicit in these criticisms is the high value we place on allowing each citizen to participate in the debate about public affairs. We might wish to encourage equality of expression among citizens by setting a reasonable limit on each one's aggregate contributions and spending. But a spending limit goes further; it blocks any spending by citizens if the candidate's limit has already been reached. Spending limits erroneously focus on the candidate's activities instead of on more or less equal participation in affairs by each citizen.

Spending limits also contradict the American preference for vigorous campaigns, for a strong crossfire of comment about public affairs, and for activating citizens. Herbert E. Alexander has forcefully put this objection to spending limits:

> If the political system is to be open and responsive to challenge, limitations are undesirable because they tend to favor the status quo. . . . One key goal of the political system should be intense competition because that helps to make the system more responsive. Limitations tend to reduce opportunities for voters to hear about candidates and issues. Periodic electioneering helps to structure and politicize society—an essential to the functioning of a democracy. Reducing expenditures reduces opportunities for voters to learn that the political season is on, that an election is coming.[25]

LIMITATIONS AND THE CONSTITUTION

Sources of National Power to Regulate Elections. Although the Constitution does not explicitly authorize the national regulation of campaigns, the Supreme Court has found ample warrant for corrupt practices legislation. In Article 1, Section 4, the Constitution provides that "The Times, Places and Manner of holding Elections for Senators and Representatives, shall be prescribed in each State by the Legislature thereof; but the Congress may at any time by Law make or alter such Regulations." The justices have taken a very broad view of what may be regulated under the "Times, Places and Manner" clause.

In 1880 the Court upheld a conviction under a federal statute forbidding fraud, violence, and other misconduct in congressional elections; it cited the time-place-and-manner provision as authority for the statute.[26] In a reapportionment case, the Court broadened its view further, stating that the clause authorizes Congress

> to provide a complete code for congressional elections, not only as to times and places, but in relation to notices, registration, super-

vision of voting, protection of voters, prevention of fraud and corrupt practices, counting votes, duties of inspectors and canvassers, and making and publication of election returns; in short to enact the numerous requirements as to procedure and safeguards which experience shows are necessary in order to enforce the fundamental right [to vote] involved.[27]

The phrase "corrupt practices" is regarded by lawyers as a term of art, encompassing financing practices generally, not merely bribery or similar conduct. Indeed, when the Court made its decision, the federal statutes already included the Federal Corrupt Practices Act of 1925, which regulated many political finance activities.

On its face, the Constitution gives less authority to regulate presidential elections than congressional campaigns. Electors were originally selected by state legislatures, and the Framers did not contemplate the need for congressional regulation of those choices. Hence the Constitution provides only that Congress may regulate "the Time of chusing the Electors, and the Day on which they shall give their Votes." By contrast, the state "shall appoint, in such Manner as the Legislature thereof may direct," its presidential electors.[28] This seems a denial of national authority to regulate the selection process.

The Supreme Court has expanded national authority to regulate presidential elections, recognizing that electors are now chosen at the polls rather than in the state legislature. The justices upheld the 1925 act's contribution and expenditure disclosure requirements by noting that:

> The President is vested with the executive power of the nation. The importance of his election and the vital character of its relationship to and effect upon the welfare and safety of the whole people cannot be too strongly stated. To say that Congress is without power to pass appropriate legislation to safeguard such an election from the improper use of money to influence the result is to deny to the nation in a vital particular the power of self protection.[29]

The Court's decision was consistent with earlier cases upholding the congressional power to regulate presidential elections. Two Reconstruction statutes punished conspiracies to intimidate a person in the exercise of his constitutional rights and to prevent by force, intimidation, or threat a citizen from supporting a candidate for presidential elector or Congress. Sustaining the laws' application to presidential contests, the justices said: "That a government whose essential character is republican, whose executive head and legislative body are both elective . . . has no power by appropriate laws to secure this election from the influence of violence, of corruption, and of fraud, is a proposition so startling as to arrest attention and demand the gravest explanation."[30]

Initially the Supreme Court held that the congressional power to regulate campaign financing, by setting limits on expenditures, did not extend to primaries, which were party affairs in which no final selection of officials was made.[31] Later decisions, however, implicitly overrule this doctrine. A conviction under federal law for falsely counting ballots in a primary was upheld on the ground that the primary was an integral part of the election process.[32] Other decisions, bottomed on the Fourteenth and Fifteenth Amendments, agreed that Congress could regulate primaries to prevent discrimination against black voters.[33]

Other constitutional provisions might also be invoked to sustain regulation of campaign financing practices. The Fourteenth Amendment provides that no state shall deny any person equal protection of the laws and allows Congress to enforce this mandate through appropriate legislation. The Supreme Court has held that the Fifth Amendment guarantee of "due process of law" against federal government intrusions includes also the concept of equal protection of the laws. It has been suggested that failure to regulate campaign contributions and expenditures advantages the rich, denies others the equal protection of the laws, and therefore is a basis for congressional regulation of political financing.[34]

It has also been pointed out that the Constitution authorizes Congress to make laws "necessary and proper" to carry out the powers given the national government.[35] If the other clauses of the Constitution do not specifically authorize campaign finance regulations, they may be regarded as "necessary and proper" to fulfill the election powers of Congress and to guarantee a republican form of government. Finally, several commentators have mentioned that the interstate commerce power, which has been broadly considered by the justices, might be a basis for campaign finance regulation.[36] Under recent sweeping decisions, Congress may regulate purely local activities if they are part of a larger class of activities, some of which are interstate in nature.[37] Because campaign financing involves both interstate and intrastate activities, it would fall under the constitutional mandate that "Congress shall have Power . . . to regulate Commerce . . . among the several States."

Contribution Limits. Making a campaign contribution is not "pure speech," and some might insist that it is therefore not protected by the First Amendment. Communicative actions closely connected to speech may, however, also enjoy certain constitutional protections. Hence the First Amendment has been held to protect refusal to salute the flag, the display of a red flag, the solicitation of legal business, wearing an armband in school, and picketing.[38] Making campaign contributions is as likely to fall within the First Amendment's ambit as these actions.

This leads one commentator to argue that "the First Amendment prohibits the setting of a legal maximum on the political activity in which an individual can engage," and that any limit on campaign contributions is therefore impermissible.[39] But the Supreme Court has not held that the freedom of speech is absolute. The justices have also allowed restrictions on speech when there was a "compelling," "substantial," "subordinating," or "overriding" governmental purpose in such regulations.[40]

When expression takes the form of action, the government may regulate it for purposes not intended to curb communication but rather to achieve some other important governmental purpose. Thus a statute prohibiting destruction of draft cards has been upheld as a necessary step toward maintaining the draft, even though the defendant burned the card to protest against the Viet Nam war.[41] Similarly, picketing and demonstrating which block streets, obstruct the doorways of public buildings, threaten the order of courthouses, or disrupt schools in session have been held subject to legislative regulation, despite claims that they were expressions of protest against racial discrimination.[42]

Supreme Court cases have established congressional authority to prevent corrupt practices, preserve the fundamental right to vote, and safeguard elections from the improper use of money to influence the result. Referring to their decision upholding campaign finance disclosure requirements, the justices later said the valid purpose of Congress was "to maintain the integrity of a basic governmental process," namely elections. Further, the Court gave Congress a wide latitude in selecting means to protect elections against the influence of money. "The power of Congress to protect the election of President and Vice President from corruption being clear, the choice of means to that end presents a question primarily addressed to the judgment of Congress."[43]

No one doubts that contributions which bribe officials or voters are beyond the First Amendment's protection. But the integrity of elections may also be endangered by contributions that have no such overt purpose. First, there is a compelling public interest in preventing rich men and wealthy interests from spending so much money that they drown out other citizens' voices in campaigns and therefore unduly influence voting. Second, there is a substantial public interest in preventing some from winning special access to officeholders by making large contributions. This access occurs before elections, when candidates may strike postures pleasing to big givers in order to solicit their financial support, and after elections, when big givers have special entrée to plead their causes with officials. A major lobbyist pointed out that heavy contributing "doesn't mean that we own them, of course. But the door is sure opened a little wider for us to get in and present our problems."[44]

These governmental purposes do not, of course, justify a prohibition against all campaign contributions, but only whatever limit on the size of contributions is necessary to minimize the threat of bribery, of undue influence on voting, and of disproportionate access to candidates and officials.[45] In setting the limit on contributions, the discretion of Congress is very broad; but Congress should resolve any uncertainty on the high side to allow as much latitude for free expression as does not endanger the integrity of elections.

Some have suggested that this rationale for contribution limits cannot apply to a candidate's own spending, since that does not create undue pressures upon him.[46] But a rich man's large personal outlays do promote his views in such high volume that he threatens to drown out other voices and unduly influence the election. A wealthy candidate, no less than wealthy interests, promotes a special viewpoint. The campaign advantages of rich candidates have been reflected in the larger number of wealthy hopefuls and in their unusual electoral successes since World War II.

A wholly different basis for regulating campaign contributions is found in the equal protection clause of the Constitution and in the sweeping congressional power to carry out that mandate.[47] Holding that state legislative districts must be of equal population, the Supreme Court said the Constitution "requires . . . that each citizen have an equally effective voice in the election of the members."[48] And, striking down high filing fees for candidates, the Court expressed concern not only with the discrimination against poor candidates but also against poor voters, because the burden of filing fees also falls disproportionately on "the less affluent segment of the community, whose favorites may be unable to pay the large costs required [by such fees]." It would "ignore reality were we not to recognize that this system falls with unequal weight on voters, as well as candidates, according to their economic status."[49]

Campaign contributions are analogous to filing fees. They give citizens of different means very different voices in elections. And they discriminate against less affluent voters as a class. It might easily follow that Congress can guarantee equal protection of the laws to citizens in elections by setting a limit on campaign gifts. Further, this reasoning would justify lower contribution limits than would the need to protect the integrity of elections. Contribution limits could be set within the means of most citizens if they made a significant effort to take part in politics. At the very least, limits could be established that would very substantially reduce the disparity between the gifts that poor and rich citizens could afford to make. This latter formula is more probable, since the justices in recent years have allowed substantial disparities in the population of legislative districts; exact equality is apparently not required.

Finally, Congress has a wide latitude to take steps to assure equal protection of the law, even to prohibit practices that the justices have not found would violate the Constitution in the absence of congressional action. And Congress is allowed to select the broadest means to protect the equality of citizens. Since Congress has special knowledge of campaign financing practices, the justices would be unlikely to challenge either the means used to regulate campaign contributions or the ceilings imposed on them.[50]

Expenditure Limits. The framework of constitutional analysis is not substantially different for expenditure limits than for contribution ceilings. Spending is a form of expression, but it may be regulated to achieve compelling state interests. It is far more difficult, however, to identify a compelling need for spending limits than it is for contribution limits. We have previously suggested that most of the goals announced by proponents of spending ceilings are, in fact, better achieved by public financing, contribution limits, or both.

Expenditure limits have been so ineffectual that their constitutionality has rarely been litigated. The Wisconsin Supreme Court sustained that state's low gubernatorial spending limit on the theory that it saved men of modest means from putting themselves under obligation to big contributors in order to raise the funds necessary for candidacy.[51] The decision applied only to a candidate's own spending; it did not curb outlays on his behalf by "voluntary committees." So-called voluntary committees soon became the major vehicle in campaigns, and over the years candidates more and more ignored the fiction that these committees were beyond their discretion and control.

The United States District Court for Hawaii recently endorsed spending limits for the same purpose—"to permit potential candidates of limited means to seek public office." The court struck down media spending limits as an unnecessary incursion upon free speech because the state's interest in promoting "equality of opportunity to participate in the political process" was fully "protected by the limitation on *total* expenditures." But the purpose of "keeping political channels open to people of limited means is a noble goal" that justifies state restrictions on free speech through the device of overall spending limits.[52]

The Wisconsin and Hawaii courts' rationale was misplaced. Democracy does not turn on the ability of every man to run for office but rather on the voters' opportunity to choose. This requires ample, not low, campaign spending. Further, candidates can be largely freed from entangling financial obligations by low contribution limits (Wisconsin has none) and public financing; spending limits are unnecessary for this purpose.

A second rationale for spending limits is similarly defective. It argues that candidates should have an equal opportunity to be heard. Apart from its erroneous focus on candidates and its unsupported assumption that all candidates will be able to raise money up to the spending limits, this argument ignores the question whether other citizens also are entitled to be heard during a campaign. If both candidates spend their full legal quota, and neither raises an issue that one or several citizens believe is significant, isn't there a free speech guarantee for those citizens to spend money to raise the issue and for the general body of voters to hear about it? If so, limits on candidates neither regulate the amounts that will be spent to discuss their candidacy nor assure that those amounts will be equal.

The Washington Supreme Court touched precisely this issue in striking down that state's expenditure limits. Spending ceilings are defective, the justices observed, because they:

> can operate to prohibit absolutely plaintiff and others from exercising their constitutionally guaranteed freedom of speech. . . . If a committee, indeed if one person, has spent the maximum allowable in favor of a [measure or candidate], plaintiff is absolutely barred from any communication which involves an expenditure.[53]

For effective control of campaign spending, most proponents have been driven to advocacy of a central treasurer system. Simply put, this requires that all expenditures on behalf of a candidate be channeled through his designated agent. It raises questions whether the central treasurer must also be the channel for all spending to criticize candidates, to make non-endorsing comments about them, and to discuss hot issues during campaigns. Quite apart from these intractable problems, any central treasurer scheme runs afoul of insurmountable constitutional objections.[54] Long ago the Wisconsin Supreme Court struck down a law preventing any citizen from directly spending campaign money outside his own county; the purpose was to channel all spending through the candidate's committee by prohibiting independent citizen outlays. The court found the statute squarely contrary to the First Amendment.[55]

Similarly, a three-judge federal district court struck down the section of the Campaign Communications Reform Act and its accompanying regulations which provided that news media could not carry advertising supporting a candidate without his certification nor allow advertising opposing a candidate without his opponent's certification if the opponent's consent to the broadside could reasonably be implied. The court found a First Amendment violation because:

> Candidates favorably named in ads, or those whose consent to derogatory advertisements may be implied, are provided with the opportunity of effectively blocking publication by refusing to make the requisite certification statements. . . . Any such candidate wields potential veto power over attempts to communicate public views.[56]

Advocates of expenditure limits often cite the Florida Supreme Court's decision upholding a central treasurer system to achieve full disclosure of campaign financing.[57] But the court did not consider the First Amendment question of whether a central treasurer could veto expenditures requested by contributors. Since Florida had no spending limit, the treasurer could take all contributions and spend any earmarked funds as requested by the giver. This would result in full disclosure of sources, amounts, and uses of money; but it would not cut off expression by citizens. The Florida precedent does not address the constitutionality of a central treasurer system to enforce spending limits.

Drafters of the original Presidential Election Campaign Fund Act and of the Federal Election Campaign Act of 1974 recognized the constitutional objection to prohibiting all independent citizen expenditures during campaigns. Both laws therefore permitted a person to spend up to $1,000 independently. These outlays were not counted against a candidate's spending limit as long as they were not authorized by him.

Even this provision for independent expenditures, however, does not cure all the constitutional problems. First, the 1974 act allows an individual to contribute $1,000 in each election, but to spend only $1,000 in any calendar year to support a candidate. It is unclear why the free speech guarantee does not protect direct expenditures at the same level as contributions—namely, $1,000 separately in each primary, run-off primary, and general election. Second, the $1,000 spending rule applies to committees as well as individuals. But committees may give $5,000 to candidates under the 1974 act. Again, permissible expenditures for direct speech about a candidate are lower than for expression that takes the form of a contribution to that candidate. Further, a committee is a combination of people, yet their expenditures for direct expression are held to the same level as those of a single individual. If each individual can spend up to $1,000 for direct expression, the First Amendment freedom of association would seem to allow all members of a group to aggregate their direct expenditures.

Expenditure limits seem far less likely than contribution ceilings to pass constitutional muster.[58] First, the compelling governmental purposes cited to support a curtailment of expression are not persuasive. They are either ineffective or can be better achieved by other means. Second, spending limits mistakenly focus on expression by candidates rather than by citizens; and a limit on candidate outlays does not permit all citizens to express themselves. Third, the central treasurer device needed to make spending limits effective gives candidates an unconstitutional veto power over the content of citizen speech. Finally, if constitutional guarantees are recognized by allowing independent citizen spending, the law must permit it at the same level as contributions to the candidate. And this permission for substantial independent spending guts the effectiveness of spending limits because when a candidate reaches his expenditure ceiling his supporters will simply make generous "independent" outlays on his behalf.

Contribution limits curb undue influence, corruption, and inequality among citizens in financing campaigns. Although protected by the First Amendment, campaign contributions may be limited to achieve these objectives. Similarly, institutional contributions may be limited to achieve the same goals. Curbs on the purposes of spending may also be useful when they ban such direct corruption of elections as the bribery of voters or election officials. But other prescriptions or prohibitions of specified campaign expenditures are not useful: they displace money to other activities, they ignore changing campaign technology, and they lack public support. Finally, overall spending limits are neither wise nor constitutional. They limit the crossfire of debate and the voter activation that are essential for democracy; they are usually unworkable; and they cannot be properly adjusted to fit the various districts and changing campaign circumstances across the nation. Further, they infringe on free expression without achieving any compelling purposes that cannot be achieved by other, less restrictive means. Spending limits relying on a central treasurer are especially defective because they threaten the opportunity for citizens to express their views about candidates and issues outside the framework of campaign organizations.

THE POLITICAL BROADCAST ACT

The practical difficulty of drafting effective legislation, the host of constitutional problems, and the decentralization of American politics have thwarted comprehensive expenditure limits. But in 1970, Congress was determined to impose some limits on escalating campaign costs and on media outlays in particular.

Limiting only this segment of campaign costs had a certain practical appeal. First, radio and television broadcasters were federally licensed; Congress could therefore use licensing to enforce expenditure limits. And newspapers, though not licensed, could also be regulated because they were a limited and identifiable number of business concerns whose books could be easily scrutinized. Second, Congress could enforce candidate media spending limits by simply requiring all such outlays to have the approval of the office seeker or his agent, thus creating a central treasurer for the media side of each campaign.

This congressional action sprang also from political motives. The mass media had begun to reverse traditional patterns of campaigning that favored incumbents. A handsome appearance suddenly became as important as a carefully developed voting record tailored to district interests. The incumbent's painstaking cultivation of party,

5

AN EXPERIMENT WITH MEDIA LIMITS

ethnic, religious, and economic organizations in a district might be overridden by a media blitz reaching those constituents more often and more effectively than their traditional institutions. High-priced outside media producers created an instant campaign that overcame the carefully maintained organizations of long-time officeholders. In a Congress elected predominantly from one-party districts, the mass media are a special menace, for media campaigning is especially effective in nomination contests where party labels do not guide voter choice. Such a cruel wrenching of incumbents' worlds won many converts for reform.

In response, Congress passed the Political Broadcast Act of 1970, limiting radio and television spending for federal offices and for governor and lieutenant governor in general elections to either $20,000 or seven cents times the number of votes in the preceding election, whichever was greater.[1] Congress halved this formula as the spending limit for primaries. The measure also included repeal of the equal time provision of the Federal Communications Act in presidential and vice presidential campaigns, opening the way for media debates between the two major party candidates in 1972. President Nixon vetoed the act, warning that broadcast limits aided incumbents, that limits on dollars rather than time discriminated against candidates in urban areas where media rates are high, and that limits on broadcast spending would simply cause a displacement of campaign funds to other media and campaign techniques. He did not mention repeal of the equal time provision, but the White House was widely known to oppose it both because Nixon had suffered politically in his 1960 debate with John F. Kennedy and because the President did not want to give his 1972 challenger any unnecessary exposure. The Senate failed to muster two-thirds to override the veto, and the Political Broadcast Act of 1970 died.

Nonetheless the struggle over the bill invited a renewed effort in 1971. First, the principle of limits just on the media segments of campaigns won wide acceptance as a practical first step toward reform. Second, the bill won large enough majorities in Congress to warrant a second try. The House had given its approval by 247 to 112, while the Senate had favored the bill 60 to 19 on original passage. Even on the vote to override, when lines tightened as the President's party rushed to his defense, the Senate favored the measure by 58 to 34.

Moreover, in 1970, the mass media had been used as never before. An unknown businessman named Howard Metzenbaum toppled John Glenn, the former astronaut, in Ohio's Democratic primary for U.S. Senate by launching a last-minute radio and television blitz. Another businessman, Milton Shapp, humbled Pennsylvania's big-city bosses by spending more than a million dollars on media to defeat their endorsed gubernatorial candidate. California Senator George Murphy was retired by handsome John Tunney, son of the boxer who beat Jack Dempsey, whose television ads featured him strolling along a deserted beach, accompanied by a pretty wife and towheaded children, and closed with the punch line "you need a fighter in your corner." In Illinois, Republican Senator Ralph Smith's ads featured Adlai Stevenson's blinking eyes close-up on the screen with scenes of 1968 Chicago rioting superimposed, and a voice-over asking why Stevenson didn't denounce student demonstrators. In neighboring Indiana, Senator Vance Hartke's opponent sponsored an ad showing a Viet Cong firing an automatic weapon while the audio attacked Hartke for supporting trade with Communist nations that might put supplies into the hands of the enemy. Spiro Agnew and Richard Nixon denouncing Democrats, demonstrators, and radic-libs on prime time television topped off one of the nation's bitterest campaigns since Joe McCarthy rode high in 1952. The Political Broadcast Act laid down policy guidelines and congressional strategy, but the 1970 campaigns demonstrated the political importance of limits on media spending.

THE CAMPAIGN COMMUNICATIONS REFORM ACT

On January 19, 1972, more than fourteen months after the 1970 election, the House of Representatives finally approved a conference committee version of the Federal Election Campaign Act of 1971.[2] The Senate had endorsed the bill more than a month earlier. On February 7, President Nixon grudgingly signed it, without the traditional signing ceremony that usually trumpets executive approval of major legislation. The President's mood was not surprising; the new law contained the same principles he had vetoed in the 1970 Political Broadcast Act.

The Campaign Communications Reform Act, placed on the statute books in 1972 as Title I of the Federal Election Campaign Act of 1971, curbed candidate expenditures for "communications media"—radio and television broadcasting, newspaper and magazine advertising, billboards and similar display facilities, and telephone banks. To enforce the spending limits, Congress provided that communications media could not accept advertising without authorization of the candidate or his agent, who was then responsible for keeping outlays under the statutory ceiling.[3]

A candidate could spend either ten cents multiplied by the number of persons in his constituency who had reached eighteen years of age, or $50,000, whichever was greater. The population-based formula resulted in a higher spending limit in presidential and senatorial campaigns; the flat $50,000 figure was the wiser choice of candidates for the House of Representatives. Sixty percent of whichever amount was chosen could be devoted to radio and television advertising.

These statutory limits applied separately to each primary, run-off primary, and general election campaign. In presidential nomination contests, the ceiling was calculated on a state-by-state basis; each candidate was entitled to spend up to the limit in each state he entered as a candidate. The act also required broadcast stations to sell time to candidates at the lowest unit cost offered any other advertiser for a comparable class and amount of time; this provision would reduce costs to politicians by 25 to 35 percent, allowing them to buy more broadcast time with the same amount of money. A similar provision controlled the cost of newspaper and magazine advertising.

To guarantee candidates access to the broadcast media, Congress amended the Federal Communications Act to provide for the revocation of broadcast licenses of stations guilty of "willful and repeated failure" either to allow federal office candidates reasonable access to media or to permit them to purchase reasonable amounts of broadcast time.

In an age of inflation, Congress also attempted to eliminate one of the most important flaws of past state and federal limitations on campaign spending by including in the Communications Reform Act a mechanism for automatically increasing media spending limits. In subsequent election years, the ceiling of ten cents per voting age resident or $50,000 would increase by the same percentage as did the Consumer Price Index over its 1970 base.

The supporters of the Reform Act expected it to curb the spiraling of political spending because broadcast media were an increasingly costly item in campaign budgets. They thought it might also reduce the "unfairness" of campaigns in which a candidate massively outspent his opponent on the communications media. The public's concern about instant, media-created candidates, blatant distortions in some radio and television spots, and the tedium of apparently endless candidate appeals also were cited by the act's supporters.

The act's proponents were particularly interested in the limits it would impose on presidential campaign spending. They estimated the 1972 ceiling on broadcast spending at $8.4 million (about $150,000 below the actual ceiling imposed by the Comptroller General). In 1968, $12.6 million had been spent on radio and television to advance the Nixon-Agnew ticket. The Humphrey-Muskie effort had totaled $6.1 million. Thus the act could be expected to reduce the GOP's broadcast expenditures and to equalize substantially the opportunity for the opposing candidates to be heard.

Democrats were, of course, moved by self-interest as well as by a desire to curb the rising tide of broadcast advertising. Even with their party $9 million in debt, the Democratic ticket might still be able to raise the $8.4 million that would match the Republican broadcasting budget under the Reform Act. If they could not, at least the limit would hold down the traditional edge held by the Republicans. Incumbency also influenced some votes on the Reform Act, as it did on the Broadcast Act.

The law imposed no restraint on the content of media advertising; up to the maximum, campaign funds might be used as readily as before for the kinds of vituperative messages that have triggered loud public complaints. The act was also unlikely to reduce the total volume of political broadcast advertising. Although it invited states to invoke the federal limitations and extended enforcement through the Federal Communications Commission to those that did so, no state accepted this invitation, and without such acceptance the act did not apply to campaigns for state and local offices. Perhaps as a result, campaign spending on the part of state and local candidates rose; aspirants for governor and lieutenant governor spent $6.2 million in 1968 and $9.7 million in 1972. (The 1970 figure of $15.9 million is not relevant because many states with four-year terms schedule their gubernatorial races in the off year to insulate state politics from presidential trends.) Further, the legislation did not necessarily curb wealthy candidates, for those with political aspirations could simply turn from congressional races to state politics where they could use their wealth unfettered.

THE INEFFECTIVENESS OF LIMITS

The effects of the act on broadcast spending were not clear-cut. From 1968 to 1972, television and radio spending did not decrease, but the increase was only 1 percent—from $58.9 million to $59.6 million. Broadcast spending in 1972, except in the presidential campaigns, did show a dramatic decrease from 1970, when the onslaught of radio and television reached its highest and most offensive point. The following figures show the trend in total non-presidential television and radio spending in recent years. Presidential broadcast spending is excluded from the figures for 1968 and 1972.

1966	$32.1 million
1968	30.5 million
1970	59.2 million
1972	45.1 million[4]

The decline in spending from 1970 to 1972 may be more apparent than real, however. Presidential campaigns usually siphon off funds that would otherwise be spent by candidates for lesser offices. The reduced non-presidential media outlays in 1972 may be more an artifact of this phenomenon than a result of campaign reform legislation. Indeed, total broadcast media spending in all races, including presidential contests, has remained nearly constant in recent years: $58.9 million in 1968, $59.2 million in 1970, and $59.6 million in 1972. The Reform Act plainly did not reduce overall broadcast spending after it took effect in February, 1972. Indeed it may have increased the volume of broadcast messages, for under the act's lowest-unit-cost rule politicians could buy substantially more advertising for the same dollars in 1972 than in 1968 and 1970.

If the congressional authors of the Reform Act hoped that it would discourage increases in the total cost of American campaigns, that hope, too, was frustrated. Scholars noted several years ago the tendency toward displacement in campaigns.[5] When new technologies emerge, they capture campaign outlays; and when artificial limits are imposed on spending for established techniques, money flows to different campaign purposes. In either case, established campaign activities are not completely abandoned. Instead, candidates spend money on both the old techniques and the new ones because, as many politicians admit, they don't know what works. The result is an increase in the overall cost of politics.

The displacement principle was alive and well in 1972. Presidential broadcast spending in the general election dropped from the 1968 level of $20.3 million to $10.8 million. The Nixon-Agnew ticket spent $4.3 million, compared with $12.6 million four years earlier. The McGovern-Shriver team spent $6.2 million, about the same as the $6.1 million devoted to the Humphrey-Muskie ticket. Despite media outlays at the same or lower levels, however, total campaign outlays soared. The Republican slate spent more than twice its 1968 total while the Democratic candidates more than tripled the outlays of their 1968 counterparts.

Nor can the drop in broadcast spending be readily attributed to the Reform Act. That neither side's spending even remotely approached the $8.55 million permitted by the law suggests that factors other than the spending ceiling were at work. The media rate reductions probably helped lower costs. So did prevailing doubts about the effectiveness of saturation radio and television advertising in 1972; many politicians believed that the public was soured by the excesses of 1970 and would resent high-intensity broadcast campaigns.

Broadcast spending in presidential primaries also declined abruptly. Although the act allowed each candidate who entered every state primary and spent up to the statutory limit to spend as much as $5,366,000 for radio and television advertising, media outlays by both parties' nomination hopefuls dropped from $8.1 million in 1968 to $3.5 million in 1972. The Republicans, of course, had no serious presidential nomination contest in 1972; hence their total broadcast spending was only a few hundred thousand dollars. The Democrats witnessed a vigorous competition for the highest office, but the candidates agreed to hold spending at a level lower than the statutory maximum. Spending was also curtailed by the staggering party deficit and by the absence from the race of any candidate able to pour enormous personal wealth and credit into the campaign (as had Robert Kennedy in 1968).

It is quite possible that, in 1976, both parties will have vigorous contests for the nomination, several wealthy candidates will figure among the contenders, the Democrats will no longer be debt-ridden, and the number of presidential primaries will grow from the fifteen in 1968 and twenty-five in 1972 to a still larger number. In these circumstances, broadcast spending in presidential primaries may rise precipitously and surpass the relatively high 1968 figure.

The act's usefulness in campaigns for the Senate and House was also limited. Its ceilings exceeded outlays even in most high-cost campaigns for Congress.[6] In 1970, before passage of the act, United States senators were elected in thirty-five states, and in twenty-six of them Democrats had nomination contests. Of eighty candidates involved in those primaries, only one spent more than the six cents per potential voter allowed by the act. And that one—W. P. Kay, who won nomination in Alaska—spent only $12,400, far less than the $30,000 (60 percent of $50,000) permitted under the other formula provided in the legislation. Republicans had nomination contests in twenty-four states, and not a single one of their fifty-three candidates exceeded the act's expenditure limits. Norton Simon, the California millionaire who challenged George Murphy, spent exactly six cents per potential voter.

The act would apparently have had a little more bite in the 1970 general election. Twenty-six of the sixty-nine major-party senate candidates reported that they spent more than six cents per potential voter. One of these—Senator Ted Stevens of Alaska—spent only $18,000. The others spent more than $30,000, but fully eighteen of them would not have had to curb their spending by so much as a nickel if they had divided their expenditures more evenly between the primary and general election campaigns. The law permits spending up to the six-cent or $30,000 limit both in the primary and in the general election. These candidates bought more broadcast time in the general election than the law would have allowed, but they spent far less in the primary. Their total spending was either less than twelve cents per potential voter or less than $60,000.

The act would have had even less impact in House campaigns. Although 254 Democrats had no primary opposition, 558 aspirants had to campaign for nomination. Only two exceeded the six-cent limit, and only one of them spent more than $30,000. On the Republican side, 246 candidates were unopposed in House primaries, while 307 faced nomination contests. Although six of these candidates exceeded the six-cent limit, none spent over $30,000. Thus among 865 candidates who actually fought nomination battles, only one—T. B. Allen, who lost the Democratic primary in Maryland's Eighth District— would have been required to curb his spending under the act, and then only to the extent of $600.

In the general election, 46 major-party House candidates exceeded the six-cent limit, but only 11 spent more than $30,000, and 3 of them exceeded that amount by less than $500. Only one House candidate— W. R. Archer, in the Seventh District of Texas—spent more than $60,000 for the primary and general election combined.

The Reform Act's dollar limitations, then, would have curbed the spending of only seven United States Senate candidates in the general election, one House candidate in the primary, and one House candidate in the November, 1970, balloting.

In 1972, with the Reform Act in operation, very few candidates for the Senate and House came close to the act's limits on their broadcast expenditures. Candidates presumably left themselves a margin for error to avoid exceeding the statutory ceilings. For purposes of analysis, we may assume that any candidate who spent more than 90 percent of the Reform Act's broadcast spending quota was constrained by the statutory limit from purchasing more radio and television time. (In fact, a well-run campaign should have been able to purchase broadcast advertising in a systematic way that would have brought it within one or two percentage points of the limit.)

The Federal Communications Commission reported that 147 major-party candidates made some broadcast expenditures in 1972 primary campaigns for the United States Senate. Only 4 spent more than 90 percent of the Reform Act's broadcast spending limit; 2 of the 4 spent less than the limit, and 2 others exceeded it. Including a special election in Vermont, thirty-five states had general election contests for the United States Senate in 1972. Seventy-one candidates in these 35 races spent some money for political broadcasting: 11 spent more than 90 percent of the maximum permitted by the Reform Act; 4 of these exceeded the maximum. These figures suggest that in relatively few cases—under 3 percent in Senate primaries and about 15 percent in general election campaigns—did broadcast spending approach the Reform Act's limits.

In 81 congressional districts, no broadcast spending occurred in the primary elections. In the remaining 354 districts, 679 Democrats and 416 Republicans made broadcast outlays. Only 9 of these 1,095 candidates spent more than 90 percent of the Reform Act's radio and television expenditure limit: 6 of the 9 exceeded it. In 31 districts there was no general election broadcast spending. In the remaining 404 districts, 393 Democrats and 361 Republicans made broadcast expenditures. Only 18 of these 754 candidates spent more than 90 percent of the amount allowed by the Reform Act, and only 2 of them exceeded it.

THE FAILURE OF ENFORCEMENT

The FCC's 1972 compilation of broadcast spending throws an interesting sidelight on the Reform Act. In fourteen cases, Senate or House candidates actually exceeded the statutory broadcast spending limits in primary or general elections. One violator was an incumbent United States Senator; five were successful contenders for federal office. Ten were Democrats and four Republicans. No prosecution was made for any violation. The prosecution of violators would involve action against six sitting members of Congress of both parties, and the Justice Department apparently had no more interest in prosecuting incumbents or candidates of its own party than it did under the Federal Corrupt Practices Act and other predecessor legislation. This failure to enforce the Reform Act's generous ceilings on broadcast spending against the handful of individuals who exceeded them made the act wholly ineffectual.

THE VARIABLE IMPACT OF
MEDIA LIMITS

If the act's broadcast limits had been less generous and had been enforced, they would have discriminated against candidates in non-metropolitan congressional districts whose radio, television, newspaper, and outdoor advertising facilities primarily serve the district's population. In metropolitan districts, communications media serve large numbers of people other than those eligible to vote in contested districts. Candidates in these districts therefore do not ordinarily use communications media. Such campaign methods as direct mail, door-to-door canvassing, window signs, bumper stickers, literature drops, street rallies or carnivals, etc. are more suited to metropolitan area campaigning, and these methods are not covered by the Reform Act.

In non-metropolitan districts, on the other hand, media campaigning may be crucial. Districts are sparsely settled, and it is difficult for candidates to reach voters directly. Candidates do not have the benefit of neighborhood organizations so typical in urban settings. Furthermore, district lines and media audiences are more nearly congruent, making media outlays a reasonable campaign expenditure. If media are an effective method of campaigning in non-metropolitan districts but not in metropolitan areas, segmental limits on broadcast outlays curb campaigning in the former districts but not in the latter. In non-metropolitan districts this might crimp the vigorous campaigning essential for democratic elections.[7] Or, from a completely opposite perspective, it leaves unfettered in metropolitan districts the excessive spending so many believe jeopardizes free elections. From either vantage point, segmental broadcast limits work discriminatory and undesirable results.

Table 5-1 compares the total general election broadcast expenditures per eligible voter in 1970 in metropolitan, semi-metropolitan, and non-metropolitan districts. Of course campaign expenditures for all purposes are higher in competitive districts than in non-competitive districts. To hold the factor of competitiveness constant, the table compares only the competitive districts in each of the three categories. It confirms that broadcast expenditures are higher in non-metropolitan districts than in metropolitan districts and therefore that broadcast spending limits would have a discriminatory effect.

The Communications Reform Act tied its expenditure limits to the Consumer Price Index (CPI) as a hedge against inflation and obsolescence. But advertising rates for most communications media were rising faster than the CPI. In the decade preceding 1970, the base year used to calculate permissible broadcast spending under the act, the index rose an average of 3.1 percent annually. The average annual increase in advertising rates per thousand during that decade was 3.8 percent for newspapers, 4.2 percent for spot radio, 5.7 percent for consumer magazines, 6.8 percent for business magazines, 7.2 percent for spot television, and 10.2 percent for outdoor advertising (billboards). Network prices averaged an annual increase of 2 percent for radio and 4.7 percent for television, but network advertising takes up only the smallest portion of campaign broadcasting outlays.

Because the cost of media messages is rising faster than the CPI, candidates for federal office would eventually have had to cut back the number of broadcast messages to avoid exceeding the act's spending limits. This would have occurred only slowly in House of Representatives races where the act's limits were generous. But in Senate contests, relatively soon—perhaps within a decade—inflation would have imposed serious restrictions on most major-party contenders in

TABLE 5-1   Total Radio and Television Broadcast Spending Per Eligible Voter in Competitive[a] Metropolitan,[b] Semi-metropolitan,[c] and Non-metropolitan[d] House of Representatives Districts in the 1970 General Election

Broadcast Spending Per Eligible Voter	Metropolitan Districts		Semi-metropolitan Districts		Non-metropolitan Districts	
	N	%	N	%	N	%
0– 4¢	18	90	19	59	23	33
5– 8¢	0	0	4	13	25	36
9–12¢	1	5	4	13	12	17
13¢ or more	1	5	5	15	9	13
	20	100	32	101	69	99

[a] Competitive districts are those in which the victor received less than 60 percent of the major-party vote.

[b] Metropolitan districts are those primarily within a Standard Metropolitan Statistical Area of more than 3 million persons. Nationwide $N = 86$

[c] Semi-metropolitan districts are those primarily within an SMSA of 1 million to 3 million persons. Nationwide $N = 114$

[d] Non-metropolitan districts are those not primarily part of an SMSA of 1 million persons or more. Nationwide $N = 235$

competitive states. Eventually, as the price of media activities outran the CPI, present levels of electioneering would have reached the act's expenditure ceilings. For a short time the ceiling would have frozen the amount of communications activity. But soon afterward the escalation of media prices would have compelled a reduction in media activities. At that point the broadcast spending limits would have faced obsolescence of the kind that doomed so many other attempts to limit political spending.

Candidates, after all, feel entitled to a "reasonable" amount of campaign broadcasting. Officeholders especially are likely to accept as reasonable the levels of campaign activity at which they have most recently won and held their offices. When broadcast limits compel them to curtail their campaign communications they begin to regard them, with some justification, as unreasonable or unworkable. The media provide the most effective means by which candidates can take their case to the people and meet democracy's requirement of vigorous campaigns. When legal spending maximums begin to curtail media campaigning by politicians on a large scale, legal restrictions will be repealed, amended, or forgotten.

Overall, the Campaign Communications Reform Act of 1971 fell far short of reformers' expectations. While it might have reduced and equalized broadcast spending in presidential races, it would not have significantly curbed radio and television spending in most presidential primary contests or in nomination and general election battles for the House and Senate. Nor did it affect communications spending in campaigns for state and local offices. The act probably would not have discouraged the emergence of instant candidates, and it did not reduce the barrage of media messages that confuse, benumb, and alienate voters.

Some equalization in communications activity by politicians might have occurred, primarily in non-metropolitan districts, in cases when the handicapped contender was able to raise a war chest that approached the media spending limit imposed by law. His well-financed opponent would not have been able to overshadow that spending effort simply by committing more and more dollars to communications activity as he otherwise could have done. But in most congressional districts the challenger is so inadequately financed that he could not have mounted a media campaign that came close to the act's ceilings. In such races the problem for democracy is to provide the challenger with adequate resources to guarantee an effective adversary campaign rather than to prevent the well-financed candidate from overmatching his opponent.

From a wider vantage point, segmental media limits must face the same challenge as other spending limits: that they are an unconstitutional abridgement of the freedoms of speech, press, and association. And there is grave doubt whether democracy is served in theory or practice by curbing vigorous discussion through every available channel about candidates and issues in elections.

From every perspective, then, the Campaign Communications Reform Act was an inadequate response to the problem of campaign finance in American democracy. Perhaps for these reasons, but certainly in part because the act did not reduce the political dangers to or pressures on incumbents, the Federal Election Campaign Act of 1974 repealed the Campaign Communications Reform Act. Its passing will be lamented by very few.

THE IMPULSE TO CONCEAL

Historically, both politicians and contributors have had good reasons to conceal campaign finance practices. They have guarded campaign ledgers with almost fanatical zeal. And where laws require disclosure of political funding, they have searched out loopholes, practiced evasions, and encouraged violations. The most common method of circumventing disclosure laws has been "laundering," the practice of channeling contributions through intermediaries to obscure the original sources of funds. The term is appropriately derived from the underworld practice of channeling money obtained from vice operations through straw men into legitimate businesses. Unlike underworld leaders, politicians do not launder funds to avoid the tax consequences of illegally earned income. They have other equally compelling motives for concealment and laundering.

First, they may wish to conceal illegal contributions. As of May, 1974, eleven American corporations and associations had pleaded guilty to making illegal campaign contributions to the 1972 campaign, and all of those gifts had been in some way laundered.

Second, they may wish to hide sources of campaign funds that, although legal, might offend

6

THE DISAPPOINTMENT OF DISCLOSURE

voters. The high-powered funding drive conducted by the Committee for the Re-election of the President prior to April 7, 1972, the effective date of the 1971 Campaign Act, was presumably intended to avoid publicity about the widespread gifts of business corporations and financial interests.

Third, politicians may want to avoid reporting large gifts, regardless of source. The public suspects, rightly or wrongly, that large givers seek a *quid pro quo*. According to the Twentieth Century Fund Survey, 35 percent of respondents mentioned only the motive of personal gain in describing large contributions, and another 34 percent described personal gain as one of several reasons for generous political gifts. Fearful that disclosure of large contributions will spark adverse public reaction at the polls, politicians frequently prefer to conceal or launder such gifts.

Finally, the contributor may demand concealment if his gift is illegal, or if he fears exposure of his attempt to influence politics, or if he wishes to avoid criticism for making large gifts. Sometimes contributors demand concealment simply because they wish to avoid being pressured for financial support by candidates and political committees who learn of their political involvement elsewhere through disclosure of their gifts.

Politicians may also want to conceal expenditures. Many feel that voters distrust heavy spending in campaigns; and a candidate who spends large sums, especially if his outlays far outdistance opposition expenditures, may conceal the full cost of his campaign. Voters also may object to particular expenses—for example, illegal campaign activities or dirty tricks; the hiring of pollsters, public relations firms, media production specialists, or other technicians who might manipulate election results; and campaign specialists from outside the district or state who might be perceived as "carpetbaggers." Cautious politicians often want to conceal these expenditures to avoid any voter backlash.

DISCLOSURE IN THEORY

When it became apparent during the 1950s that expenditure limitations were a failure, attention turned back to the old idea of reform through full disclosure of the sources, amounts, and uses of campaign funds. Many states already had statutes that required some reporting of political finances. In the 1930s, the leading commentator on political finance had set down the tenet that disclosure was essential for free elections.

> Publicity of contributions as of expenditures—pitiless, continuous and intelligent publicity, extending to [candidates and] nonparty

as well as party organizations—is the least that a democracy should demand.[1]

In 1960, a scholar of political finance elaborated the purposes that would be served by this "pitiless, continuous, and intelligent publicity" of financial arrangements:

An effective publicity system will create financial accountability, increase public confidence in the electoral process and curb excesses and abuses by increasing political risk for those who would undertake sharp practices.[2]

These arguments influenced later reform groups. Conceding that "we see no sure way by statute to restrict the amount of money individuals may put into campaigns" and despairing of limiting candidates' expenditures, the President's Commission on Campaign Costs turned to full disclosure as the best answer.

Full and effective disclosure is the best way to control excessive contributions, on the one hand, and unlimited expenditures, on the other. Publicity has a cleansing and policing power far more powerful that that of limitations.[3]

The Twentieth Century Fund's independent Task Force on Financing Congressional Campaigns made the strongest case yet for full disclosure. It foresaw that full disclosure might encourage small contributions as well as impose curbs on shady practices. In *Electing Congress*, the task force affirmed that

full disclosure and publication of all campaign contributions and expenditures are the best disciplines available to make campaigns honest and fair. We also believe full public reporting will tell the public where political contributions are going, where they are needed, and thus encourage more people to make contributions to political campaigns.[4]

These claims address virtually every problem of political finance. Politicians would restrict the amounts they spent and the sources from which they took money in anticipation of adverse public reaction. The public itself would be able to pass judgment on candidates with full knowledge of their financing practices. And, full disclosure would encourage small gifts by pointing up the reality of campaign costs.

STATE AND FEDERAL LAWS: PRE-WATERGATE

This optimism concerning disclosure could not be contradicted from prior American experience with full disclosure laws. The trouble with the existing laws was thought to be in their operation, not in the theory behind them. The Twentieth Century Fund Task Force observed that thirty-one states either had no reporting laws whatever or required reports of varying degrees of completeness only after an election, when disclosure would neither deter candidates, inform the public, nor spur giving.[5] A 1971 study showed that in seven states the reporting requirements applied only to candidates, leaving committees free to receive and disburse funds without public scrutiny. In two states, the disclosure laws applied only to primary elections; in one, only to the general election; in three states, while disbursements were subject to reporting laws, receipts were not.[6]

Until Watergate loosed a flood of new laws, state disclosure codes were weak, and their enforcement was even weaker. For example, in the forty-one states with some kind of disclosure laws, only seventeen provided by statute that the filing officer, typically the secretary of state, report to a public prosecutor those candidates and committees failing to file political finance statements. In only eleven states was the filing officer required to inspect statements for completeness, accuracy, and other basic compliance with law. And in only thirteen did the law mandate that the filing officer report illegal or excessive expenditures to the public prosecutor.[7]

Even where reporting requirements were relatively complete and enforcement provisions realistic, few prosecutions actually occurred. The tacit understanding of politicians was that no one would kick open the lid of the Pandora's box of financing practices. Individuals and groups were discouraged by the long, tedious, and costly litigation necessary for enforcement. And prosecution often appeared useless because in reality it seldom could be concluded in time to affect the election in which the alleged violations occurred.

The weakness of full disclosure laws can be illustrated by the Federal Corrupt Practices Act of 1925, which until 1972 was the major federal law regulating political finance. It required reporting of receipts and disbursements only in general election campaigns, ignoring the financing of primaries altogether. It covered committees operating in two or more states, thus excluding the vast majority of committees supporting congressional aspirants. Even where funds were transferred from one state to another, the law was easy to evade. A committee would be formed, either for general fund raising or on behalf of a congressional candidate, in the District of Columbia, which had no disclosure laws whatever. Money raised from a wide variety of sources would then be transferred as a lump sum to the candidate's home-state committee, where it would be reported simply as a receipt from the District of Columbia committee. Nowhere along the line was it necessary to name the actual contributors.

Candidates for federal office and committees that supported them and operated with their knowledge and consent were required to report. But if candidates took care not to seek information about the operations of committees supporting them, they were not required to report those expenditures. Since most of these support committees operated on an intrastate basis, they were not required to report as multi-state committees. Candidates adopted the practice of spending little or nothing personally, leaving virtually all expenditures to be made by non-reporting intrastate committees. In a typical case, reports filed in Washington in 1970 showed no personal spending by any general election candidates for the United States Senate in Connecticut, but reports filed in Hartford by various state support committees revealed expenditures of more than $1,153,000. Similarly, Washington reports showed outlays of $23,662 in contests in Kentucky for the United States House of Representatives, but state reports detailed disbursements of more than $205,000.[8]

The law required senatorial candidates and their committees to file with the secretary of the Senate and all others with the clerk of the House. It was not enforced vigorously because the secretary and the clerk did not wish to embarrass their present or potential employers. The law did not require these supervisory officers to audit the reports or to file complaints if they appeared inaccurate; and of course they did not take such initiatives on their own. Without audits, politicians became sloppy or deliberately evasive in the books they kept and the reports they filed. Moreover, hours when the reports were available to the public, working space, the use of adding machines, typewriters, and photocopying equipment were all closely restricted, thus frustrating attempts to summarize and publicize the campaign finance reports.

All these practices stimulated a general belief that the reports were a very imperfect reflection of reality, and they discouraged most potential watchdogs such as the press, citizens' groups, and the political opposition from trying to monitor political finance practices and disseminate information about them during campaigns. The Citizens Research Foundation made vigorous post-election efforts to compile and issue comprehensive summaries of these reports, providing a continuing and useful albeit rough description of political finance in the United States. But despite voluminous scholarly and journalistic literature on these evasions and widespread knowledge of them in political circles, no one was ever prosecuted under the law.

Reformers advocating full disclosure wrote off these state and federal experiences as the failures of particular laws and of the men responsible for enforcing them. They cited, as a contrast, dramatic improvements in public reporting under Florida's "who gave it, who got it" law, enacted in 1951.[9] That law provides that candidates for major offices such as governor and senator must file receipts and expenditures weekly during the campaign, while aspirants to lesser offices and political committees report monthly; all funds must be spent through a treasurer and depository bank designated by each candidate; receipts must be filed within twenty-four hours; and no funds may be received within five days of the election, preventing delayed reporting of gifts and last-minute saturation campaigns.

Florida's law sharply improved reporting of expenditures and receipts. Immediately prior to the law's passage, two candidates for the United States Senate reported spending somewhat less than $100,000 apiece; after the reporting law went into effect, publicly acknowledged spending rose to more than $500,000 in the 1952 Democratic gubernatorial primary and to more than $2,240,000 in the same contest in 1966. The most attentive commentator on the Florida law observed in 1962 that "it is the informed judgment of those who should know . . . that Florida voters have been given an excellent profile of the financial support of all candidates before the lever is pulled in the voting booth."[10]

The success of the Florida law led Massachusetts to attempt to follow a similar format in its Campaign Fund Reporting Act, passed just before the 1962 election. Yet, in 1965, the Massachusetts Crime Commission concluded that "There is almost universal circumvention of the provisions of our Campaign Fund Reporting Act in the reporting of contributions and expenditures."[11] With the ink scarcely dry on the new law, both Edward McCormack and Edward Kennedy and their treasurers reported far less income and spending in their bitter 1962 contest for the Democratic senatorial nomination than was estimated by close observers.[12] The commission reported that

> loans to candidates were not fully reported; that candidates delayed the reporting of debts; that disclosure was avoided by persons who paid candidates' bills rather than undergo the publicity of making donations directly; that several candidates concealed types of expenditures and names of payees by channeling large sums to advertising agencies for undisclosed uses; and that cash contributions were not fully reported.[13]

The widely acclaimed Florida law may have had less effect than was originally believed for, in recent years, there have been occasional reports of substantial unreported spending. And, rather than educating the voters to the reality of political finance, the disclosures required by law apparently scandalized them. The result was that in the late 1960s, Florida enacted a new expenditure limitation law in response to the massive sums that had been reported spent. Although the limitations are more realistic than elsewhere—$350,000 for nomination and election campaigns for governor and senator, $250,000 for campaigns for statewide offices, $75,000 for congressional campaigns, and $25,000 for local offices—some were nonetheless low by the standards of spending that had occurred in Florida in the 1960s, and they are all characterized by the inflexibility that has made other limitation laws obsolete.

THE FEDERAL ELECTION CAMPAIGN ACT

The Florida law, notwithstanding its weaknesses, was vigorously advanced as an example of what could be achieved at the national level with tightly drafted legislation and effective enforcement. President Nixon's pledge to support comprehensive campaign finance reform, made through Senator Scott during the Republican campaign to sustain the President's veto of the Political Broadcast Act of 1970, ironically laid the groundwork for a federal full disclosure law. In 1971, citizens groups renewed their activities in behalf of campaign finance reform, strengthened both by the President's pledge and by growing unrest about political finance in the country and among congressmen, many of whom had just been through the incredibly expensive and oft-times foul 1970 congressional elections.

Against this background, Congress enacted the multi-purpose Federal Election Campaign Act of 1971.[14] Title III of the act rewarded the efforts of disclosure advocates by providing a surprisingly comprehensive scheme for reporting campaign receipts and expenditures.[15] In its main outline, Title III:

- Covers candidates and committees involved in election campaigns for president, vice president, senator, representative, and delegate to Congress or resident commissioner.
- Designates the clerk of the House of Representatives to receive political finance reports of candidates for the House and committees seeking to influence House elections; the secretary of the Senate for Senate candidates and involved committees; and the comptroller general (the head of the General Accounting Office) for presidential candidates and committees as well as various other committees.
- Defines elections to include general, special, primary, and run-off elections; nominating conventions and caucuses; delegate selection primaries; presidential preference primaries; and constitutional conventions.
- Defines candidates broadly to include those who qualify as candidates under state laws and those receiving or spending money, personally or through others, to seek election.

- Defines a political committee as any association spending more than $1,000 in a calendar year. By federal regulation, if any portion of a political committee's funds are spent to influence an election for a federal office, the committee must report.
- Defines contributions to include gifts, subscriptions, loans, promises, and political committee transfers of money or anything of value, including the pay of personnel whose services are rendered to a candidate (but not including volunteer workers).
- Defines expenditure broadly to include purchases, payments, distributions, loans, and other transfers of money or other things of value to influence elections or express preferences in election campaigns.
- Requires each political committee to provide its name and address and to register its officers and finance committee members, affiliated organizations, the names and addresses of candidates or party committees it supports, the names and addresses of banks and other fund repositories, and the disposition to be made of unused funds. By federal regulation, affiliated organizations include those forming political committees to influence federal elections, supporting primarily the political committee, or having generally the same membership as the political committee.
- Requires each political committee to keep records of all contributions and expenditures; to maintain on its books the name, mailing address, business address, and principal occupation of any person contributing more than $10 and of any person to whom an expenditure is made; and to retain a receipted bill of all expenditures which in the aggregate amount to more than $100 to any person in any calendar year.
- Requires candidates and political committees to file reports of receipts and expenditures on the tenth of March, June, and September, annually as well as on the fifteenth and fifth days preceding the election and on January 31. By federal regulation, these filings must be either hand-delivered on the specified date or deposited as certified airmail at a post office before midnight two days prior to the specified filing date. The purpose of these regulations is to assure the availability of reports on the filing date itself so that the reports due five days prior to election can be scrutinized and publicized before voters go to the polls.
- Requires Senate and House candidates and committees supporting them to file duplicate copies of their reports in each state with the secretary of state or comparable official in charge of elections.
- Requires that each candidate's and political committee's report include cash on hand, total receipts, and the sum of individual contributions since the last report as well as the cumulative

amount of receipts and individual contributions for the calendar year.

- Requires that each report itemize the name, mailing address, occupation, and principal place of business of those persons contributing more than $100, making or receiving loans, and making transfer payments. The date and amount of such transactions must also be reported. By federal regulation, reports must include each transaction since the last report and the cumulative amount contributed by each person during the calendar year.
- Requires that each report include total expenditures and the name, mailing address, occupation, and principal place of business of persons to whom expenditures of more than $100 are made. The date, amount, and purpose of expenditures must also be reported. By federal regulation, reports must include the cumulative amount for specified purposes, such as communications media and personnel, for the calendar year.
- Requires candidates and political committees to make continuing reports on the amount and nature of debts and the name, mailing address, occupation, and principal place of business of those to whom debts are owed until the debts are extinguished.
- Requires full reporting of all receipts and expenditures in connection with conducting national party conventions within sixty days after their adjournment.
- Provides that the supervisory officers shall report "apparent violations" to the Justice Department for prosecution and shall determine, after notice and hearing opportunity, whether any complaint made by any person alleging a violation of the law should be forwarded to the Justice Department for action.
- Requires the supervisory officers to prepare annual reports for each candidate and committee and to make such reports available for sale to the public.
- Requires the supervisory officers to prepare and publish an annual report showing total expenditures by candidates and committees, specified for nomination and election contests, for party, nonparty, and candidate groups, for national, state, and local levels, and for various purposes; and showing total receipts, specified by categories of amounts, by the level (local, state, national) at which the contributions were made, and by the particular contributors of more than $100.

THE STATES AFTER WATERGATE

Congressional enactment of the Federal Election Campaign Act of 1971, Watergate, a growing public outcry, and new finance scandals in the states loosed a torrent of legislation. The rich variety of state laws reflects the states' role as laboratories for public policy experimentation. The overall impact has been to tighten disclosure rules, impose expenditure and contribution limits by various creative formulas, and install widely differing public financing plans. All have strengthened campaign finance regulation.

A report in June, 1974, counted reform laws enacted in twenty-five states in the first six months of the year. The magnitude of state reform may be suggested by mentioning several of the most widespread changes. Although thirty-one states had either no reporting requirements or only post-election disclosures as recently as 1971, by September, 1974, only three states had no laws and only eleven retained post-election reporting. In thirty-six states disclosure was required both before and after elections.

Similarly, in 1971 only three states vested campaign financing authority in a separate agency. By 1974, twenty-three states had adopted elections boards or similar independent bodies, and virtually all these agencies had independent enforcement powers.[16] Many states also moved toward a central treasurer system—formerly effective only in Florida, Massachusetts, and a handful of others—to facilitate comprehensive reporting as well as to make spending and contribution limits enforceable. The Federal Election Campaign Act of 1974 will undoubtedly spur a new round of state reforms, adopting some of the federal rules and devising still new regulations that suit state purposes.

THE 1974 AMENDMENTS

The Federal Election Campaign Act of 1974 has mainly been praised for its low contribution limits, its sweeping expenditure ceilings, and its public financing of presidential primaries and general elections and of national conventions.[17] Several of its provisions, however, bear on the disclosure rules established in the 1971 act. These amendments:

- Substitute reports ten days before and thirty days after elections for two pre-election reports and modify the dates for quarterly and annual reports.
- Repeal the requirement for recording the occupation and principal place of business of contributors over $10, but not for those over $100 aggregately, to certain committees.
- Repeal the requirement for reporting the occupation and principal place of business of those to whom expenditures are made, leaving them identified solely by name and address.
- Prohibit cash contributions of more than $100 to a candidate or committee.

- Require expenditures, other than petty cash outlays not exceeding $100, to be by check.
- Require each candidate to designate a national or state bank as his campaign depository and make all financial transactions through that depository, but allow candidates for president to maintain a separate depository in each state.
- Require candidates to designate a principal campaign committee, which shall be responsible for financial transactions on the candidate's behalf.
- Provide that other committees supporting a candidate file their campaign finance reports with the principal campaign committee, which then compiles all reports and files them together.
- Reduce the size of late gifts that must be specially reported from $5,000 or more to more than $1,000.
- Eliminate the requirement that annual summaries of contributions and expenditures be published by the supervisory officers and make this effective in 1973 and 1974 as well as for future years.
- Create a Federal Election Commission with responsibility for administering the law but retain in the clerk of the House and secretary of the Senate the duty to receive statements on campaign finances.

These amendments both strengthen and weaken the 1971 act. The requirement of a principal campaign committee will centralize financing and facilitate disclosure by eliminating the confusion caused by a flurry of different reports from committees supporting the same candidate. The rules compelling candidates to designate depositories, banning payments except by check, and limiting cash contributions will make money more easily traceable and will thereby deter concealment of political funds. Much greater disclosure of large last-minute contributions will occur.

Not recording the occupation and principal place of business of certain small contributors will not significantly jeopardize disclosure, and lifting the same record-keeping and reporting requirements for expenditures will diminish disclosure only slightly. The continued division of responsibility between the clerk, secretary, and Election Commission, however, bears the seeds of confusion and of uneven enforcement despite the overall supervisory authority of the commission. Most important, the repeal of the statutory mandate that supervisory officers publish summaries of receipts and expenditures and a complete listing of contributions in excess of $100 will make enforcement more difficult and will reduce the ability of the people and the press to correlate officials' post-election conduct with their campaign funding sources.

THE CONSTITUTIONAL ISSUE

Serious questions have been raised about the constitutionality of these full disclosure provisions. The national government clearly has the authority to regulate federal elections,[18] but this power may be limited when legislation invades First Amendment rights. In the 1960s, the Supreme Court held that Southern states could neither compel teachers to disclose all their organizational memberships for the past five years nor force the NAACP to submit its membership lists to state officials as a condition of operating in those states.[19] The justices warned that these regulations would invade the freedoms of speech, association, and perhaps assembly. Disclosure of NAACP membership might lead to harassment, community hostility, and economic reprisals, which would "chill" freedom and discourage citizens from exercising their First Amendment rights. Similarly, a Los Angeles ordinance prohibiting distribution of any handbill that did not identify its sponsors was struck down because disclosure might discourage the authors and tend to restrict freedom to distribute information.[20]

On the other hand, the Supreme Court has sustained disclosure where there is a compelling government or public interest. The threat of subversion was held to warrant investigation into citizens' political ties; enforcement of criminal laws was found to be sufficient reason to force reporters to disclose confidential sources; and public concern with backgrounds of community leaders has supported revelation of teachers' and lawyers' organizational ties and of newspapers' financial backers.[21]

Critics of full disclosure laws argue that revealing the names and addresses of campaign contributors will deter citizens from taking part in politics.[22] Some point out the possibility of government reprisals, a danger more plausible after the Watergate revelations. Others suggest that contributors might "fear . . . harm to social, business, employment, and professional relations from private kinds of retribution; these are just as much a part of the deterrence that is to be protected against as are official reprisals."[23] Most critics argue that, even if disclosure is necessary to safeguard against corruption in elections, revealing contributions of $100 goes too far because that small sum is unlikely to lead to undue influence or to wrongdoing.[24]

Proponents of disclosure point out, however, that campaign contributions are not speech, association, or assembly. They are actions that are related to these constitutional guarantees but go beyond them. Such actions are less entitled to protection, especially when they influence politics and set the course of government actions affecting other citizens' rights. Moreover, there is a First Amendment argument for disclosure; it provides a free flow of information that helps voters make decisions about politics, candidates, and programs.[25] It is also difficult to insist on privacy for campaign contributors when others who influence elections—by posting a sign on their lawn or car, attending a political rally, or canvassing their neighborhood—hold themselves up for scrutiny by the public nature of their activities. The argument that contributions of $100 are too small to require disclosure ignores the need to examine many moderate-sized gifts from associated individuals or interests to detect the aggregate pattern of their giving. Also, the disclosure of smaller gifts is necessary to enforce the limits on a person's total gifts to various committees supporting the same candidate and to all political committees of every kind.

The Supreme Court upheld the disclosure requirements of the Federal Corrupt Practices Act of 1925, but it did not consider the First Amendment issues in that case. Later it sustained the Federal Lobbying Act's disclosure rules against a challenge based squarely on First Amendment guarantees.[26] Both these cases, however, occurred before the right of political privacy had been extended in the NAACP cases. Nonetheless, campaign contributions are probably sufficiently different from pure speech, there is probably a sufficient public interest in knowing who is contributing to candidates, and the need for disclosure to allow enforcement of campaign laws is probably great enough to sustain the 1971 act and similar disclosure laws. A final determination, of course, must await the justices.

A United States district court recently upheld the Georgia Campaign Financing Disclosure Act against challenges that its provisions requiring disclosure of contributions in excess of $100 violated the constitutional freedom of association. The court noted that such revelations impinge upon First Amendment rights, but such restrictions are permissible if they advance a compelling state interest. Disclosure is justified by the state's urgent need to preserve the democratic process from corruption and to ensure fair elections. Although not every giver of more than $100 threatens the integrity of elections, the disclosure threshold represents a rational attempt by the legislature "to establish a level of contribution that will attract the attention of the candidate" and might therefore allow a contributor to make claims upon him. Disclosure of contributions exceeding $100 therefore serves the state's compelling interest and is constitutional.[27]

LOOPHOLES AND EVASION

Despite its sweeping provisions, the amended 1971 act is not foolproof. Common Cause and alert members of the press have discovered loopholes and evasions. The "laundering" of campaign contributions has been the most prevalent of these practices.

In one instance, an American business transferred funds to an inactive foreign corporation. It paid "legal fees" to an attorney. The attorney made "loans" to certain Americans, who in turn contributed equal sums to the Nixon campaign. The original donor was well concealed, and the Committee for the Re-election of the President was able to "report" the direct sources of the campaign contributions. Laundering through foreign corporations or individuals is particularly difficult to trace.[28]

Transfers of funds through many committees, all reporting their financial activities, may have the same effect as laundering funds.[29] In a relatively simple case, an international labor union's political action committee transferred funds to one of its affiliated state groups. The state group contributed to a congressional candidate, who duly reported receipt of the funds. Only a diligent searcher would have discovered that the contribution actually came from out-side the state; he would have been compelled to trace the sum back to the state labor group and then back to the Washington-based international union, which filed its report only in the nation's capital.

A far more sophisticated arrangement of the same kind involves transfers through a series of committees, the earlier ones filing in Washington and the later ones locally. The newsman, citizen, or opposition researcher would find it necessary to trace a contribution back through several committees in the state capital to discover it had originated in Washington and then to examine several Washing-ton committees to identify the initial donor.

If local political committees become involved, the record of a chain of transactions may be obscured completely. A gift made to a local committee can be routed to a second group, which effects still a third local transfer. The third committee makes a contribution to a Washington political committee, and that group transfers it to a state-based congressional campaign committee. That campaign com-mittee either spends the money or transfers it one more time to a congressional candidate's organization. Because the first political committee in the chain does not directly support candidates for federal office, it need not report under federal law. If state law requires it to report, that filing is likely to be in an obscure court-house or, at most, in the state capital. Tracing the gift to its source involves searching federal reports in Washington and then state reports filed with state or local officials.

In many instances, laundering can only be inferred or suspected. In 1972, a number of special interest groups made very large con-tributions to the congressional campaign committees of the two major parties, but no earmarking of funds to specific candidates was acknowledged. One method of carrying out this practice is for the special interest to write a check to the party committee but to give it to the candidate for delivery to that committee. Its delivery then creates an understanding that the committee will subsequently give a like amount to the candidate. The obligation is wholly tacit. Indeed, this procedure is hardly distinguishable from the normal method by which congresssional campaign committees raise many of their funds.

A number of methods of dealing with loopholes exist. All committees and candidates could be required to acknowledge transactions involving earmarked funds. But the decentralization of American politics leaves even that remedy defective. Most money raised in American politics, especially at the local and state levels, does not involve earmarking. Big donors and special interests that give to party committees or *ad hoc* fund-raising organizations know what candidates will be supported. Often they also expect that the fund raisers will subsequently plead their case with the officials they supported. The United Fund financing organization in the Republican party is the clearest example: although there is no earmarking, the giver knows where his money will go and who the financial middlemen are when he needs to do some special pleading.

An apparent expenditure loophole in the 1971 act's full disclosure scheme can be traced directly to the regulations set up by the supervisory officials rather than to the law itself. The law provides simply that expenditures of more than $100 shall be reported, but these officers have the option of requiring either that candidates and committees report each outlay in excess of $100 in a reporting period or that they report the aggregate sum paid a person during the current period and in previous periods. By choosing the former option, the officers have made it difficult to discover the full amounts paid out for particular goods and services or to specified individuals. A picture of outlays can therefore be obtained only by examining as many as ten different reports of a candidate or committee in a twelve-month period.

One last loophole is the $999 political committee, which would spend just under the $1,000 statutory cut-off point for filing reports. A manageable collection of such committees might be feasible in House and Senate races. Furthermore, they could be used to conceal sources of funds, since contributions to them need not be reported and the same individual could give to several of them. No systematic use of the $999 committee has yet come to light, but since their purpose would be to avoid reporting they may simply have escaped notice.

COMPLIANCE

In 1974, the General Accounting Office was still auditing the reports of the 1972 presidential campaign committees and the congressional supervisory officers were still compiling their reports. Thus the extent of compliance and the vigor of enforcement under the Federal Election Campaign Act was still unknown. Reports flooded into Washington and the state capitals in huge waves, and the supervisory officers certified a host of "apparent violations" to the Justice Department for prosecution. Although an early appraisal would be tentatively favorable, serious shortcomings are already visible.

The clerk of the House estimated at one point that more than six hundred congressional candidates, mainly those defeated in primary election contests, and almost a hundred presidential committees had failed to file. But the *Washington Post* reported it had been told informally that violations would run two or three times that number.[30]

Another reporting problem involves the identification of contributors. At a minimum, campaigns for federal offices receive several hundred thousand gifts of more than $100. Many are received by mail or in other circumstances that do not easily permit the candidate to obtain the required information about the contributor—his name, address, occupation, and principal place of business. Philip Hughes, director of the Office of Federal Elections, has reported finding a large number of these technical and probably irremediable violations in both the Nixon and McGovern campaigns.[31] Because these violations were not deliberate attempts to conceal the identities of contributors, Hughes suggested that they could not be considered serious. Their effect was, nonetheless, to deny to the electorate information that the proponents of disclosure maintain is necessary for wise voter choice at the polls.

Candidates also frequently failed to comply with the statutory rule requiring reporting within forty-eight hours of contributions of $5,000 or more received after the last pre-election report is filed. An unreported election eve contribution of $50,000 to the Nixon campaign by Frank Sinatra captured press attention when noted by the General Accounting Office in mid-February, as did a similarly unreported $5,000 contribution by Mr. and Mrs. Paul Newman to McGovern. In all, the McGovern campaign failed to file reports of ten last-minute contributions of $5,000 or more, and the Nixon committee did not give forty-eight-hour notice of an unspecified number of such gifts totaling more than $1 million.[32]

Although the GAO and its congressional counterparts made exceptional efforts to facilitate full reporting, many 1972 campaign finance statements were improperly completed. A manual of instructions, relatively simple forms, full and plain federal regulations, and several briefings for politicians and press were all sponsored by the supervisory officers. But these well-intentioned and extensive efforts were frequently thwarted by the amateurism that marks much of American politics. The few professionals in a campaign are primarily involved with major campaign decisions, and the filing of campaign finance statements is shifted downward to the volunteers or to young, inexperienced paid workers, who were swamped by the flood of record keeping required by the 1971 act.

Even when no intentional violation and no deliberate concealment were meant, the purpose of the law can be frustrated. One small example will suffice. The Keep Kastenmeier in Congress Committee, the main political arm in the re-election campaign of Representative Robert Kastenmeier of Wisconsin's Second District, did not carry over its expenditure totals from one report to another on its seven filed statements. The volunteer who filed the reports, and perhaps the local campaign staff backing her up, intended no violation. In fact, the reports are in every other way models of care and completeness. But the result of unsophisticated bookwork in this case was incorrect disclosure. Newsmen perusing the reports, acting quickly to meet deadlines, picked up the total expenditure listed on these reports and included them in their news stories. What was really reported was the expenditure in a single filing period, not the cumulative expenditures for the calendar year.

The 1971 law, in short, may be unintentionally violated in a large number of instances because too much information is asked for and too little account is taken of the amateurism of American politics. Yet workable full disclosure requires that statements be technically correct because they are only a first stage in transmitting the information to the public for its evaluation. Under the theory of full disclosure, the opposition politicians and press who are responsible for publicizing the information cannot be expected to conduct extensive reviews of the reports and figures for accuracy and completeness.

ENFORCEMENT

Faced with a new and complex law requiring an unprecedented amount of information, the Office of Federal Elections in the General Accounting Office proved to be a vigorous watchdog. It systematically audited political committee reports and dispatched auditors to examine the books of committees operating outside Washington. It filed a series of reports critical of presidential campaign committees whose sloppy financial procedures caused unintentional violations. And it certified apparent violations to the

Justice Department when it discovered substantial or intentional breaches of the law.

Nevertheless the overall enforcement mechanisms had serious shortcomings, including the role of the Justice Department. Recent attorneys general not only have been partisan appointees of presidents, they have also been chief political officers. Under such leadership the Justice Department is unlikely to be considered neutral in enforcing election laws. In campaign finance cases less visible than Watergate, where media and political pressures are not so intense, the discretion and potential partisanship of the Department of Justice is almost unlimited. That fewer than a dozen non-Watergate prosecutions have followed the supervisory officers' certification of more than 10,000 apparent violations may be taken as an indication that the Justice Department is, at the very least, an unenthusiastic agent of enforcement.

The 1974 amendments created a Federal Election Commission with independent power to receive complaints and to investigate violations. It has independent authority to go to court for civil remedies to prevent or correct violations. A Senate provision to allow the commission also to bring criminal actions was deleted, and criminal prosecutions remain in the hands of the Justice Department. The commission may refer both civil and criminal actions to the attorney general. He is required by law to report his disposition of these referrals within two months. These provisions promise somewhat stronger and more independent enforcement; but they do not create a fully independent agency, as the Senate bill recommended.

An additional weakness in enforcement was the three-way division of responsibility among the clerk of the House, the secretary of the Senate, and the comptroller general. Since the clerk and secretary are political appointees of the majority party in the respective houses, their designation to administer the law is tainted. Republicans on the Senate Commerce Committee warned of this taint in their minority report. "The Secretary and the Clerk will find it difficult to take firm steps in gaining compliance from incumbent Senators and Representatives ... who are responsible for their selection to their office," they argued; and "every impulse ... will be for the Secretary and the Clerk to do the minimum required by a new law."[33]

Subsequent negotiations between the GAO and the congressional officers illustrated the weak posture of the clerk and secretary. The clerk, for instance, argued unsuccessfully that "filing" should be defined as mailing; thus reports mailed five days in advance of elections would have constituted compliance even though they would have been received too close to the election for even the modest scrutiny that now occurs. The GAO urged that social security numbers be required to identify contributors, a measure that would eliminate much of the present uncertainty; it was overruled by the congressional officers. It also proposed that gifts of $500 or more be returned to the donors if all required identification was not obtained by the political committee. The regulations finally adopted require only that a campaign treasurer use his best efforts to obtain such information and keep a record of those efforts.

The effect of divided responsibility and political pressure also surfaced in the issuance of summary reports, which are helpful to the media and the public as they try to grasp patterns of political financing. In mid-September, 1972, the GAO issued a 760-page computer printout of gifts of $25 or more to presidential campaign committees from the act's effective date on April 7 to September 10. Neither of the congressional supervisory officers followed GAO's lead. On August 23, 1973, the GAO released a computer printout of 84,337 contributions by 70,000 persons who gave in excess of $100 in the 1972 presidential campaign. On March 24, 1974, it followed up with a report showing direct expenditures and transfer payments to influence the presidential nomination and election by 1,786 political committees filing with the Office of Federal Elections. Both reports were consistent with the 1971 act's requirement that filing officers issue summary reports. Not until mid-1974 did the clerk and the secretary issue any report required by the act.

The reluctance of the secretary and clerk to construe the law broadly and enforce it vigorously has been reinforced by the harassment of the clerk by Representative Wayne Hays, chairman of the House Administration Committee. One report says that "When [House Clerk W. Pat] Jennings went before the Hays committee to request funds for personnel and equipment to administer the law, the hearings became a donnybrook of name-calling and threats."[34] Jennings' request for thirty-eight additional staff positions was cut to twelve, and his budget application of $399,030 was pared to $156,984. Hays also ordered that the price of photocopying copies of reports be raised from ten cents to a dollar a page, although he backed down on this requirement in the face of a Common Cause lawsuit. In a final attempt to cripple enforcement, he threatened legislation to move administration of the law from the clerk's office to his Administration Committee.[35] These overt pressures, added to the ever-present and subtle constraints of the employment relationship, cast serious doubts on the capacity of the clerk and the secretary to administer the law effectively.

The Federal Election Commission created by the 1974 amendments is composed of two members appointed by the speaker of the

House, two by the presiding officer of the Senate, and two by the president. In addition, the Senate secretary and House clerk serve without voting power. While the commission has general supervisory authority, the clerk and the secretary are authorized by statute to receive the campaign finance reports of candidates for their respective houses. This arrangement could lead to substantial centralization and coordination of the disclosure functions, or it could continue the previous confusing division of authority.

The fact that the vigilant Office of Federal Elections in the GAO was disbanded rather than transferred to the new commission has created the impression that the new body may not be as militant as many had hoped. This impression is reinforced by the apparent intention of Congress to have appointees who are personally and politically close to the members and who therefore, like the secretary and clerk, are unlikely to enforce the campaign finance laws vigorously. Congressional reluctance to create an effective enforcement agency is also signaled by the 1974 act's provision that the commission's regulations be submitted to Congress, where either house can veto them within thirty days. Even if rarely exercised, this power is an implicit deterrent to the commission's zealous enforcement of the law. The future of enforcement is uncertain, but some believe that the 1974 amendments are in fact a retreat from the strong stance taken earlier by the GAO.

Finally, the penalties provided by law may not be strong deterrents. The statutory penalties are light: fines up to $1,000, imprisonment of not more than one year, or both. Where only a fine is imposed, the crime is a misdemeanor only. An early conviction under the act, involving eight counts of mishandling $30,000 by the Committee for the Re-election of the President, resulted in the maximum fine of $8,000, scarcely a severe penalty. The Senate version of the 1974 act proposed that any violation be a misdemeanor carrying penalties of up to $10,000 or one year in jail or both and that wilful violations be felonies with penalties of up to $100,000 or five years' imprisonment or both. The House conferees rejected this proposal, and it was stricken from the final version.

Light penalties are accompanied by the likelihood that they will not be imposed on the primary beneficiaries of the violations. Prosecutions usually involve political committees, as in the eight-count conviction of the Nixon re-election group, rather than individuals. This state of affairs encourages campaign strategists to calculate whether they wish to pay the fines as overhead for doing some politically advantageous act. Even if individuals rather than committees are convicted, as has happened in the aftermath of Watergate, underlings will usually take the rap.

Because prosecutions will almost always occur after the election, any adverse publicity surrounding convictions does not threaten immediate voter reaction at the polls, which is supposedly the most effective deterrent to improper conduct. By the time his aides are prosecuted, the candidate who has benefited from violations of the act may well be already in office.

TOO MUCH INFORMATION?

So much information is required, so many sources of information report, and so much information is forthcoming that the primary objective of full disclosure legislation, providing the public with political finance information that can be worked into the electoral calculus, is thwarted. The flood of information under the Federal Election Campaign Act so inundates newsmen, the opposition, and the reporting officers themselves that no one knows before election day what the state of political finance is, even though a law that actually commands substantial reporting has replaced a wholly ineffective law.

Too much information is coupled with too little time to analyze it. The fault is not in the law, which in 1972 required disclosure fifteen and five days before elections, but in the inherently conflicting requirements of full disclosure. Full disclosure of receipt and expenditure information requires that filing deadlines be set close to election day not only to assure completeness but also because so many financial transactions occur in the last hectic days of political campaigns. But full disclosure produces mountains of political finance information that must be exhaustively analyzed to reveal significant patterns of giving and spending; time also is needed to publicize these patterns, to allow debate and discussion about them, and finally to permit voters to ponder them and to calculate what weight political financing shall have in their ballot choices. The demands of disclosure, then, are simultaneously for massive reporting close to election day and for plenty of time before election day to assess what has been massively reported. It is scarcely surprising that disclosure disappoints its proponents and falls short of their promises.

The scope of the problem of organizing the information becoming available under the Federal Election Campaign Act is seen in an estimate made by Philip S. Hughes, who was director of the GAO's Federal Elections Office, that he was receiving materials from approximately 725 separate committees supporting Senator McGovern's presidential candidacy and from 250 committees supporting President Nixon's re-election bid.[36] The GAO's summary report for 1972 reflected reports from 1,785 committees. This number does not include the thousands of committees that supported congressional candidates or influenced congressional elections; those groups reported to the clerk of the House and the secretary of the Senate.

The formation of hundreds and perhaps thousands of local and special committees throughout the nation manifests the traditional American interest in presidential politics and is one of the great vehicles for citizen participation in electing the chief executive. Yet any group that spends as much as $1,000 must report under the 1971 act. A similar, although smaller, proliferation of committees occurs in congressional campaigning. The multiplicity of committees hinders effective disclosure of campaign financing, yet it is essential for widespread grassroots participation.

The 1974 act moves toward greater centralization of reporting by candidates. Each designates a principal campaign committee through which most funds are channeled. Other committees authorized by the candidate file their reports with the principal campaign committee, which then compiles and files them. The Election Commission could promulgate regulations that would bring order to the many committee filings incorporated into the principal campaign committee's report. If it does so, the scrutiny and publicizing of campaign finance information will be much easier and faster. Even these measures will not, however, simplify the morass of special interest committee reports.

Beyond the large number of committees that must report is the enormous volume of reports filed by those committees. At the end of 1972, officials of the House of Representatives estimated that the campaign finance reports received by the clerk would fill 110,000 published pages. Through November, 1972, Senate officials had received an estimated 60,000 pages of reports.[37] The Office of Federal Elections cautioned that its March, 1974, report on committee receipts and outlays was not error-free because of the quantity and irregular quality of the source documents—about 10,000 separate reports containing about 95,000 pages of information.

The overload of information becomes even more acute when the spotlight shifts from committees to contributors. The mid-September, 1972, report of the GAO, mentioned above, contained more than 36,000 names of contributors of $25 or more. The final report of August, 1973, listed more than 84,000 contributions from 70,000 persons who had given more than $100. These reports include no contributions made to House or Senate candidates or to committees influencing congressional elections in 1972. The number of contributions finally reported will certainly be several hundred thousand. This volume of information simply cannot be systematically reviewed in time for election day.

Additional problems occur when a single giver sends money to several or many committees. Since there is no centralized reporting, the true magnitude of his activities shows up only upon examining all the committee lists or waiting for a computer to sort and alphabetize all the givers to the various committees. Even then, however, identification of contributors is not certain. Names are misspelled; addresses may be different; and occupational descriptions may vary. *Congressional Quarterly* illustrated the problem by showing that Angier Biddle Duke, a well-known Democratic contributor, was listed by four different McGovern committees, under two different names, and at three different addresses. For less well-known figures, the tracking problem becomes insurmountable.

The tidal wave of information plainly discouraged newsmen. Conversations with reporters from major papers assigned just to follow the political financing story in 1972 revealed their sense of helplessness and frustration. Most newspapers, the broadcast media, and the wire services did not, of course, assign full-time staffers to cover the political finance beat.

The effectiveness of press coverage of campaign finance in 1972 is not clear. The press often was honestly perplexed about how to handle political finance coverage and about what its role should be. Candidate preferences of newspapers may have colored their reporting of political finance practices just as they did coverage of the far-more-salient Watergate story. Ben Bagdikian reported that Nixon-endorsing papers carried early Watergate stories on only 48 percent of the potential opportunities and only 21 percent of the time on the front page, while McGovern-endorsing papers ran the stories 77 percent of the time and on the front page on 46 percent of the opportunities.[38]

The nature of the coverage also varies. A major round-up story can be filed after political finance statements become available. Certain follow-up stories may also be carried when they make some special, newsworthy point. But most newspapers would be hard pressed to justify more coverage than this, since campaign finance reporting then occurs at the expense of other, more current news.

The impressions gained from a year's clipping from major national newspapers attentive to campaign finance news tends to confirm these patterns. Post-filing stories typically ran from nine column inches to several dozen, and they highlighted latest expenditure totals and a handful of the largest contributors. Follow-up stories explained how gift taxes were avoided by multiple small gifts and reported concentrated interest group giving. Where news stories identified big givers ("Nixon's 10 Top Contributors Gave Campaign $4.1 Million"),[39] the detailed listing of who and how much must have struck most readers as incomprehensible or trivial. The *New*

York Times' response to the Nixon Re-election Committee's release of pre-March 9 contributor lists, as a result of a Common Cause lawsuit, was to print thirty-six column inches of contributors' names, addresses, and business affiliations in the paper's tiniest type.[40]

Even such revelations as those carried by the *Times, Washington Post,* and other papers about the massive financial contributions of the dairy interests to the Republican campaign are newsworthy only once. When they appear on the inside pages, they cannot make much of a dent on the public consciousness. Yet the theory of full disclosure assumes just such an impact—specific knowledge sufficient for voters to make decisions about particular candidates, not overall impressions of the evils of big spending, big giving, and special interest manipulation. If the nation's major papers are overwhelmed by the torrent of data unleashed by disclosure and are unable or unwilling to give the kind of repeated, in-depth coverage needed, political finance reporting in smaller papers, which serve most voters and do not have Washington or state capital correspondents, must conform even less to the model required for a working disclosure system.

IS ANYBODY LISTENING?

If the scrutiny of political finance virtually broke down from the overweight of disclosure, it was nonetheless true that in 1972 more was learned and transmitted about money in politics than during any recent election campaign. And if the media have neither the resources nor the format to publicize political finance practices, as envisioned by disclosure advocates, they nonetheless gave far more attention to money in politics than in the past.

The public is the link in the chain of disclosure that can retaliate against politicians who spend too much or whose campaigns are excessively beholden to special interests and big givers. But only the sketchiest indicators of voter reaction to political finance revelations during the campaign are available. Watergate was the most-reported episode; but it was a political finance issue only in the non-reporting of funds and the use of the money to hire and equip burglars, disclosures that would not be made under the law in any case. It was the break-in, bugging, links to the White House, and cover-up that made Watergate important, not the failure to report campaign funds. Further, some voters' reactions to Watergate, which got much more publicity than political finance, showed the limited extent to which public knowledge of practices sways opinion. Although at least 75 percent of the public knew about Watergate by mid-October and agreed that a basic violation of civil liberties occurs when a party wiretaps the opposition headquarters, by 70 to 13 percent people viewed Watergate as "political spying"; by 62 to 26 percent they weren't worried about the civil liberties aspect of the case because it was "mostly politics"; and by 57 to 25 percent they thought that such political spying was a common occurrence in American politics.[41] More than eight in ten did not see Watergate as a reason to vote for George McGovern.[42]

The electoral impact of the complex political finance issue was non-existent. Despite the highly publicized $9 million Democratic debt as the year began, the continuing reports of vast Nixon fund-raising successes, and periodic news about McGovern's difficulty keeping his campaign from floundering financially, 47 percent of the people thought neither party had "an unfair money advantage over the other."[43]

The Twentieth Century Fund Survey, taken soon after the election, reinforces the view that public opinion is not likely to be an effective check on campaign finance practices. Fully 62 percent of people surveyed answered affirmatively when asked, "Did you happen to hear or read anything about the campaign money being raised or spent by any of the political parties or candidates during this election year?" But what was heard, or at least remembered, was so indefinite and unclear that it was unlikely to prompt much attitude change or electoral judgment.

Only 55 percent of those polled had heard or read anything about Republican campaign financing, and recall among that group was sketchy. Fifty percent of the whole sample could relate something they had heard about the way Republicans raised money in 1972; the most common recollection was about the failure to report contributions (presumably those occurring before the law's effective date, April 7, 1972). Only 29 percent mentioned anything about the sources of GOP funds, and only 22 percent noted anything about the amounts of Republican spending. Even fewer people—51 percent —had heard about Democratic financing. Only 11 percent mentioned anything about the method of Democratic fund raising, despite the nationwide telethon and McGovern's pleas for twenty-five dollars from one million voters. Fifteen percent recalled something about the source of Democratic funds, usually about the large number of small givers. Twenty percent related information about the amount of Democratic spending, but more than half of those responses involved the oversized Democratic debt remaining from 1968. The same person often recalled several pieces of information, but many of those who said they had heard something could not remember anything specific at all. Thus knowledge that might be useful in assessing candidates or parties was very scattered in the electorate.

Most respondents said that the information they had gotten about political finance practices had not prompted any change in their

TABLE 6-1   Political Finance Information and Attitude Changes toward the Two Major Political Parties

"Did [what you heard about the money raised and spent by any of the political parties or candidates during this election year] cause you to feel more favorable toward the (Democratic/Republican) party or candidate than before, less favorable, or did it make a difference?"	
Hadn't heard anything[a]	38%
Made no difference	37
Caused more or less favorable feelings toward one or both parties	21
Other[b]	4
	100

SOURCE: Twentieth Century Fund Survey (see Chap. 3, n. 1, above).

[a] Includes those who didn't know or didn't respond to the question of whether they had heard any campaign finance information.

[b] Had heard about other than the major parties.

attitudes toward the two parties. The figures in Table 6-1 indicate that only 21 percent of the whole sample believed any change had occurred as a result of campaign finance information. In a close contest, of course, attitude changes among 21 percent of the population could be decisive, and disclosure might therefore be praised as an effective potential sanction against politicians employing questionable finance practices. Since our figures refer to attitude changes toward parties generally, they do not describe the attitude change in any particular race, which is the more critical factor in affecting political conduct. Of course, all party politicians have some stake in maintaining conduct within the party that will not offend public norms.

A more serious difficulty with this analysis is that changing attitudes are heavily related to party affiliation. Selective perception, an attempt to reconcile the conflict between personal beliefs or allegiances, on one hand, and adverse information or competing beliefs, on the other, is the way most people respond to information. They hear or at least remember only that which conforms to pre-existing beliefs; or they reinterpret what they hear so that it fits their established beliefs.

As we have seen, information about the political finance issue in 1972 was generally less favorable to the Republicans than to the Democrats. Watergate, concealed pre-April 7 contributions, special interest giving, and heavy expenditures were all linked to the Republicans by publicity. Unfavorable attitude changes toward Republicans substantially outnumbered favorable changes (Table 6-2, column 8).

When overall attitude changes are examined more closely, however, they show a high degree of selective perception by party iden-

TABLE 6-2 Political Finance Information, Attitude Change, and Party Identification

Those who heard campaign finance information about Republicans became:

	Strong Dem. (col. 1)	Weak Dem. (col. 2)	Ind. Dem. (col. 3)	Ind. (col. 4)	Ind. Rep. (col. 5)	Weak Rep. (col. 6)	Strong Rep. (col. 7)	Total (col. 8)
More favorable to Rep.	3%	1%	1%	4%	7%	4%	12%	4%
No different	49	71	50	81	79	87	84	70
Less favorable to Rep.	48	28	50	15	13	9	4	26
	100%	100%	101%	100%	99%	100%	100%	100%

Those who heard campaign finance information about Democrats became:

	Strong Dem. (col. 9)	Weak Dem. (col. 10)	Ind. Dem. (col. 11)	Ind. (col. 12)	Ind. Rep. (col. 13)	Weak Rep. (col. 14)	Strong-Rep. (col. 15)	Total (col. 16)
More favorable to Dem.	33%	14%	24%	5%	8%	5%	4%	14%
No different	61	70	65	82	77	82	74	72
Less favorable to Dem.	6	16	11	13	15	13	22	13
	100%	100%	100%	100%	100%	100%	100%	99%

SOURCE: Twentieth Century Fund Survey (see Chap. 3, n. 1, above).

tifiers. Overwhelmingly, Democrats became more favorable to their own party (columns 9–11) and less favorable to the Republicans (columns 1–3). Despite the damaging information about the Nixon campaign's financing, Republicans became more favorable to their party than did the whole population (columns 5–7); and they became more hostile to the Democrats as a result of political finance information (columns 13–15). Independents tended to have fewer attitude changes and they split more evenly between the parties than did those who professed party affiliations.

Despite the interest in the new law, the special effort by some media to cover political financing, and an unusual array of newsworthy campaign finance events touching both parties, the voters seemed largely inattentive and unmoved by full disclosure. Many said they had heard something about political finance issues, but the quality of their information was poor. Few said their attitudes toward the parties had changed as a result of what they learned. And although the Democrats gained somewhat greater popularity as a result of the issue, which may have benefited them more at the House and Senate levels, most attitude changes were heavily conditioned by pre-existing party affiliations.

DISCLOSURE AND THE DEMOCRATIC CITIZEN

If the public won't pay attention to political finance practices revealed under effective full disclosure laws, some will say that it deserves the kind of political process it is getting. Since the pollsters first discovered that more Americans could identify Dick Tracy, Joe Louis, and Elizabeth Taylor than prominent members of the Cabinet and Congress, there have been protests from scholars about the incompetence of the public. Only 43 percent of Americans know their congressman; only 30 percent know the length of his term; only 19 percent know where he stands on any issue; only 40 percent regularly read about the campaign during a presidential race; only 9 percent take time to attend any political meeting during the presidential contest; and so forth.[45] The system cannot be made workable, the critics say, if a democratic citizenry will not do its civic duty, especially in the curbing of money in politics through disclosure.

This censure of the American citizenry has been denounced as resting on a false theory of knowledge about democracy, indeed about life. It assumes that democratic citizens must know the details of politics in order to govern themselves. Such a standard of citizen performance is impossible: "there is no escape from the problem of ignorance [in a democracy], because nobody knows enough to run the government. Presidents, senators, governors, judges, professors, doctors of philosophy, editors and the like are only a little less ignorant than the rest of us."[46] Hence, in self-government, as in every aspect of life, individuals must accommodate themselves to dealing daily with an incredible number of matters about which they know very little.

The nature of modern mass democracy and of our complex post-industrial society stretches even thinner the obligations that can reasonably be imposed on citizens. In the Greek city-state, life and politics were relatively simple; the community was small and government had few duties; citizens devoted ample time to this uncomplicated process because a slave class supported them. In modern democracies the issues are complex and technical; the community is large and government is involved in every aspect of life; the average citizen gives more than two-thirds of his day to the basic necessities of sleep, work, and eating and additional hours to his family and private pursuits. To hold such citizens responsible for detailed knowledge about government or about the names, identities, and special interest affiliations of campaign contributors imposes an incredible and impossible test for self-government.

But self-government is not therefore impossible. There is, for instance, considerable consistency between the way people vote and how they stand on the overriding issues before the nation. Announcing, in 1963, that "the perverse and unorthodox argument of this little book is that voters are not fools," the late V. O. Key, Jr., demonstrated that the same kinds of poll data used to condemn voters also showed that the electorate was capable of governing intelligently. On such issues as social security, business regulation, farm programs, the conduct of World War II and Korea, and the recognition and policing of labor unions, voters who shifted from one party to the other in succeeding presidential elections overwhelmingly agreed with the policy of the party they shifted to. Those who remained with the same party from one election to the next mainly agreed with the most visible programs of the party they voted for.[47]

Similarly, surveys from 1956 to 1968 showed supporters of the Democratic party to be substantially more liberal than others on federal aid to education, government provision of medical care, government guarantees of jobs for those willing to work, federal enforcement of fair employment and housing, federal enforcement of school integration, and, to a lesser extent, foreign aid. Large majorities perceived differences between the two parties and correctly understood the Democrats to be more liberal. During these four presidential elections, issue orientation among the public rose measurably.[48]

Together with knowledge about highly salient issues, voters use party labels to bring order from the chaos and complexity of public affairs. By correctly perceiving the Democrats as liberal or as favorable toward government intervention to address social or economic problems, and by correctly perceiving the Republicans as conservative or as hostile toward governmental solutions to societal problems, voters can match their own general preferences with a major party and vote accordingly. Further, voters identify those holding power by their party label and then vote for or against a party to show their approval or disapproval of the way the nation is run.

In every aspect, voters look only broadly at politics. On issues, their preferences are mainly limited to such general terms as "the government in Washington ought to help people get doctors and hospital care at low cost." When they do not know about issues, they use the party label to identify candidates whose general ideas or whose conduct of government they wish to mandate or reject.

These realistic perspectives on the capacity and limits of the American electorate dim the prospects for full disclosure of political finance. It is improbable that citizens in a modern mass democracy will learn the details of the financing of particular campaigns and then base their electoral decisions on them. Even the most attentive among us cannot govern ourselves if we are required to know the details of national health insurance legislation rather than merely to hold a general preference about government-sponsored medical care. Nor can we govern ourselves if legislation puts the burden on us to clean up campaign financing by understanding the complex web of financial transactions that occurs in campaigns. Nor can we rely on party labels to clarify this issue for us, because both parties are irrevocably caught in that web of big money and special interest money by which we finance our political campaigns.

THE CALCULUS OF VOTING
Even if the American voter did grasp the information revealed by full disclosure of campaign finances and did incorporate it into his calculus of ballot choice, the success of disclosure in curbing our political money ills would be doubtful. The theory of disclosure insists that voters will reject candidates at the polls when disclosure shows too much spending, misdirected spending, unsavory or disfavored financial sources, or excessive contributions. In elections, however, a citizen cannot express himself solely on campaign finance practices; his vote for a candidate is a decision about many other issues as well.

In all our elections, issues of war and peace, domestic social welfare, national economic policy, race relations, and civil liberties are at stake. Will an ideally informed citizen give much weight to campaign finance practices when the other issues he must decide are so momentous? To put it directly, would a 1972 voter who favored a hard line in Southeast Asia and on college campuses have cast his ballot for George McGovern because of the way Richard Nixon financed his campaign?

The answer is made more difficult because political finance practices do not usually offer a clear choice between competing candidates. All are typically involved with big money and special interest money. In 1972, Nixon raised massive sums from business interests; but McGovern had the support of many elements of organized labor as well as big gifts from the ideological left. Nixon's spending topped $50 million, almost double his 1968 total; but McGovern's outlays approached $40 million, more than triple the expenditures of his party's 1968 standard-bearer. Even if an informed voter had thrown the momentous issues of 1972 to the winds, basing his vote solely on the lesser criterion of campaign financing, would his choice have been a clear one, especially if that choice had not been confused by association with the Watergate bugging and break-in?

THE DISAPPOINTMENT OF DISCLOSURE

The sponsors of the Federal Election Campaign Act of 1971 assumed that past failures of disclosure legislation resulted from defects in the disclosure laws, not weaknesses inherent in the theory of disclosure. Like its predecessors, the 1971 act has defects. And it has been further weakened by the 1974 amendments. Laundering remains possible under certain circumstances, long chains of transactions make tracing funds difficult, small committees need not report, supervision is divided, enforcement is problematic, and penalties are light. Further, the natural decentralization of American politics and the fund-raising role of political parties thwart effective disclosure of candidate finances.

The question remains, however, whether a more tightly drafted law, accompanied by vigorous enforcement and heavy penalities, would produce the results claimed by advocates of disclosure. We doubt it. First, contradictory demands are inherent in the theory of disclosure. Everything must be revealed; but everyone's revealing everything produces so much information so close to election day that it cannot be analyzed, publicized, and then understood by the public.

Second, the effectiveness of disclosure depends entirely on the transmission of political finance information to the voters. The media may simply find this too burdensome, or they may cover it in ways consistent with editorial preferences. Nor can candidates be relied on to transmit campaign finance information. When competing candidates are well funded, both are likely to count big givers and interest groups among their contributors; neither then has an interest in raising the political finance issue. If one candidate is well funded and the other is not, the impoverished candidate simply does not have the resources to discover and publicize the amounts and sources of his opponent's funds.

Third, even if the information is available and transmitted, the general public cannot and will not comprehend and use it. Mass democracy does not rest on the voters' detailed knowledge of issues but rather on their ability to choose leaders and parties whose general outlook coincides with their own. Yet full disclosure assumes that voters want and can use detailed knowledge and analysis of amounts, sources, and expenditures of campaign funds. Further, voters frequently avoid information that does not harmonize with their party or candidate preferences; they selectively perceive facts that confirm their choices and screen out hostile information.

Fourth, voters do not and should not give campaign finance practices a heavy weight in making ballot choices, and therefore candidates rarely need fear that disclosure of such practices will result in political penalties at the polls. In the present political financing system, both parties and virtually all candidates receive and use funds from big givers and interest groups. Voters usually do not have a choice between clean money candidates and dirty money candidates; all are soiled. More important, the vote is each citizen's way of influencing the nation's direction on issues of war and peace, taxation and economics, government programs and expenditures, civil liberties, race relations, environment, and other profound national questions. He would waste his vote if he gave more weight to the sources of campaign funds than to a candidate's posture on these great issues.

Finally, of course, disclosure fails because it does not provide enough money from untainted sources or distribute it evenly enough to make possible vigorous adversary campaigns for all major offices in all districts throughout the nation. Indeed, instead of generating more money, clean money, and evenly distributed money for politics, disclosure probably dries up funds by highlighting how unsavory and unfair our financing system is and turning citizens away from participation in a seemingly dirty business.

There is not the slightest indication that the massive disclosures under the 1971 act changed the course of the 1972 presidential election, although revelations of big and dirty money were made well in advance of the election. Nor did citizens respond to these revelations by making small contributions to offset the dangerous money that has long flowed into politics. The 1971 act's weaknesses were demonstrated in practice in 1972; but disclosure's inherent defects as a reform policy mainly caused the act's failure to curb the scandalous funding practices that will mark the 1972 campaign in the pages of history.

We do not conclude, however, that disclosure is wholly without merit. Although it is not likely to alter the role of big and interested money during campaigns or to stimulate mass giving to politics, disclosure may very well be useful during inter-election periods if the media and attentive groups wish to monitor official conduct. Official postures toward big and interested contributors should be known. Between elections there is more time to analyze campaign finance practices, to transmit them to citizens, to capture public attention, and to persuade at least attentive citizens that on certain issues financial links between officials and groups may bear on policy decisions.

Most important, however, is the negative role of disclosure. The story of American campaign financing is a shabby one. Disclosure educates the public, perhaps slowly, about the reality of campaign costs, the sources of money, and the uses of funds. Telling that story, especially between elections, serves to spur the search for new campaign finance policies that provide clean money, enough money, and well-distributed money. Disclosure, in short, heightens the demand for reform and almost invariably points reformers toward public financing of political campaigns. It is no accident that the revelations under the 1971 act have, together with Watergate and other events, impelled many citizens, reform groups, and members of Congress toward sweeping public financing measures.

Reformers in the United States have emphasized limits on contributions and expenditures, and disclosure of political financing. Although Theodore Roosevelt urged public financing of American campaigns in 1907, there was little serious consideration of the idea and almost no experimentation with it until the last decade. Until Lyndon Johnson endorsed the check-off plan in 1967, no other American president had expressed support of the cause. In the aftermath of Watergate, Congress adopted the Federal Election Campaign Act of 1974, which provides public financing of presidential primaries and general elections and of national party conventions. The Senate also adopted public financing of congressional races, but the House rejected the idea by a narrow margin. Since 1972, eight states have adopted direct public financing schemes, and others have enacted indirect tax subsidies.

This rush of reform occurred against an American background featuring very few experiments with direct public financing. Indeed, as Watergate sent the nation lurching toward campaign reform, serious political consideration of direct public subsidies was scarcely ten years old in America, dating from the tentative endorsement of matching grants by President Kennedy's Commission on Campaign Costs. In foreign democ-

7

AMERICAN EXPERIMENTS WITH PUBLIC FINANCING

racies, however, public financing had become a commonplace. We reserve consideration of post-Watergate American legislation and of foreign public financing schemes for successive chapters so that here we can consider the indirect and direct tax-supported campaign reforms that have molded the present American debate and have often seriously misdirected it.

Viewing the government's role in electoral politics, Americans have usually distinguished between elections and campaigns. Government, they say, may safely engage in election administration. The mechanics of voting do not, in the main, involve advocacy; and in general, despite the stubborn recurrence of ballot fraud in some American locales, government can maintain and operate the apparatus for recording voters' choices and counting ballots more efficiently and more fairly than politicians or parties. But in a constitutional system resting on the principle that competition both sharpens voter choice and checks the excesses of leaders, campaigns should be managed entirely by contending politicians, not the government. The assumption of competitive politics is that those striving for office can state their case and criticize the opposition more effectively than anyone else. Americans have worried that if government became involved in campaigns, it would inevitably—despite good intentions—find itself judging the merit of campaign appeals, usurping the prerogative of the voters in a democracy.

ELECTION ADMINISTRATION

Historically, political parties paid many of the costs of election administration, including ballots, polling places, and election workers. In this century, however, state and local governments assumed that responsibility. Today, taxpayers generally pay the costs of ballots and voting machines, lists of electors, election clerks, vote tabulations, polling places, and some recount activities. In the state of Washington, in the late 1960s, these activities cost an estimated $3.00 per registered voter in each election year. An Oregon study found, however, that election expenses varied widely from one locale to another; the range was between $1.00 and $1.50 per registered voter.[1] Few of these estimates include the full costs of government personnel (such as county clerks) involved part-time and seasonally in election administration. But the Oregon figures do conform closely to estimates by Canadian officials that, in the 1960s, national election costs, excluding the provincial elections, ran about $1.25 per eligible voter.[2] Including a margin for hidden personnel costs, for inflation, and for the multiple costs associated with the long ballot, one might fix election administration expenditures in the range of $1.75 per eligible voter. In 1972, this outlay would have been about $244 million for an electorate slightly exceeding 139 million. Election costs therefore ran about 57 percent of campaign costs, which were an estimated $425 million in 1972.

One aspect of election administration that touches directly on the vote-seeking activities of candidates is the availability of lists of electors, which are used for mass mailings, voter registration drives, and get-out-the-vote activities. Where government prints and distributes such lists free of charge or for a nominal fee, candidates and parties save substantial sums that would otherwise be devoted to copying or compiling voting rolls. Practices vary from jurisdiction to jurisdiction. Politicians benefit most when registration lists are computerized and when mailing stickers as well as voter rolls can be purchased for a nominal fee from election boards.

North Dakota does not require voters to register before election day; some small communities in other states also do not require voters to register in advance. But although prior registration requirements vary widely from one jurisdiction to another, in most places the public treasury pays the cost of maintaining the voting rolls. A controversial issue is whether government should also foot the bill for getting voters registered, as it does in most other democratic nations. Certainly the process has inevitable political effects, altering the balance in a district's party alignment and perhaps changing the prospects of certain candidates, including incumbents or those from particular economic or ethnic groups. Recognizing the campaigning element in voter registration, parties and candidates often devote substantial financial and manpower resources to getting their adherents on the rolls.

But most other democratic countries view registration as part of orderly election administration, intended to limit the voting in a given district to its residents and to prevent voters from casting multiple ballots. The Committee for Economic Development has argued that "all necessary election and primary costs that do not benefit one candidate or party or position on election issues against any others are properly a public responsibility and should be conducted at governmental expense."[3] The CED includes government-financed, universal voter registration among those responsibilities.

Idaho is the only one of the United States with government-conducted voter registration. It authorizes a deputy registrar in each precinct to keep registration rolls up to date, and it permits door-to-door canvassing for this purpose. Although such social characteristics as its small and settled population also carry some weight, Idaho's universal, government-sponsored voter registration system undoubtedly is a large part of the reason why this state consistently ranks among the top three in both percentage of population registered and percentage of population voting. California law provides for the appointment of large numbers of deputy registrars, who receive twenty-five cents for each voter registered; these provisions have led to vigorous voter registration canvasses both in busy public places, such as shopping centers, and door to door. At least one study shows that these efforts can substantially increase a party's voting strength.[4] In most states, though, the individual citizen must take the initiative in order to register. These arrangements discriminate against those who move frequently, who live far from registration centers, whose employment overlaps the office hours of the registration officials, or whose sophistication about politics is limited by low educational attainment or other socio-economic factors.

On May 9, 1973, the United States Senate invoked cloture and, by a vote of fifty-seven to thirty-seven, passed a bill allowing postcard voter registration in national elections. A new Voter Registration Administration in the United States Census Bureau would mail postcard forms to all postal addresses and residences. Citizens returning cards to local voting registration agents within thirty days would be enrolled for federal elections. The Voter Registration Administration would pay the costs of processing the cards. The bill also provided an incentive to postcard registration for state and local elections; 30 percent of costs of processing the cards would be paid by the federal government. Cost estimates for this universal voter registration vary widely; supporters claim it would run about $120 million, while opponents have cited figures as high as $300 million. But a Wisconsin legislative official puts the cost of computerized, statewide postcard registration at approximately $1.33 a head for approximately 1.2 million unregistered voters. A 1970 estimate, probably on the low side, put the number of unregistered Americans at 30 million, and approximately 5 million must be added to that figure to take into account the unregistered among the newly enfranchised eighteen- to twenty-year-olds. On May 8, 1974, the House of Representatives narrowly rejected the Senate measure by a vote of 204 to 197.

Governmental voter registration would have a substantial impact on campaign finance. Total campaign costs in 1968 ran $300 million and in 1972 approximately $425 million. Voter registration was important among these costs, and under the proposed legislation the government would be devoting substantially more money to registration than parties and candidates have been spending. The low level of expenditures on registration undoubtedly reflects the short supply of private resources available for this purpose and the inadequacy of party and candidate registration drives. A national voter registration system would, therefore, have two effects: it would free millions of party and candidate dollars for other purposes, and it would provide more dollars for a vastly more effective registration of American voters.

SERVICES IN KIND

The most notable of the advocacy services to parties and candidates is the voters' information pamphlet, authorized at one time or another in fourteen states and actually used in twelve of them. The voters' information pamphlet ordinarily contains information about referendum and initiative propositions (six states), candidates (two states), or both (four states). At this writing only five states still have voter information pamphlets in use—three for referendum and initiative measures and two for both measures and candidates.[5]

The best-known of these is the Oregon Voters' Pamphlet, distributed by mail to each of that state's voters in each primary and general election.[6] It includes information about political parties, candidates for party offices (such as committeeman and national convention delegate), candidates for public office, and ballot measures. Contenders may buy space in the pamphlet for a nominal fee, ranging from $15 per page for state legislative candidates to $150 per page for presidential aspirants. Circulation of the pamphlet was over 1 million in both the primary and general election in 1970. To provide voters with information about legislative and other candidates in their own areas, the pamphlet was published in seventy different regional editions in the primary and thirty-six in the general election.

The pamphlet's combination of low price, wide circulation, and apparently high standing encourages wide candidate use. In recent elections, 100 percent of the candidates for Congress and state office have bought space in general elections and about 80 percent in primaries. In contested campaigns for county offices, at least one candidate purchased space in the pamphlet in about 80 percent of the 1970 races. Even in judicial elections, about 42 percent of the candidates in contested races bought space in the decade from 1960 to 1970.

The pamphlet is primarily subsidized by the state. The gross cost for the 344-page pamphlet in the 1970 general election was $126,839, or 12.6 cents apiece. Fees from candidates averaged 1.3 cents apiece; hence the state paid 11.3 cents per item.

The value of the Voters' Pamphlet to Oregon politicians may not be great; campaign costs do not seem to be rising more slowly in Oregon than elsewhere.[7] Doubts about its vote-winning effectiveness are surely among the reasons why politicians have not altered their spending practices despite the state subsidy provided by the Voters' Pamphlet. In general, television is the medium most widely used by Americans to obtain political information about national and statewide offices; newspapers are slightly more often used for local political information. Dense print media, like magazines, rank far behind television, newspapers, and radio as information sources about politics. And television is a far more believable medium to most people, with newspapers, radio, and magazines trailing far behind, in that order.[8] The 300- to 400-page Voters' Pamphlet is comparable to a magazine; Oregon politicians apparently calculate—probably correctly—that it is of only slight use in getting their case across to the public. They will not reduce spending for other media in reliance on it.

Surveys about voter use of the Oregon Voters' Pamphlet indicate that 45 percent of the respondents read all or most of it and another 39 percent read some of it. Only 11 percent thought the information in the pamphlet was excellent; 59 percent rated it pretty good, and the remainder gave it lower marks. Voters also were asked to rate the influence of the pamphlet on election decisions. As Table 7-1 shows, only on ballot measures, about which voters probably have few alternative sources of information, did respondents give the pamphlet much credit for helping them make their choices.

Estimates of the usefulness of the pamphlet for this purpose corresponded to income level; only 21 percent of respondents in the lowest income group (under $3,000), as opposed to 61 percent in the highest income group ($25,000 and over), found it very helpful. Perhaps the upper income groups, better educated and more interested in politics, are able and willing to invest intellectual energy in studying complicated ballot propositions, and use the Voters' Pamphlet for this purpose largely because few other information sources are available. In selecting candidates, however, a higher percentage of low-income than of high-income people (15 percent and 10 percent respectively) found the pamphlet useful. No single medium that can influence even this percentage of an electorate is likely to be ignored; but the reluctance of politicians to limit spending for other activities and to rely on the pamphlet alone to get their messages to the voters seems well founded.

Recognizing the preference of the public for broadcast over print media, several states have simply extended the principle of services in kind to television and radio, providing free time for candidates on the publicly owned educational radio and television networks. But these networks, too, generally win the attention of only highly select audiences and do not seem to have enough impact to encourage politicians to reduce their campaign expenditures. In any case, only a few states provide these services, and in none of these states has the impact of free time been systematically evaluated.

A more ambitious proposal to provide candidates with access to

TABLE 7-1 Usefulness of the Oregon Voters' Pamphlet in Making Electoral Decisions

Usefulness on[a]	Very Useful	Somewhat Useful	Little or No Use	Not Sure	Total
Ballot measures	41%	38%	19%	2%	100%
Statewide and congressional races	16	43	37	4	100
State legislative and county races	19	48	30	4	101[b]

SOURCE: Donald G. Balmer, *State Election Services in Oregon* (Princeton, N.J.: Citizens' Research Foundation, 1972), pp. 58–60.

a "How useful would you say the Voters' Pamphlet is in helping you to make up your mind (on how to vote on ballot measures?) (what candidate you will vote for in statewide or congressional/state legislative or county offices?)"

b Does not total 100 percent because of rounding.

television and radio is "Voters' Time," prepared by the Twentieth Century Fund Commission on Campaign Costs in the Electronic Era.[9] Under this proposal, the government would purchase half-hour segments of television time, paying the networks 50 percent of the lowest commercial rate. These segments would then be allocated to the presidential and vice presidential candidates. Candidates would qualify for Voters' Time if their names appeared on the ballot in three-quarters of the states whose electoral votes were sufficient to elect a president. Presidential aspirants whose party had ranked first or second in popular votes in the last election would be given six prime-time half-hours in the thirty-five days before election; candidates whose parties had received one-eighth of the popular votes would receive two half-hour segments; those simply qualifying in the required number of states would be entitled to one half-hour slot. These programs would be broadcast simultaneously on all networks and would be held to a format standard that would promote rational political discourse, including substantial live appearances by the candidates for president and vice president.

The commission's recommendations fall short on a number of counts. First, they do not provide media time in primary campaigns, when the party label is absent and the impact of media exposure is consequently greater. Second, the commission acknowledges that if the Voters' Time approach were extended to senatorial or congressional races, the broadcast channels would be overwhelmed with political shows. Yet presidential campaigns are already extensively covered by media, both on news programs and in paid advertising. It is lower-level candidates who more acutely need full exposure.

Third, public interest in live performances by politicians is very limited. A 1968 study revealed that audiences quickly fell to about two-thirds of normal when presidential campaign broadcasts were substituted for the usual program fare.[10] Simultaneous broadcasts will discourage the television audience from switching channels, but they cannot prevent Americans from simply ignoring or turning off long presentations by politicians. When the number of programs reaches twelve half-hours, as it would have in 1972, or thirteen, as in 1968, inattention may turn to alienation. Certainly the availability of substantial amounts of free television time would reduce a candidates's need to raise money for broadcast media, but it would not necessarily reduce campaign expenditures. Money might simply be applied to other campaign activities.

Other recommendations for in-kind services include reduced postal rates and the franking privilege. If parties and candidates were permitted the lowest postal rate presently available to charitable organizations, they could increase their solicitations for funds and volunteer workers as well as their appeals for votes. Granting the franking privilege to congressional challengers would offset the free "non-political" mailings of incumbents during their terms.[11]

Mailing privileges might increase the level of political activity and might have a multiplier effect by bringing more resources into campaigns. But both gains in all likelihood would be minimal. Even now, citizens' mail-boxes are overflowing with appeals and advertising; additional political solicitations would probably get scant attention. The public's relative inattention even to a well-established mail appeal like the Voters' Pamphlet argues against the effectiveness of vastly increased political mailings. Steadily expanding solicitations have not led to a proportional increase in giving. Again, the campaign funds saved by services in kind are likely to be displaced to other activities. Overall, then, free mailing service would increase the level of political activity only slightly, would have little effect on voters, and would not significantly reduce the candidate's incentive to raise and spend large sums of campaign money.

INDIRECT SUBSIDIES

The Irrelevance of Tax Incentives. In recent years, tax incentives for campaign giving have been a favorite legislative recommendation of reformers.[12] Any tax incentive for political contributions is of course a subsidy of candidates by all taxpayers, since they must make up through taxes the sums lost when contributors write off gifts against their taxes. In theory, tax incentives serve the purposes of reform in at least three ways. First, it is claimed, more people would make campaign contributions if the government, by providing tax incentives, assumed a substantial part of the cost. Presumably, if more people made campaign contributions, contributors would be more representative of the whole population than they are now, and the disproportionate influence of large contributors and special interests on candidates would be reduced.

Second, tax incentives would increase the flow of money into politics and encourage a more vigorous adversary process. New contributors would provide most of this additional money. But tax incentives might also lead those who have contributed in the past to be even more generous. At the very least, a contributor could increase his political gift at no extra cost to himself simply by adding to his usual contribution the amount subsidized by the government through tax deductions or credits. Some givers undoubtedly would increase their gifts by still more.

Third, tax incentives may, in the vision of one reformer, "dignify political contributions by signifying state recognition of their usefulness, as in charitable and educational giving."[13]

The most general objection to the tax incentive device is that, even if it achieved its sponsors' goals, it would not alter the present maldistribution of political funds. A larger and more representative contributor corps is as likely as the present one to give money to high-visibility campaigns such as those for president, senator, and governor, leaving lesser but equally important office seekers, such as congressional and state legislative aspirants, still so impoverished that truly vigorous contests are beyond their financial reach. Nor would tax incentives reverse the present tendency of givers to allocate their funds to sure winners or hotly contested races. Minority-party candidates in one-party districts and challengers facing strongly entrenched incumbents would still be orphans in the private financing system, and the largest number of races for the House of Representatives, state legislatures, city and county councils, and many other governmental bodies would still lack the kind of effective competitive campaigning that poses alternatives for voters.

Despite these flaws, a 1974 count showed that tax incentive plans had been adopted by twenty-seven states and, in the Revenue Act of 1971, by Congress. Twenty-two states allow tax deductions for political contributions ranging from $25 to $100. Four states allow a small tax credit. And one state and the federal government offer both options. The Revenue Act of 1971 permitted a contributor to a candidate or political committee to deduct up to $50 ($100 on a joint return) or to take a tax credit of one-half on gifts up to $25 ($50 on a joint return).[14] In late 1974, Congress doubled both the deduction and the credit for political donations.

A tax credit, of course, allows each taxpayer the same benefit for each dollar contributed regardless of income or tax bracket. Every dollar given to politics, up to the limit provided by law, can be subtracted directly from the individual's tax liability.

The tax credit does not benefit—and thus does not provide an incentive for—those who have no taxable income. In 1972, there were 139 million Americans over eighteen years of age and only 121 million taxpayers. At least 17 million voting-age Americans—and probably more, since some taxpayers are under eighteen—could not take a tax credit. Softening this exclusion is the fact that non-taxpayers are probably the least likely portion of the electorate to make contributions.

The tax deduction is far more controversial. Too few voters can take advantage of it; only 48 percent of tax returns itemize deductions, and those who do itemize are disproportionately drawn from high income groups. Fully 75 percent of those reporting adjusted gross income of $10,000 to $15,000 and 85 percent of those above $15,000 are itemized. Finally, of course, the dollar benefit gained from a tax deduction is proportional to one's tax bracket. A contributor in the 70 percent bracket wins a $35 tax reduction by deducting a $50 political gift; a taxpayer in the 20 percent bracket receives only a $10 reduction. Since tax incentives are a subsidy by all taxpayers, even the relatively small inequality demonstrated by this example may be objectionable: the candidates supported by large givers receive a larger subsidy than others do.

The credit-or-deduction option of the federal law reduces these disparities but does not eliminate them. A low bracket taxpayer could make a political contribution of $50 at a personal cost of $25, because he would receive the other $25 in the form of a tax credit. A taxpayer in the 70 percent bracket could make the same $50 contribution at a personal cost of only $15; the remaining $35 (70 percent of his contribution) would be offset by his tax deduction. Or the 70 percent bracket taxpayer could make a total contribution of $83.33 at a personal cost of $25, while the maximum gift a low bracket taxpayer can make at the same personal cost is $50. Hence, the high bracket taxpayer can make a political contribution more cheaply than a low bracket taxpayer; or he can exercise greater political influence at the same personal cost that a low bracket taxpayer incurs to have a smaller impact on politics.

Of course, the deductions and credits allowed in American jurisdictions are so small that the disparities in tax savings and in political influence are very slight and may not have much impact in practice. Those in 70 percent tax brackets are not likely to alter their political activity in order to save $35. If they are interested in politics, they will contribute, and contribute very substantially. The tax benefit is just a minor windfall received for doing what they would do anyway. On the other hand, the tax credit may well give a family in a lower bracket the incentive to contribute. But this family must then provide the full sum from their own pockets at the time the gift is made, and only half of it is returned at tax time.

A more general objection to tax incentives is that they are irrelevant. Most studies show that political activism is most closely associated with socio-economic class, strength of partisan identification, intensity of feelings about issues, competitiveness of electoral contests, and similar socio-political conditions. Although they may have some positive effects on campaign giving, tax incentives alone are not likely to make activists out of the cynical, the apathetic, or the uninformed.

In fact, the vastly widened participation in financing campaigns predicted by tax incentive advocates has failed to materialize. Despite the federal credit-or-deduction option available in 1972, the percentage of voting-age Americans making campaign contributions was the same 12 percent as in 1960 and 1964.[15]

The insignificant impact of tax incentives for political contributions is confirmed by the small number of taxpayers using them. Only 2.5 percent of individual taxpayers took the federal credit in 1972 and only 1.3 percent took the deduction. The total of 3.8 percent is not only far less than the 12.4 percent who gave, it is probably exaggerated because many taxpayers tend to falsely claim hard-to-trace tax breaks. The number of households participating is even smaller, measured by returns rather than individual taxpayers claiming the incentives. The credit was claimed on only 2.1 percent of the returns and the deduction on only 1 percent. State tax incentive experiments confirm the tendency toward low participation. In 1972 only 2.1 percent of California taxpayers took advantage of the Golden State's deduction of up to $100 for political contributions. And in the 1970 congressional elections only 0.5 percent of Oregon taxpayers claimed that state's tax credit for one-half of campaign gifts up to $10 (see Table 7-2).

Moreover, tax incentives do not reduce the disproportionate representation of high income groups among campaign givers by encouraging lower-income people to participate. In 1972, those with adjusted gross incomes of $20,000 or more were 27 times as likely to claim a political tax incentive as those with incomes under $5,000. Yet these high-income people were only 9 times as likely to give as their lower-income neighbors (compare columns 3 and 5 in Table 7-2). High-income Californians were 46 times as likely as their state's low-income citizens to claim a deduction, and in Oregon the well-off were 290 times more likely to take the tax credit than those at the bottom of the income ladder (columns 1 and 2 in Table 7-2).

TABLE 7-2 Political Tax Incentive Users and Campaign Contributors by Income Class

Income Group[a]	Percentages of Returns in Each Income Class Using Tax Incentives			Percentage of U.S. Population Contributing		
	California 1972[b] (col. 1)	Oregon 1970[c] (col. 2)	U.S. 1972[d] (col. 3)	1968[e] (col. 4)	1972[f] (col. 5)	Change (col. 6)
$ 0– 4,999	0.2%	0.2%	0.4%	3.0%	3.7%	0.7%
5,000– 9,999	0.7	0.1	2.2	7.3	11.5	4.2
10,000–14,999	1.7	0.4	4.1	8.4	11.7	3.3
15,000–19,999	3.3	1.2	6.2[g]	14.3	19.8	5.5
20,000 and more	9.2	5.9	10.8[g]	24.1	32.0	7.9
Total	2.1	0.5	3.0	7.6	12.4	4.8

[a] Adjusted gross income in cols. 1–3; total family income in cols. 4–6. These figures are roughly comparable in most cases.
[b] Information provided by California Franchise Tax Board.
[c] Information provided by Oregon Department of Revenue.
[d] Information provided by United States Internal Revenue Service; includes both credits and deductions.
[e] SOURCE: Survey Research Center of the University of Michigan.
[f] SOURCE: Twentieth Century Fund Survey (see Chap. 3, n. 1, above).
[g] Estimated. Includes proportionate distribution between the two income classes of IRS information provided for the two combined.

The small number of taxpayers taking advantage of tax incentives suggests that the increase in campaign giving from 7.6 percent in 1968 to 12.4 percent in 1972 should not be attributed to these revenue breaks, especially since 12 percent of Americans gave in 1960 and 1964 when there were no tax incentives. Further, from 1968 to 1972 the increase in giving was 0.7 percent in the lowest income group and 7.9 percent in the highest (see column 6 of Table 7-2). If tax incentives inspired increased giving, they promoted it eleven times more often among upper-income persons than among the poor.

Finally, some will argue that in 1972 Americans were not yet aware of the federal tax incentives and that they will be encouraged to make contributions as they become familiar with the credit-or-deduction system. State experiments contradict this reasoning. California has offered its tax deduction since 1957, and 1972 participation was only 2.1 percent of tax returns.

The Twentieth Century Fund Survey asked whether tax incentives for political contributions were available. Only 39.6 percent of respondents gave the correct, affirmative, answer. Another 21.3 percent said no, and 39.1 percent didn't know or didn't answer. These figures confirm that Americans generally did not know of the tax incentives. To test the possibility that if Americans knew of tax incentives they would use them, a further question was asked those who had not contributed in 1972 and either did not know tax incentives were available or did not believe they were. Those who said they would give if a tax incentive was available were only 5.7 percent of the sample. Taking their answers at face value, they would have added only marginally to the American contributor base, increasing it from 12.4 percent to 18.3 percent. And while these self-professed tax-inspired givers are somewhat more representative by income of the general population than is the actual contributor corps, the highest income classes are still almost three times as likely to give as the poorest group (see Table 7-3).

Counter-Reform: Two Tax Incentives That Work. The failure of the deliberate legislative effort to increase participation and small gifts by offering tax deductions and credits for modest contributions contrasts with two administrative decisions by the Internal Revenue Service (IRS) that successfully and vastly increased big giving in 1972. First, in June, 1972, the IRS ruled that a political committee was to be considered separate and independent for gift tax purposes if one-third of its officers were different from those of other committees supporting the same candidate.[16] The ruling was made retroactive to cover the massive fund raising from big givers that occurred before the Federal Election Campaign Act went into effect

TABLE 7-3   Contributors and Potential Contributors under a Tax Incentive Plan, 1972

Income Class	Percentage of Income Class Contributing in 1972	Percentage of Class's Potential Contributors in 1972[a]	Total
$ 0– 4,999	3.7	8.2	11.9
5,000– 9,999	11.5	8.0	19.5
10,000–14,999	11.7	4.4	16.1
15,000–19,999	19.8	2.5	22.3
20,000 and more	32.0	0.8	32.8
Total by income[b]	12.4	5.9	18.3
Total[c]	12.4	5.7	18.1

SOURCE: Twentieth Century Fund Survey (see Chap. 3, n. 1).

[a] Non-contributors responding that they would contribute if they could obtain a tax break for doing so.

[b] Totals of those respondents who reported family income (N=1332).

[c] Totals of full sample, including respondents who did not report family income (N=1481).

on April 7, 1972. Simply by dividing his large contribution into the maximum non-taxable units of $3,000 and distributing them to many separate committees supporting the same candidate, a big giver could have avoided gift taxes entirely. The tax rate for gifts is relatively steep; avoiding the tax may have made the big giver an even bigger giver. Or it may have created new big giving by eliminating a cost they would otherwise have incurred. Whether the benefit of this subsidy went to the recipient candidates or their donors, it ran into millions of dollars.

In 1973, Tax Analysts and Advocates, a public interest law firm, brought suit against the Treasury Department to knock out the IRS ruling. The United States District Court for the District of Columbia agreed that the candidate received the "benefit" of the contributions to various committees operating in his behalf and that the gift was therefore the total of all the smaller contributions, not each $3,000 contribution separately. This effectively eliminated the multiple committee dodge for big givers. Declaring the IRS ruling null and void, the court nonetheless allowed collection of the gift tax on these multiple committee gifts only after the date of its decision, June 7, 1974.[17]

Second was the 1972 ruling that stocks given to a political committee are to be valued at their purchase price rather than their market price. A taxpayer who made his contribution in stock did not have to pay income tax or capital gains tax on the increased value. A gift of stock purchased for $1,000 and then valued at $3,000 earned the donor credit with the recipient for a $3,000 contribution that actually cost the donor only $1,000, since he was not taxed for the appreciation in value. But because the political committee was a non-taxable entity, when it sold the stock at the appreciated market value, it did not pay taxes on the $2,000 difference between the purchase price and the sale price. Hence nobody paid the income tax or capital gains tax on the increased value of the stock; yet both the giver and the political committee could make use of the increased value. The uproar following media reports of this IRS ruling caused its withdrawal in 1973.

Both major-party presidential candidates made extensive use of the gift tax avoidance device in 1972. The General Accounting Office (GAO) reported to the Commissioner of Internal Revenue that "we have widespread use of the device of multiple committees to facilitate avoidance of gift tax liability by major contributions." According to one source, there were more than 750 McGovern committees and 250 Nixon committees.[18] According to another, 650 Nixon committees were in operation before the April 7 date when the Federal Election Campaign Act required each to register.[19] One public relations executive reported that he alone had set up 150 separate Nixon committees to allow contributors to avoid gift taxes.[20] They bore such obscure names as the United Friends of a Balanced Society and the Dedicated Volunteers for Government Reform.[21] Similar McGovern groups were called Mental Health Workers for McGovern and Sixth Street McGovern for President Committee.[22]

The effects of this device show up in the giving patterns of particular donors. Richard M. Scaife, heir to the Mellon fortune, gave Nixon $990,000 distributed among 330 committees, thus avoiding any gift tax. If his whole contribution had been regarded as a single gift for tax purposes, his gift tax liability would have ranged between $244,000 and $590,000, depending on the extent of his other gifts. W. Clement Stone, the Chicago insurance magnate, and his wife reportedly gave $2 million in small, tax-avoiding gifts; his tax liability would have run as high as $1.4 million if his contribution had been aggregated for gift tax purposes.[23] McGovern received more than $300,000 in gifts and loans that were later converted to gifts from Max Palevsky and his former wife. Palevsky is the largest shareholder in the Xerox Corporation. All his gifts were in multiples of $3,000 or less. Stewart Mott, a General Motors heir, was listed as having contributed or lent at least $340,000 in similar small sums to McGovern.[24]

The contribution of stock to avoid taxes was probably less widespread than the gift tax dodge, but both presidential campaigns employed both devices. Dr. Alejandro Zaffaroni, developer of a birth control pill, contributed $207,400 to Senator McGovern in blocks of stock in his company valued at less than $3,000.[25] Almost $350,000 in stock contributions to the Nixon campaign came to light when bank records of fourteen pre-April 7 Nixon committees were filed with the federal district court in a lawsuit by Ralph Nader's Public Citizen, Inc., and other consumer groups, alleging that a milk price support increase by the Department of Agriculture had been triggered by dairy group campaign contributions to the President's reelection campaign.[26] All these gifts were in sums of $3,000 or less.

Opportunities for gift tax and income tax avoidance provide additional incentives for the very rich to influence the direction of American politics. The sums involved are large enough, the financial acumen of the donors is great enough, their tax advice is good enough, and their interest in government is high enough to make such incentives effective. If the policy goals of political finance regulation include encouraging broad-based citizen participation on a more or less equal footing, preserving the integrity of government, and restoring confidence in politics, special tax incentives to big givers must be eliminated.

PUBLIC FUNDING IN THE CONGRESS

Not until 1966 was serious legislation to provide subsidies for presidential campaigns a subject of debate on the floor of Congress. The sponsor of this legislation was Russell Long, senator from notoriously corrupt Louisiana, long allied with the oil and gas interests that are so well known for their lavish political contributions.

Long's motives and sincerity were widely questioned. Reformers, inherently suspicious of power and especially of powerholders who do not pay frequent lip service to their causes, had thought of him as a wheeler and dealer, not as one of their own. Seeing the chairman of the powerful Senate Finance Committee suddenly and imperiously attaching a public funding amendment to an unrelated bill did little to allay their suspicions, nor did his flamboyant and bitter but unsuccessful rearguard effort to prevent its repeal. Some accused Long of having set back the reformist cause for years.[27]

But Long has deep populist roots. His father, Huey Long, had fought the big interests in Louisiana and, as governor, vigorously elaborated, though he did not invent, the oldest form of what might be called "quasi" public financing—systematic collections from government employees and contractors to counter the wealth of the business establishment. The means were atrocious, but the purpose and intended effect were not altogether dissimilar. (The comprehensive public financing of politics in Puerto Rico arose from similar circumstances. Collections from public employees became a counter-force to wealthy interests in politics, and discomfort with these collections led finally to tax support for parties and campaigns.) Hence it was the populist instinct that led Russell Long to public financing of campaigns; and his efforts forced Congress to act in 1966, propelled public financing to the public's attention, and laid out the path that Congress would follow again in the Revenue Act of 1971.

The provisions of the original Long Plan never became effective and do not need cataloguing here. But Russell Long's advocacy of a taxpayer check-off established the principle of public funding of campaigns. Each taxpayer with an income tax liability was allowed to designate $1 of his taxes for the Presidential Election Campaign Fund. This money would be paid out to the national party commit-tees to support the general election campaigns for president. It distinguished between major parties, those receiving 15 million or more votes in the last presidential election, and minor parties, those receiving 5 to 15 million votes. Each major party would receive $1 per vote for the average vote of all major parties, minus $5 million. A minor party would receive $1 for each vote in excess of 5 million received by the party's candidate in the last election. Rigorous audit-ing procedures and other safeguards were provided.

The check-off device had tactical significance because, as a public financing proposal tied to the tax system, it fell within the jurisdic-tion of the Finance Committee, where Long had leverage to push the bill. It was touted as a means of assuring citizen participation, giving each taxpayer the opportunity to decide for himself whether to contribute a dollar to presidential election campaigns. It was not the taxpayer, however, but Congress that determined who would get how much of the money. The check-off gave citizens the choice of whether or not to participate, but it did not permit them to direct the dollars they allocated.

In the form of an amendment to the unrelated Foreign Investors Tax Act of 1966, the Long Plan passed the Senate, survived the House-Senate conference, was approved by both houses, and was finally signed by the President. This success gave eloquent testimony to Long's power as chairman of the Senate Finance Committee, his parliamentary skill, his persuasive advocacy, the desire of Congress and the President to pass the parent tax legislation, and the urgency in Congress to adjourn for the upcoming election campaign. It also showed that the idea of public financing of campaigns was not totally repugnant to Congress, and it reflected the growing concern of many congressmen as well as the President about the dangers of the prevailing private financing system.

The congressional opponents of the Long Plan directed their criticisms primarily to its allocation provisions. They pointed out that the plan did not specify what election expenses could be paid from the Presidential Election Campaign Fund. It applied only to general election campaigns, leaving contenders for nomination still fully reliant on private money. The plan also provided what was regarded as too much money—about $30 million to each major party in 1968, a sum then unprecedented in presidential election politics.

Republicans opposed it, as they would probably have opposed any public financing system that would equalize the financial resources of the two parties and eliminate the Republicans' traditional financial advantage. Anti-Johnson Democrats joined in the opposition, some to express displeasure with the President's foreign policy by generally opposing what Mr. Johnson endorsed, and some for fear that these vast sums in the hands of a Johnson-dominated Democratic National Committee would be used to influence the 1968 nomination contest. Supporters of Robert Kennedy, for instance, suggested that state delegations would be influenced to support Mr. Johnson or his hand-picked candidate at the national convention by promises that large sums of check-off money would be allocated to the presidential campaign in their states, where it could also help state and local candidates.

Members of both parties feared that putting large sums of money into party organizations would transform our current, candidate-oriented system and lead to "bossism" on a national scale. A few senators, including Albert Gore of Tennessee, cited constitutional objections to the plan. Others warned that it discriminated against minor parties and that it did not provide for funding of new parties at all.

In May, 1967, Senator Gore, a Senate liberal, sponsored a measure to make the Long Plan inoperative. His bill was passed, but Long, refusing to accept defeat, kept the debate going for more than a month and pushed the Senate to five different roll calls, many decided by hair-thin margins. His efforts were often supported by the Johnson administration, which displayed the zeal of the newly converted. In the end, the opposition prevailed. But Long's efforts did produce evidence that public funding was gaining ground in Congress.

The 1967 defeat of the check-off did not discourage Russell Long in his quest for reform. Supported by the Johnson administration, he guided through the Senate Finance Committee the Honest Elections Act of 1967. It included a deduction-or-credit tax incentive provision, a tightly drawn full disclosure scheme, and another attempt at public subsidies for campaigns. Now, however, the subsidies would be provided in direct flat grants not to parties but to candidates in general elections for president and United States senator. The Finance Committee intended that candidates for representative should also be supported, but it left the formula open so that the House could write in what it thought appropriate.

Again, the proposal distinguished between major parties and minor parties, using the same yardsticks provided in the original Long Plan. It required that candidates using public funds eschew all private money, a provision that Albert Gore insisted on. It also allowed candidates to choose either public or private funding, a provision perhaps intended to still Republican fears that their fund-raising advantage would be eliminated by mandatory public financing. (They nonetheless continued to oppose public financing.) Although the proposed grants were generous, the bill did not include an escalator clause to guarantee that public funding would rise with inflation.

The funding formulas in the bill provided subsidies for new parties as well as for the major and minor parties that had garnered the requisite vote in preceding elections. Major party presidential candidates would receive a sum equivalent to twenty cents times the total number of votes for president in the last election. The approximately $14.1 million each major-party presidential candidate would have received under the plan in 1968 was more than the roughly $9.5 million spent by Democrats and labor in 1964 or the $11 million they spent in 1968, but less than the approximately $16 million spent by Republicans in the former year and far less than the $25 million spent on behalf of Richard Nixon in 1968.

Senatorial support was based on the higher total vote for senator in the last two elections or on the total vote for president in the preceding presidential contest, depending on which yielded the largest grant. Senatorial contenders would be eligible for a grant of fifty cents times the number of votes up to 200,000, plus thirty-five cents times the number of votes between 200,000 and 400,000, plus twenty cents times the number of votes over 400,000. Or they could choose a flat subsidy of $100,000 if that was higher.

Minor-party support was based not on the total previous vote but on the vote for that party. A minor-party presidential candidate would receive forty cents for each vote received by the candidate of his party in the last presidential campaign. Senatorial candidates could claim a dollar a vote for the first 100,000 votes, seventy cents for the next 100,000 votes, and forty cents for each vote beyond 200,000; and they could choose their vote base from among the same three elections available to major-party candidates. To accommodate legitimate claims of new parties, the Honest Elections Act permitted a presidential candidate to make a post-election claim for forty cents per vote received in the current election if he received 5 percent or more of the total vote. New-party senatorial candidates could apply the minor-party funding formula after an election in which they received 5 percent or more of the votes. Minor- and new-party candidates could also accept private contributions equal to the difference between the amount of their government grants and the amount of a major party grant for the same office.

The Honest Elections Act of 1967 never reached the floor of the Senate. But the hearings once again aired the case for public financing, and the introduction of general appropriations instead of the check-off plan appeared to enlarge the options available to Congress. The Finance Committee's extension of the public funding idea to congressional campaigns was another major breakthrough toward a public financing system.

TOWARD PUBLIC FINANCING:
THE CHECK-OFF PLAN

On November 17, 1971, Senator John Pastore of Rhode Island introduced a revised version of the income tax check-off as an amendment to the Revenue Act of 1971, President Nixon's vehicle for a tax program to reverse the downward trend in the national economy. This legislation had been carefully planned by national Democratic party leaders, including Chairman Lawrence O'Brien, Senator Long, and Democratic presidential aspirants in the Senate; and it was strongly supported by almost all the Democrats in Congress.

Senator Edward Kennedy articulated the principled Democratic argument for the tax check-off; he called it "the best investment the American taxpayer can possibly make to end the most flagrant single abuse in our democracy, the unconscionable power of money." Many in Congress and the nation agreed. But in the background was the $9 million Democratic party deficit, carried over from the 1968 presidential campaign. As the Democrats entered the election year, Edmund Muskie was the nomination front-runner, and opinion polls credited him with a fair chance to defeat the President. The party's debt and inability to finance the 1972 campaign seemed the only black clouds on the horizon. The check-off might disperse those clouds.

For the Republicans, too, principle and politics merged, inspiring strong opposition to public funding. The Republicans had fought the Long Plan in 1966 and 1967. Indeed, Republicans had often balked at measures involving federal regulation of elections—lowering of the voting age, universal government-sponsored registration, the Voting Rights Act of 1965 and 1970, for example. As in other areas, they preferred state regulation to centralization. Republican opposition to the increased use of tax money for such activities was generally consistent with the Republican preference for smaller budgets and limited government. Senator John Tower denounced the check-off as "an attempt by a group in Congress to grab taxpayers' money for their own end."

But principle was not the only force behind the Republican opposition. In the upcoming campaign, the check-off would neutralize an important Republican advantage. The GOP has spent more than the Democrats in every modern presidential election except in 1960. Finally, the Republicans were publicly estimating a 1972 campaign budget between $30 and $40 million; but the check-off formula would give them only $20.5 million. If they accepted public funds, they would have to curtail their plans for the campaign. If they refused and used private contributions instead, Democrats would denounce them as big spenders and creatures of special interest groups.

From this senatorial morass of partisan advantage and policy preference, an amended check-off plan emerged and passed by a fifty-two to forty-seven vote, largely along party lines. Fifty Democrats, joined by Republicans Charles Mathias and Clifford Case, made up the majority. Forty-two Republicans, four conservative Southern Democrats, and Independent Harry F. Byrd, Jr., were in opposition. To gain the two liberal Republican votes, the Democrats accepted an amendment by Senator Mathias which, for the first time in the United States, installed in a public financing bill the principle that the level of funding of a party's candidate should be proportionate to a measure of popular support. This amendment, killed by the Democrats in an amendment to the Debt Ceiling Act on July 1, 1973, gave the taxpayer the option of earmarking his checked-off dollar for the candidate of a particular party.

Ten days after Senate enactment, the check-off plan was shelved for 1972. Presidential press secretary Ronald Ziegler warned that Mr. Nixon would veto the entire Revenue Act unless the check-off and a series of "budget-busting" Senate Democratic amendments providing tax relief for individual taxpayers were removed from the bill. Business feared a presidential veto of the measure, which included substantial tax breaks for industry, and business lobbying against the check-off was fierce.

On the eve of the Senate-House conference committee's action on the bill, presidential spokesmen announced that Republicans had enough Southern Democratic votes to beat the check-off plan on the House floor. Whatever the accuracy of this report, Representative Wilbur Mills, chairman of the Ways and Means Committee, led House conferees demanding that the effective date of the check-off plan be deferred. As finally passed, the Revenue Act kept the check-off on the statue books, but it would not take effect until 1973, and the money could not be used in a presidential campaign without a specific congressional appropriation of the checked-off funds. On the other hand, the 1971 act did allow taxpayers to begin in 1973 checking off tax dollars for presidential campaigning; and this provision, its supporters said, would serve as a referendum that might lead to public endorsement of public funding through the check-off.

The Presidential Election Campaign Fund Act tried to address many of the most troublesome problems of regulating political finance. It allowed a citizen to participate in public affairs or not by marking or ignoring the dollar check-off on his tax form. It also provided citizen choice by inviting each taxpayer to earmark his dollar for a specific party. It skirted major policy and constitutional difficulties by permitting candidates to choose either public funding through the check-off or private funding in the traditional way. Finally, it hedged against free speech and association issues by allowing "unauthorized" political committees to spend up to $1,000 beyond the spending limit applied to publicly funded candidates. This measure was intended to protect the rights of citizens who wanted to express themselves about candidates but who were not affiliated with a candidate and could not therefore use his check-off dollars for that expression.

But a number of weaknesses had already become apparent when the act was passed; some of its most attractive provisions had Achilles' heels. The most important objection was that taxpayers must earmark presidential campaign dollars on tax forms they file long before they know who the candidates will be. As the 1972 election results eloquently tell, many Democrats would have bitterly resented the allocation of their checked-off dollars to George Mc-Govern. And a good many citizens who might have contributed to the general fund would not have wanted any of their money to go to either candidate.

Second, the check-off excludes from participation large numbers of Americans who do not pay taxes. Third, the check-off does not fund congressional campaigns, which are as undernourished financially and as severely affected by big and special interest giving as presidential races.

Fourth, no provision was made for financing nomination contests. The problem of too little money and the dangers posed by big givers and special interest money were therefore simply pushed back one step in the political process. The number of states with presidential primaries has increased sharply in recent years—from sixteen in 1968 to twenty-three in 1972—and nomination costs have spiraled accordingly. In the 1968 pre-convention contests, the personal wealth of Robert F. Kennedy and Nelson A. Rockefeller visibly raised the ante in nomination politics.

Fifth, events in 1972 demonstrated again two recurring shortcomings of expenditure limits such as those attached to the Presidential Election Campaign Fund Act. Spending ceilings were set too low, and no escalator clause was provided to raise the ceilings as prices increased. A candidate accepting public money was limited to spending fifteen cents multiplied by the population that had reached eighteen years of age. In 1972, the spending limit would have been $20.5 million. By 1976, that limit would rise to about $22 million. Yet in 1972, the McGovern-Shriver ticket spent between $35 million and $40 million and the Nixon-Agnew ticket nearly $50 million. Inflation and new campaign technologies will undoubtedly drive costs up again in 1976. The aspirant who accepted check-off dollars in 1976 would have been required to wage his campaign with, at most, about two-thirds of the budget of the losing 1972 ticket, which was not exorbitantly financed.

A candidate in 1976 might opt for public funding if he calculated that he would be better off not devoting time and energy to private fund raising and that he would reap substantial electoral advantage from receiving only "clean" tax dollars while his opponent was accepting large amounts of special interest money. But the level of taxpayer participation in the check-off plan in 1973 was discouraging. Total participation was under 3.1 percent, producing $4 million for the Presidential Election Campaign Fund. If this rate had repeated itself in 1974, 1975, and 1976, and assuming some increase in the number of taxpayers, the total check-off dollars accumulated by 1976 would not have exceeded $20 million. A major-party candidate who opted for public funding in 1976 might only have expected to receive about $9 million. He would then have found himself in a hopeless position. He would have accepted a $22 million spending limit while his opponent engaged in unlimited spending. And he would still have been required to devote time and energy to private fund raising to make up the $13 million difference between $9 million he received from the Presidential Election Campaign Fund and his $22 million spending limit. Finally, criticism of his opponent for receiving special interest money would be blunted, because he, too, would be raising substantial amounts from private sources.

Low participation by taxpayers in 1973 touched off a storm of congressional criticism of IRS. Democrats asserted that the check-off, which required filing of a separate schedule found at the back of tax booklets, was deliberately made inconvenient because of

President Nixon's opposition to the scheme. Further, IRS was accused of providing inadequate information in the tax booklet and of failing to mount a publicity campaign to alert taxpayers to the Presidential Election Campaign Fund. Only 36 percent of respondents to the Twentieth Century Fund Survey, for instance, had "heard anything" about the check-off plan almost a year after its passage. Some congressmen and several newspapers also reported that the special tax schedule was unavailable in the locations usually distributing tax forms.

The IRS responded that the separate schedule prevented its auditors from knowing a taxpayer's party preference. But taxpayers reveal other information which is as likely to promote auditing bias. Returns may indicate a taxpayer's religious affiliation by the church and charitable contributions he makes; similarly a number of deductible contributions, such as those to the NAACP's Legal Defense Fund, tell something about a taxpayer's political views.

If the fear is that government will amass files on the political affiliations of citizens, the means were already at hand. Contributors desiring tax credits or tax deductions for political donations may have these gifts audited. Most states require voters to register party membership in order to participate in primaries; and the Federal Election Campaign Act of 1971 requires political committees participating in campaigns for federal office to the extent of $1,000 to report all contributors of over $100 and to maintain records of all givers of more than $10. The check-off plan's increment to the already ample political information available to the government seemed too slight to warrant such scruples.

If the IRS was concerned solely with auditor bias rather than some larger question of political privacy, information could easily have been hidden from auditors and others by simple design changes in the basic tax forms. The check-off option could have been included on a special section of forms 1040 and 1040A that would simply be torn off the main forms and filed before the returns are audited. The IRS had ample time to make such revisions in the tax forms after passage of the Presidential Election Campaign Fund Act in January, 1972. Its inaction invited the conclusion that IRS had little interest in this and similar tax form revisions that would expand participation.

In early 1973, Senator Long took the occasion of hearings on the appointment of new IRS commissioner Donald C. Alexander to extract a promise that the check-off would appear on the face of the 1974 tax forms, as Congress had originally intended. Common Cause successfully sued the IRS in the United States District Court for the District of Columbia to compel inclusion of the check-off on the 1040 form, to force adequate publicity about the plan, and to permit taxpayers to file the check-off retroactively. To accommodate this last condition, IRS included on the 1974 tax form a box for 1973 taxpayers to check off if they had not done so in that year.[28]

The 1974 tax returns showed a fivefold increase in participation, to 15 percent. This added $17.5 million to the Presidential Election Campaign Fund. Still another $8.4 million came from 1974 taxpayers who marked an additional dollar because they had not done so in 1973. By July 1, 1974, a total of $29.8 million had been collected in the Fund.[29] At the 1974 participation rate, almost $65 million would be collected before the 1976 presidential election—far more than the $40 million to $45 million needed for presidential campaigns under the statutory formula.

A number of critics hold the view that a 15 percent participation rate is still a popular rejection of public financing. Proponents point out, however, that Watergate cast a cloud over all campaigning and may have discouraged participation. They also argue that participation will continue to improve as citizens become aware of the tax check-off and its purposes.

These predictions draw support from other evidence. H&R Block, Inc., the nation's largest tax preparation firm, accounting for 10 percent of 1974 tax returns, carefully explained the check-off to each taxpayer. Taking no position on the check-off, it nonetheless emphasized that the check-off did not cost the taxpayer an additional dollar but rather was taken from his pre-existing tax liability. A sample of the firm's returns showed that 35 percent of taxpayers participated.[30]

When the check-off plan was explained to respondents in the Twentieth Century Fund Survey, 40 percent said they would be likely to check off one dollar, 42 percent said they would not, and the rest did not pay taxes or were undecided. The H&R Block figure of 35 percent and the Twentieth Century Fund Survey finding of 40 percent are close enough to suggest that the check-off's ultimate potential lies in that range. At those rates, ignoring any increase in the number of taxpayers, the check-off's potential is $48 million annually. During the two-year congressional and four-year presidential election cycles, this level of participation would produce enough money to publicly finance not only presidential campaigns but a substantial share of congressional canvasses as well.

The Twentieth Century Fund Survey also reveals that potential check-off participants are far more representative of the whole population than is the present private financing corps. Fifty-three percent of those polled identified themselves as Democrats, 14 percent as independents, and 33 percent as Republicans. Potential check-off

TABLE 7-4   Income Class of 1972 Givers and Potential Givers under the Check-Off Plan[a]

Income Groups	Percentage of Income Class Contributing		Income Classes' Percentage	
	Actual 1972 (col. 1)	Potential Check-Offs (col. 2)	of General Population (col. 3)	of Potential Check-Offs (col. 4)
$ 0– 4,999	3.7%	37.5%	16.6%	20.0%
5,000– 9,999	11.5	45.2	31.4	31.4
10,000–14,999	11.5	45.7	26.1	25.8
15,000–19,999	19.5	50.9	14.6	13.0
20,000–24,999	23.4	52.2	4.3	3.8
25,000 and more	36.8	52.0	7.0	6.1
	12.4[a]	40.2[a]	100.0	100.0

SOURCE: Twentieth Century Fund Survey (see Chap. 3, n. 1).
[a] Percentage for the whole population.

participants were 58 percent Democrats, 11 percent independents, and 31 percent Republicans.

At 40 percent participation, the check-off plan would virtually eliminate the traditional class bias in campaign giving. Table 7-4 shows that high-income persons give ten times as often (36.8 percent) as low-income persons (3.7 percent). But under the check-off, high-income groups are less than half again as likely to participate as low-income people (see column 2). A somewhat different perspective reveals that low-income people would actually be overrepresented under the check-off system; they constitute 16.6 percent of the population but would make 20 percent of the contributions. High-income people comprise 7 percent of the population but would make only 6.1 percent of the contributions (compare columns 3 and 4). Since all taxpayers would contribute the same amount—one dollar— under the check-off, both the amounts allocated and the number of participants would be roughly proportionate to each income group's strength in the population.

The 1974 increase in check-off participation and the even higher potential shown by the H&R Block sample and the Twentieth Century Fund Survey are consistent with evidence showing that popular attitudes have become far more favorable toward public financing of campaigns. In June, 1973, 58 percent of Gallup Poll respondents agreed that the tax money should pay for presidential and congressional campaigns and that all private contributions should be prohibited. In September, the same questions gained 65 percent support. Further, the Twentieth Century Fund Survey shows that those willing to participate in a public financing plan are mainly representative of party and class divisions in the nation.

Overall, the Presidential Election Campaign Fund Act had too many defects to address effectively the nation's campaign financing needs. It did not cover congressional campaigns or primaries; and it excluded at least 18 million eligible voters who are not taxpayers. Its reliance on prior election returns did not allocate money on a current support index to aid new or emerging parties and to avoid artificial support for dying causes.

Americans have moved only gradually toward public financing of campaigns. They have done this most willingly to support the costs of election administration, although government funds are still not used to put voters on the registration roles. Various indirect subsidies to politics have been tried or urged from time to time. Voter pamphlets, the franking privilege, and free media time are only marginally helpful in supporting vigorous campaigning. They do not provide enough support for underfinanced candidates, and they do not significantly reduce a candidate's need to obtain private contributions. Tax incentives for giving have failed entirely; few Americans participate, and those who do are even more disproportionately from high income groups than is the class-biased contributor corps.

The tax check-off was the best pre-Watergate step toward public financing. When the check-off option was placed on the face of tax returns, it drew 15 percent participation; and surveys show a much higher potential citizen interest. The check-off does not, however, solve the policy problem of how to allocate public funds. If taxpayers earmark for particular parties, they must do so long before candidates are nominated. If the money is channeled to a general fund, a legislative allocation formula must be devised that will distribute funds according to a current index of support.

The tax check-off was significant, then, because it demonstrated the willingness of American officials and citizens to raise campaign funds through the tax system. It left unresolved the question how to distribute those funds.

Discovery of the break-in at the Democratic National Committee headquarters in the Watergate complex precipitated a two-year series of revelations of burglary, illegal wiretapping, extortion, bribery, and abuse of power through attempted misuse of the Internal Revenue Service, the Central Intelligence Agency, and the Federal Bureau of Investigation. Also revealed was a widespread pattern of illegal contributions and "laundering" of campaign funds.

Most of the crimes had nothing to do with campaign financing and might have been committed by persons so disposed whatever laws regulated the collection and use of political money. Richard Nixon was not forced to resign under threat of impeachment for campaign financing abuses. Nor were the defendants at most Watergate trials accused or convicted on such grounds. But the scandals coincided with and fed growing public and legislative sentiment for radical change in the methods of funding campaigns, and they had a sufficient taint of financing abuses to enable issue groups such as Common Cause and the Center for Public Financing of Elections to lobby for government spending as an "answer to Watergate."

The climate was more propitious for reform than at any other time in modern American

8

WATERGATE AND PUBLIC FINANCING

history. In consequence, the omnibus Federal Election Campaign Act of 1974 was passed overwhelmingly (60 to 16 in the Senate and 365 to 24 in the House) by a Congress intent on at least a symbolic exorcism of Watergate, and it was signed by a reluctant President Ford unwilling to veto it three weeks before the midterm elections. It completed the effort begun in 1966 by Senator Long, and renewed in the Presidential Election Campaign Fund Act of 1971, to establish a check-off system for funding presidential elections. It also instituted matching grants to publicly finance contenders for presidential nominations and provided federal funding for party nominating conventions. Attempts to include public financing of congressional candidates were beaten back in the House, its opposition encouraged by threats of a presidential veto. Meanwhile, under the influence of the same events and pressures, eight states also adopted public financing systems for their elections.

THE FEDERAL ELECTION CAMPAIGN ACT OF 1974

The sweeping Federal Election Campaign Act of 1974 imposed limits on contributions and spending, modified requirements for full disclosure of campaign financing, and established a Federal Election Commission to administer the law.[1] These conventional reforms build on past regulatory schemes in the nation and the states (they are discussed in Chapters 4 and 6 above). The sharp break from the past is the public financing scheme which, although enacted in principle as early as 1966, was never allowed to take effect. The new law moves from statutory endorsement of the principle of public financing to legislative creation of an operating system of public subsidies for campaigns.[2]

Presidential General Elections. The 1974 act builds on the previously existing Presidential Election Campaign Fund Act of 1971[3] which mandates public financing of general election campaigns for president. The new act's modifying amendments:

- Appropriate money to the Presidential Election Campaign Fund for each fiscal year in amounts equal to the amounts designated by check-offs during that year, eliminating the 1971 requirement that funds be appropriated separately.
- Provide optional funding for presidential candidates of major parties in the amount of the spending limit ($20 million); define major parties as those that receive 25 percent or more of the vote in the preceding presidential election; make the payment to major-party candidates at the beginning of the campaign.
- Provide optional funding for minor-party nominees in the pro-

portion of a major-party grant that their party's vote in the last or the current election was of the average major-party vote; define minor parties as those receiving between 5 and 25 percent of the vote in the preceding election; and make minor-party grants available at the beginning of the campaign.

- Allow independent candidates and nominees of new parties or parties receiving 5 percent of the vote in the current election, but not in the preceding election, to opt for proportional grants calculated in the same manner as minor-party grants, but based on current election returns; make these grants payable after the election.
- Adjust maximum public grants as the presidential campaign spending limit is adjusted to conform to changes in the Consumer Price Index.
- Prohibit candidates who receive full public funding from accepting private contributions, and limit other candidates to accepting private contributions which, when combined with their public grants, do not exceed the spending limit.

Presidential Nominating Campaigns. The 1971 act was severely criticized for supplying public funds in general elections but not in nomination campaigns. The abuses of the present private financing system would simply move from general election contests to nomination races, the critics argued. Furthermore, private money is usually more difficult to raise at the nomination stage, crippling vigorous competition; and public financing was therefore at least as urgently needed in primaries as in general elections. Some commentators also pointed out that money is more important in primaries than in general elections because voters do not have the guidance of party labels, the media give less coverage to primary campaigns, and the larger number of candidates is often confusing to voters. Hence public money to increase the visibility of primary campaigns was strongly urged.

Congress responded to these arguments by supplying public money for presidential nominating campaigns. The 1974 act:

- Provides matching funds for candidates for presidential nominations out of the Presidential Election Campaign Fund (the checkoff fund).
- Makes candidates eligible for this funding when they raise a minimum of $100,000 in matchable contributions, of which $5,000 must be raised in each of twenty states.
- Sets $250 as the maximum private contribution that can be matched with public funds.
- Provides that these contributions will be matched on a dollar-for-dollar basis.

- Imposes a limit of $5 million—one-half the $10 million nomination spending limit—on the amount of public matching funds any candidate can receive.
- Adjusts the limit on public financing to any candidate as the presidential nomination campaign limit is adjusted to conform to changes in the Consumer Price Index.
- Establishes priorities for payments from the Presidential Election Campaign Fund, with all funds necessary for anticipated payments for nominating conventions and to general election candidates set aside in that order and with nomination matching grants taken from whatever balance remains in the fund. If only limited funds are then available, the secretary of the Treasury will prorate them among nomination candidates to achieve an equitable distribution to contenders of the same party, taking into account the sequence in which they qualify and receive certification.

Presidential Nominating Conventions. The offer of ITT funding support for the Republican convention at the same time that company was involved in antitrust questions with the Justice Department highlighted the sordid way in which national party conventions might be financed. Further, the national party conventions are as much a part of the nominating process as the presidential primaries, and the arguments for funding them are equally strong. The combination of scandal and need prompted Congress to include public financing of presidential nominating conventions in the 1974 act, a widely praised innovation. The law:

- Provides optional payments of $2 million to each major-party national committee to finance its nominating convention, and provides proportional grants to minor parties based on the proportion of the average major-party vote received by their candidates in either the past or the current election.
- Takes these grants from the Presidential Election Campaign Fund.
- Limits expenditures of any party for convention expenses to $2 million.
- Authorizes the Federal Election Commission to raise these limits in its discretion.

The 1974 Act in Perspective. In some of its goals, the 1974 act is a great advance over previous American public financing proposals. Public grants for primaries as well as general elections acknowledge the importance of nominations, the potential for financing abuse, and the great impact of money in primaries. The decision to publicly finance national conventions recognizes the role these meetings play in the nominating process; and it may also signal congressional willingness to finance significant party activities, respecting the delicate balance between parties and officials in America. Providing public financing for independents and new parties both accepts their potential to win electoral mandates and honors their historic role in America as vehicles for voter protest.

In other ways, however, the act falls far short in addressing the campaign financing problems with which Americans have lived more and more uneasily in recent years. The public financing arrangements threaten to distort important and intricate balances in American politics, and some of the law's specific provisions will unintentionally produce confusion and unfairness. Most important is the act's failure to provide public financing for congressional elections. Presidential candidates funded fully with tax dollars may use their awesome fund-raising potential to solicit and channel private money for Senate and House races. This already happens in midterm elections and reached a zenith in Richard Nixon's White House, where key staffers secretly directed money in 1970 to help the President's friends in Congress and punish his enemies. The deployment of even greater presidential influence in campaign finance in both midterm and presidential elections will increase the president's clout in Congress and further undermine the already badly eroded separation of powers.

A shift in public confidence is also likely when presidential candidates are "cleanly" funded with tax money and congressional aspirants are still dependent on tainted private sources. Finally, public funding of presidential elections makes candidates both more responsive and more visible to the public. But Congress, meanwhile, remains in a shadowland, where it is not as accountable to voters because a well-financed opposition is lacking in elections and where it is not as visible to citizens.

Basing eligibility for presidential general election grants on past election results will produce distortions and unfairness in American politics. These are aggravated by the requirement that new-party and independent candidates must wait until after the votes are counted before receiving public grants while others receive theirs for use during the campaign. Under these rules, formerly significant parties whose support has decayed may nonetheless claim full grants in later elections and newly emerging parties with strong citizen support may not receive grants in a timely or useful fashion.

These effects can more readily be appreciated by reference to critical transitional points in the history of American elections. It seems unlikely that the Whig party would have gone out of existence after the election of 1852 if its leaders had known that they would be forfeiting a full funding entitlement in the next election; that so many Republicans would have supported Teddy Roosevelt's decision to run as a Bull Moose candidate in 1912 had they known that this might depress the level of public funding for their party's nominee in 1916; or that John Schmitz, the 1972 nominee of the American Independent party, would have made such an insignificant showing if he had received the more than $6 million of public money to which he would have been entitled based on George Wallace's vote in 1968.

Moreover, by deferring measurement of the strength of new parties and independent candidates until after the election in which they cross the 5 percent threshold, while funding other candidates before the election, the act deprives the former of effective use of the money they do receive. Post-election grants cannot help very much in enabling a candidate to make his case to the voters. They will not spare a new-party candidate and his associates the time-consuming efforts at fund raising that other candidates are now relieved of, nor the pressure to compromise the inevitable conflicts between the need to campaign on issues that will attract voters and the temptation to campaign on those that will attract money.

At best, post-election grants enable a new party candidate to pay off election debts. But an outsider is unlikely to have significant borrowing capacity unless he is a candidate of the very rich—and of very many of them, since the new law also limits loans to $1,000 per lender. To meet campaign costs, new candidates will necessarily pay for them with private contributions during the campaign. And these contributions may not be adequate even in the case of those candidates who reflect significant voter sentiment. Hence a new party candidate will not be awarded public funds during a campaign nor be able to use those he receives after the election.

A troublesome question is the disposition of these post-election payments, which a candidate could not use because he was unable to borrow money before the election. George Wallace, for instance, would have been granted about $6 million after the 1968 election; but it is unlikely that he would have been able to use this for any 1968 campaign purpose. The act empowers the Federal Election Commission to write regulations, subject to congressional veto, governing such questions. But the commission's alternatives are apparently to require a future Wallace to return the money he cannot use, which would mean almost all of it, or to allow him to apply it to his next campaign, in which case he might then receive a total of $12 million in public funding rather than the intended $6 million.

The provisions for federally funding presidential nomination contests are as questionable as those for general elections, although on different grounds. Matching grants do provide a more current index for determining entitlement to public financing, and they allow all candidates to be financed at the same time. But they are an index only of support among contributors rather than among voters generally. The matching grant limit of $250 is far too high, and it creates substantial inequalities among citizens. A donor of $250 triggers $250 additional dollars of public money for his candidate, while a poor donor's $1 triggers only $1. A mere 20,000 wealthy donors can command the full public nomination grant of $5 million that it will take 5 million $1 givers to trigger.

Even admitting that the difference between the $1 donor and the $250 donor is less than presently occurs between rich and poor givers, the inequality as a trigger of public subsidy is still too great in a political system that strives for a one-man, one-vote principle in its politics. This inequality is more objectionable because the Presidential Election Campaign Fund is raised on a one-man, one-dollar basis from the tax check-off. It is unacceptable for citizens to give equally to the fund and then for them to participate so unequally in allocating it to candidates. Ironically, a contributor who did not check off a dollar could nonetheless command $250 by making a matchable grant to a candidate.

Also doubtful are the threshold provisions for public grants in primary campaigns. To be eligible, candidates must raise a minimum of $100,000 in matchable funds, with at least $5,000 coming from each of twenty states. This is intended to hedge against public funding for frivolous candidates. At the outset, the disparity between small givers and $250 contributors is again too high. Whether a candidate is "serious" turns on his backing by a small number of wealthy givers or by a very large number of $1 supporters. The disparity between 4,000 contributors of $250 and 100,000 donors of $1 makes eligibility turn too much on wealth.

The twenty-state requirement is apparently intended to discourage favorite sons or regional candidates. This is a doubtful goal, since these candidates have sometimes emerged as national leaders after starting in their home areas. In particular, it discriminates against governors, whose initial constituencies for the presidency are likely to be local rather than national. In addition, the twenty-state rule ignores the distribution of voters in favor of a peculiar "state equality" theory of presidential politics. The Constitution does not require a candidate to carry, or even to run in, twenty states in order to be elected president. In fact, an electoral college majority could be achieved in only eleven states. Put a different way, New York and California together have twice as many voters as do the twenty smallest states combined, but the law gives them only one-tenth the weight of those states in launching presidential candidacies. At the extreme, a citizen of a state is disenfranchised in triggering public support for a presidential candidate if others from his state have already given $5,000 in matchable gifts.

The provisions for allocating the fund to general elections, conventions, and primaries were hastily drafted. Since there was no assurance at the time of passage that sufficient amounts would be checked off to cover all contemplated grants for the 1976 or subsequent elections, the act provides priorities and guidelines for the disbursement of funds. The secretary of the Treasury is first to set aside the amounts necessary for grants to the parties for nominating conventions, then the amounts required for the prescribed grants to presidential nominees, and the remainder of the fund is to be available to finance candidates seeking nominations. In the last case, the secretary is admonished to "seek to achieve an equitable distribution of funds available" among candidates of the same party and to take into account the sequence in which candidates qualify.

The actual and prescribed sequence of payments will not conform to these priorities, however. Parties will be permitted to draw upon their convention grants as early as July of the year preceding the election. Candidates for nominations will be able to receive matching grants as early as the beginning of the election year. And nominees will receive their flat grants only a few weeks before the election, following the conventions.

To determine how much money will be available for matching grants, the secretary will first have to make an assumption as to the number, and major- or minor-party status, of the candidates who will run in the general election. For 1976, only the Republican and Democratic nominees will be eligible for the full $20 million major-party grants based on the results of the 1972 election. No minor-party candidates will be eligible. But if the secretary assumes that he need reserve only $40 million for general-election purposes and disburses the remaining amount in the fund to primary candidates, there will be nothing left to reimburse a new-party candidate should one emerge after the conventions. In such circumstances, George Wallace in 1968 or Teddy Roosevelt in 1912 would not have been able to get their contemplated post-election funds until the new Congress convened early the following year and might not have gotten them at all if Congress refused to make supplementary appropriations.

A significant inter-party fund distribution issue occurs during the nomination campaign. The House of Representatives proposed that no party's nomination candidates could claim more than 45 percent of the available matching money. This was struck out in the final bill. The drafters apparently believed that there would be insufficient check-off money to provide full nomination funding under a 45 percent rule. Where one party had a heated nomination contest and the other had none (as frequently happens when an incumbent president seeks re-election), it would be necessary for the fund to contain huge sums, if the candidates of the party with that contest were to receive full matching grants without in the aggregate drawing more than 45 percent of the fund.

As drafted, however, the act raises the converse issue: is it fair for a party with a heated nomination contest to draw most of or all the matching money? Since all the party's hopefuls are likely to campaign against the opposition party, especially against a sitting opposition party president, the nomination grants have general election implications. Yet during the nomination stage, one party's many contenders will claim vastly more of the public funding than the uncontested nominee of the other party.

The act is equally careless in its assumption that the secretary will in fact be able to "achieve an equitable distribution of funds" to candidates for a party's nomination. The different strategies of candidates, and the inevitable unforeseen political eventualities that cause people to become candidates, may make it impossible for the secretary or for any formula dependent upon a predetermined amount of money in the fund to achieve an equitable distribution. Candidates enter nomination contests at different times and for different reasons. The unexpected withdrawal of President Johnson in 1968, for example, precipitated the candidacy of Vice President Humphrey at a time when all available matching funds might already have been distributed to Senators Kennedy and McCarthy and to Johnson himself. And the only way to be sure of preventing such a premature and inequitable distribution under this act might be for the secretary to withhold funds until so close to the convention as to render them relatively useless to the candidates.

PUBLIC FINANCING IN THE STATES

Eight states responded to the public's post-Watergate mood by enacting public financing plans.[4] These laws embody a rich diversity of fund-raising methods, eligibility requirements, and distribution formulas. They mainly do not follow the federal pattern, adapting themselves to the various roles of political parties and to the long ballot for executive offices in the states.

Two states' "public financing" schemes are in fact income tax surcharges, where the taxpayer adds one or two dollars to his tax liability. Here the state does no more than provide a collection system. Five states use a check-off plan, and one funds campaigning from general appropriations. Three states allocate money by formula to candidates, four states channel money to parties, and one directs it to parties for use in gubernatorial campaigns. Only one state contemplates the use of public funds in primary elections; the other seven either specify that funds are for general elections or time the distribution of funds to discourage their use in primaries.

State Experiments. Iowa allows taxpayers to check off one dollar to parties only. Those parties whose gubernatorial candidate received more than 2 percent of the vote in the last election are eligible. The state party distributes the money in its discretion. But it cannot allocate the money to presidential or vice presidential candidates; and if it supplies money to congressional or state legislative candidates, it must give equal grants to each of the party's general election candidates for the same kind of office. Fourteen percent of Iowa taxpayers checked off in 1974, with 39 percent of these allocating funds to the Republican party and 61 percent to the Democrats.

Maine employs a surcharge scheme, which allows taxpayers to add one dollar to their income tax liability for the party of their choice. Eligible are political party state committees whose gubernatorial candidates received 1 percent or more of the vote in the last election. The traditional fiscal conservatism of Maine residents and the additional tax liability of the surcharge combined to reduce participation to 1.3 percent in 1974.

Maryland also uses the surcharge device, but its elaborate allocation formula provides money to candidates in the primary as well as in the general election, to local and state candidates, and to minor as well as major parties. It also uses a multiple matching formula for fund distribution.

Twenty-five percent of the surcharge dollars in Maryland are allocated for statewide races, 40 percent for legislative campaigns, and 35 percent for local, judicial, and other contests. Up to two-thirds of the funds may be used in primary elections. Candidates become eligible by raising the greater of $250 or 15 percent of the spending limit for the office they seek. Contributions up to $50 to major-party candidates are matched on a three-for-one basis in statewide races and a two-for-one basis in other contests. Parties whose hopefuls for an office in the last election received less than 25 percent of the vote or that got on the ballot through a petition procedure are regarded as "minor parties," and their candidates receive proportional matching grants. In statewide races, the public funds may not exceed 75 percent of the candidate's spending limit; in other races this limit is 67 percent.

Minnesota allows a taxpayer to check off for a specific political party or for a general fund. Any party that ran a candidate in the last election or that files 2,000 petition signatures is eligible to get on the tax form for the taxpayer check-off. Public funds are distributed in general elections only. After the primary, the funds in each party's account are allocated 40 percent to statewide office races, 20 to 30 percent for state senate races (depending on the year), and 30 to 40 percent for lower house contests. Within the statewide allocation, the candidate for governor (and lieutenant governor jointly) receives 40 percent of his party's account, the nominee for attorney general 24 percent, and for secretary of state, state auditor, and state treasurer 12 percent each. Candidates within each legislative category receive equal grants. After the election, the general fund is divided among executive, senate, and assembly categories by the same formula, and each statewide candidate receiving 5 percent of the vote and each legislative candidate receiving 10 percent is entitled to an equal grant with others seeking the same office.

Each Montana taxpayer is allowed to check off one dollar for a general fund. These funds are then given to the parties whose candidates received 5 percent or more of the vote in the last gubernatorial election. Funds may be used in general election campaigns for governor only.

Rhode Island allows taxpayers to check off funds either to political parties receiving 5 percent of the vote for governor in the last election or to a general fund. The party check-offs are given to the respective party committees. The general fund is divided between the parties in two stages: (1) a party receives 5 percent of the fund for each of the five statewide officers elected on its ticket in the last election, (2) the remainder is divided so that each party receives a percentage equal to its candidates' percentage of the vote for all statewide offices in the last election. Allocations are made for the general election only. On the 1974 returns, 17 percent of Rhode Islanders checked off a dollar; 34 percent of them for the Democrats, 6 percent for the Republicans, and 60 percent to the general fund.

New Jersey is the only state that uses direct appropriations for public financing. Candidates for governor become eligible by raising $40,000 in contributions of $600 or less. All contributions in those amounts are then matched by two public dollars for each private dollar, until the candidate's total receipts reach the expenditure limit. Public financing is available only in general elections.

Utah's tax check-off is the only public financing system that provides funds to local political party organizations. Taxpayers may check off one dollar to the party of their choice. One-half of each party's earmarked funds go to the state central committee, and the other half is distributed to county committees in proportion to the percentage of total check-offs for the party originating in that county.

State Plans in Perspective. These public financing arrangements reflect state efforts to provide enough money for vigorous campaigning and to minimize the undue influence, extortion, and corruption that often accompany private fund raising. Although state campaigns are usually less visible to citizens than presidential races, taxpayers have shown as much support for public financing in the states as at the federal level. Fourteen percent check-off participation in Iowa and 17 percent in Rhode Island compare favorably with the 15 percent citizen support for the Presidential Election Campaign Fund. Maine's experience suggests, however, that citizens will not contribute through a surcharge device.

States have had the same difficulty as Congress in striking balances within our complex political arrangements. Four states allocate public funds to parties and four to candidates; in each case balances between the party organization and the party in government are altered. Similarly, only one state has funded primaries as well as general elections, portending the shift of campaign finance abuses more heavily to nomination contests. New Jersey and Montana have ignored separation-of-powers issues by following the federal pattern of financing only campaigns for chief executive. Minnesota, by contrast, provides public funds in races for both legislative houses as well as for five executive offices. And Maryland has gone even farther, channeling public money to local, judicial, and other races in addition to state executive and legislative contests.

The states have tried a variety of requirements to test eligibility for public financing. Like the 1974 federal act, each is flawed. Matching grant systems in New Jersey and Maryland provide a current index of support for candidates, but like all matching schemes the index measures financial rather than voter endorsement. This objection is stronger in New Jersey, where the matchable contribution is $600 and is therefore well beyond the means of most citizens. Maryland, on the other hand, matches only up to $50, so that most citizens can participate equally if they wish to. And Maryland wisely curbs the danger that a low matchable contribution will supply insufficient public funds for vigorous campaigning: it provides a three-for-one multiple match in statewide races and a two-for-one in others.

The eligibility thresholds in both states seem rather high. A New Jersey gubernatorial candidate must obtain $40,000 in matchable contributions and a Maryland statewide candidate about $42,000 (15 percent of the spending limit). Further, Maryland allows full matching only for candidates whose parties received more than 25 percent of the vote in the last election and gives proportional matching to "minor" parties. This diminishes the usefulness of matching as an index of current support.

Minnesota has taken the most impressive steps to adapt the check-off to changing political circumstances. A new political party can get onto the tax form by filing a nominal number of signature petitions (2,000). Maine and Iowa have kept eligibility requirements low by permitting parties whose candidates received 1 and 2 percent of the vote in the last election to be listed on the tax form. But all check-off plans have the inherent defect of soliciting citizen participation before voters know who the party candidates will be. Furthermore, the listing of parties that obtained the necessary vote in the last election may channel money to those parties after they have lost strength, especially where a four-year gubernatorial term requires some citizens to make some check-off decisions more than three years before the next election.

Both the national and state governments have shown remarkable willingness to enact public financing of campaigns. This is an essential step to provide enough money for vigorous competitive politics and to curb the abuses that now afflict fund raising. But the measures so far enacted fall far short of what is needed. Often they ignore essential balances in American politics: the comparable importance of nominations and elections, the separation of powers, the relationship between the party organization and the party in government. Frequently they do not go far enough to ameliorate unequal citizen influence in financing politics. Almost without exception they discriminate against minor parties, newly emerging parties, and independent candidates. And they tend to favor established political groups by making eligibility turn on past voting performance rather than on a test of current voter support.

The public financing measures already enacted will be severely criticized for these weaknesses. They will be challenged in the courts, especially where they establish inequality among citizens and discriminate against new, minor, or independent candidates. And they will surely distort significant relationships in American politics. These events may well discredit not only specific public financing plans but the idea of public financing itself. The best hope to avoid this result is for proponents of reform themselves to become the most vigilant guardians of the equal standing of citizens in the political process and of the rights of new, minor, and independent candidates.

Neither the public financing measures already enacted nor those seriously proposed have faced up to these challenges. An examination of political financing in other nations, which have had far longer experience with public financing, reveals a variety of provocative legislative arrangements; but it does not discover a system which fully addresses the grave defects that mar contemporary American experiments with public financing of political campaigns.

In the late 1950s and early 1960s, Puerto Rico, West Germany, and Sweden independently initiated comprehensive programs for direct public financing of politics.

After Sweden adopted public financing, neighboring and politically similar Norway and Finland did likewise. But the nearly simultaneous inauguration of public financing in the Caribbean, middle Europe, and Scandinavia seems due not to propinquity or a common outlook but to other, less obvious factors.

Many politicians in most democracies shared an awareness of both the inadequacies of private financing and its corrosive effect on political integrity. But circumstances in these three countries compelled their leaders to devote fresh thinking to the values and processes of the policies they headed. Puerto Rico was developing a modern economy and a new commonwealth relationship with the United States. Germany, after a decade and a half of tyranny, war, and truncation, was re-establishing a democratic system. And Sweden was embarked on what its government regarded as the creation of a new kind of society. Facilitating the process in each country was a dominant party headed by a charismatic "founding father" personality—Luis Muñoz Marin of the Popular Democratic party in Puerto Rico, Konrad

EXPERIMENTS ELSEWHERE

Adenauer of the Christian Democratic Union in Germany, and Tage Erlander of the Social Democratic party in Sweden.

Once the idea had been tried, politicians afflicted by rising costs and fund-raising problems in other nations could more readily consider it. Norway, Finland, and the Province of Quebec soon adopted similar systems. In 1971, the United States enacted its check-off system for financing presidential elections. In 1972, Austria began to experiment with limited public financing via subsidies to party publications. In the last two years, Canada, Israel, and Italy have also adopted systems of public financing of politics.

Today, including the United States, ten of the major democracies assume some public responsibility for paying political costs. All these other countries have party and electoral mechanisms quite unlike our own. Parliamentary systems vest the choice of the chief executive in the legislature instead of in the people through direct election. The parliamentary leader thus becomes the head of government as well, combining in one person two functions that are separate in our system. As a rule, his principal lieutenants also share responsibilities in both branches. This system infuses the party organization with a single overriding purpose—to win the requisite number of parliamentary seats to form a government; and it links the fortunes of every elected officeholder in both branches to the achievement of this purpose. As a result, the political parties in parliamentary systems are much more coherent and responsible than ours.

The importance of these parties and their strength as institutions are further enhanced where there is proportional representation and election depends on position on party lists rather than on success in single-member constituencies. In many European countries, parties tend to represent a particular ideology. Much of their money comes from large and active dues-paying memberships (particularly on the left); they may also have sizable capital investments in newspapers, magazines, publishing houses, and educational facilities.

In parliamentary systems, the direction and policies of legislative committees are closely linked to the programs of related ministries; these programs and policies must constantly be renegotiated in terms of overall government and/or party needs. So it is extremely difficult, if not impossible, for a special interest to buy assured protection or favor through campaign contributions to a single individual, even if he is chairman of a relevant committee. Instead, the interest must attempt to buy, or at least to influence, the whole party. Since other interests must overcome the same difficulty in expressing their claims, the cacophony can be resolved only through the formation of alliances. The bigger the alliances, the greater their influences. But the more participants in each alliance, the more indirect the effect of their money becomes, and the more generalized and ideological its expression must be.

PUERTO RICO

Ever since its accession from Spain in 1898, Puerto Rico has confronted two major questions: whether its ultimate political status should be independent or connected to the United States, and the degree to which its original Hispanic culture would be transformed by contact with the United States.

Puerto Ricans were given United States citizenship in 1917; but they did not gain substantial formal control over their own affairs until 1950, when cultural adaptation and modern political leadership persuaded federal authorities to grant the island commonwealth status. Meanwhile, cultural change, while making independence more feasible economically, also made it less attractive to a people aware of their favored position relative to their Caribbean neighbors and increasingly comfortable with their identity as "Americans." Today, differences in language and outlook still are strong enough for many Puerto Ricans, and apparently for mainlanders as well, to prefer that the question of ultimate status remain unresolved.

At the time of its accession, Puerto Rico was characterized by rural isolation, extreme poverty, illiteracy, and a rigid authoritarian class structure sustained by a deeply ingrained paternalistic value system. Within two years, the island was given democratic structures and universal suffrage, and shortly thereafter began its intensive, continuing investment in education for all children. The island's economic development was slow at first, but it has accelerated greatly in recent decades. Today, more than 65 percent of employment is in the modern sectors of the economy, and less than 35 percent is in the traditional sectors. Land tenure changes, crop diversification, industrialization, tourism, urbanization, a growing middle class, massive emigration to the continental United States, and travel back and forth between the island and the mainland have substantially changed the life styles and attitudes of the Puerto Rican people.

Many of these changes were accomplished under the leadership of Luis Muñoz Marin, a Puerto Rican aristocrat who, as a young writer in New York during the 1920s, had characterized the island's economy as "the triumph of after dinner delicacies—coffee, sugar, tobacco—over the dinner itself." Muñoz Marin's purpose was to liberate the common people of Puerto Rico from traditional deference to landed interests and to enlist their participation in modernizing the island's economy and society.

The campaign that brought Muñoz's Popular Democratic party

to power in the legislature in the 1940 election involved an assault on the traditional practice of massive vote buying (at two dollars a head), with campaign funds donated principally by the sugar industry. The campaign's slogan was "Verguenza contra Dinero" (Self-Respect versus Money). Muñoz told voters: "If you sell your votes, somebody has got to put up the money. . . . After that whoever wins is tied to the fellow that gave the money. . . . That is why you have seen so many political parties win, while you have never won."[1]

Rather than take money from big interests, the Popular Democratic party (PDP), in the years that followed, supported itself largely through contribution "quotas" levied on government workers. Those employees who did not contribute a fixed percentage of their monthly wages to the party (as much as 5 percent in election years) risked forms of harassment up to, and including, loss of jobs.

Although the party defended this practice as less of a threat to party and governmental integrity than "selling out" to major economic interests, it leaders grew increasingly uncomfortable with quotas. But it was not easy for the PDP to contemplate abandoning them. Political costs were rising, and the growth of a rejuvenated and strongly funded Statehood Republican party (SRP), under the dynamic, media-oriented leadership of millionaire businessman Luis Ferre, was creating new competition for the PDP.

The idea of public financial support for party activists matured among Muñoz Marin's associates during the mid-1950s. Since the abandonment of "quotas" would mean an automatic percentage increase in the take-home pay of government workers, it may have occurred to PDP leaders that the quota system had been a form of indirect government subsidy all along.

In 1956, when Ferre first ran for governor, the PDP made public financing part of its platform. In 1957, following an election in which the Statehood Republicans had doubled their voting strength (from 12.8 percent to 25 percent), PDP legislators introduced and enacted public financing legislation.

The Election Fund Act of 1957 was directed not only at the elimination of the quota system but also at limiting the advantage derived by the SRP from the support of wealthy interests. The institution of public financing was justified as a means of correcting two kinds of undemocratic abuse. The act made solicitation of contributions from government employees on government premises, or by fellow government employees anywhere, a felony. It also limited private contributions to $200 to local and $200 to central committees of a party per year ($300 each in election years).

The loss of party revenues resulting from these provisions was to be made up by the establishment of a commonwealth election fund on which all "principal" parties (those that had received at least 10 percent of the vote for governor in the preceding election and had "participated in all election precincts in Puerto Rico"— later reduced to 5 percent in the previous election, or obtaining petitions signed by 5 percent of the eligible voters) could draw. The parties could use these funds for a very broad range of approved "maintenance and operation expenses," but the money would not be payable to the parties themselves. Each party would keep a detailed record of expenses chargeable to the fund and submit a monthly expense report, including the date, the name and address of the payee, and the reason for each expense, to the commonwealth's secretary of the Treasury and controller. The party would submit vouchers for each expenditure to the secretary of the Treasury, who would then order direct payment to the creditor. An eligible party might use up to $75,000 in each non-election year and up to $150,000 in each election year, and the party could accumulate unspent balances in non-election years for use in election years.

Overwhelming PDP majorities in both houses of the legislature assured passage of the act, but the SRP also supported it after the acceptance of amendments that stiffened the proscriptions against soliciting government employees. The SRP, which stood to benefit equally with the much larger PDP in the receipt of public funds, calculated shrewdly and presciently that complete elimination of the quota system would have a greater effect on PDP resources than nominal and unenforced restriction of private contributions would have on those of the SRP.

The Independence party (PIP) was the smallest legislative party eligible for government support under the act, and it stood to gain proportionately the most from the provision of equal funds to eligible parties. But it unanimously opposed passage. Opposing commonwealth status on principle, the party was reluctant to accept commonwealth funds; some members also feared that public financing, rather than assuring freedom for parties, would substitute the coercion of government for that of economic interests.

The PIP did not draw any money from the fund in 1957, and the other parties became concerned that Independentists might change policy in the 1960 election year and claim their unspent balance of $225,000 in addition to the $150,000 that they would be entitled to receive for that year. In 1958, therefore, the legislature amended the act to provide that no party could accumulate more than half its annual allotment for use in future years and that no party could begin to accumulate unspent balances until it had begun to draw upon the fund. The PIP drew its first money from the fund in December of the following year, 1959.

In the 1960 election, in addition to the $150,000 they each were entitled to draw for that year, the PDP had accumulated a balance of $95,754.61, the SRP a balance of $106,035.29, and the PIP a balance of $6,250.00. Although all three parties used up all their credits at least a month before the election, they continued to spend large sums from other sources. The absence of reporting requirements for political committees, and of enforcement procedures, made it easy to evade the limitations of the 1957 act. *Ad hoc* committees of the kind familiar on the mainland did not appear to be covered by the act at all; they began to proliferate on the island. And the PDP succeeded in bypassing the prohibitions intended to eliminate "quotas" by calling off-premises meetings of government workers at which they were solicited for contributions, in the presence of departmental supervisors, by party officials who were not employees of the government.

These practices led to further revision of the Election Fund Act a few months prior to the 1964 election. The new amendment attempted to impose effective limitations on private contributions by requiring, for the first time, the filing of quarterly reports on receipts and expenditures and by imposing this requirement on all political committees having any kind of relationship to an election. But the amendment established no enforcement procedure, and party and other political committees have filed their reports at best fitfully and carelessly.

The 1964 amendment also tightened the prohibition against quotas by making it illegal for government employees to be asked for political contributions by "any person directly or indirectly" except through mail, newspaper advertisement, television and radio programs, or billboards, all of which presumably are directed at other people as well, and none of which allow for easy supervision by departmental chiefs. This provision has been generally effective, and quotas have all but disappeared from Puerto Rican politics.

The amendment greatly increased the amount of public money available for political activity. In addition to the PDP and the SRP, which were principal parties under the terms of the 1957 act, the no-longer-principal PIP and the new non-principal Christian Action party (CAP) received funds "for the sole purposes and effects of the election year 1964" (perhaps because the PDP wanted to ensure that its opposition in the 1964 campaign would be divided among as many parties as possible). The PDP and SRP were each given a credit of $75,000 for overhead expenses which, for 1964, could also be applied to campaign expenses. The two smaller parties, because their entitlement did not begin until after passage of the amendment in March, each received a credit of $57,500. Each of the four parties also received a basic advance credit of $75,000 for general campaign expenses and a *pro rata* share of a total of $1 million in credits (from which their initial $75,000 would be subtracted) based on their percentage of the straight ticket vote, to be available for payment after the election. A third credit of $12,500 was advanced to each party for transportation of voters, to be deducted from a percentage share of a total of $250,000 in credits for transportation, also based on the straight ticket vote and available after the election.

A total of $1,368,229.12 was withdrawn from the Election Fund in 1964 and 1965 in connection with the 1964 campaign: $688,526.50 by the PDP, $399,477.62 by the SRP, $140,500 by the PIP, and $139,725 by the CAP.

The possibilities for third party emergence under the Puerto Rican system were illustrated in 1968, when Governor Sanchez Vilella, who had come to office as Muñoz Marin's hand-picked successor upon the latter's retirement, failed to win renomination by the PDP, and ran for re-election with a *pro rata* share of government funding as the candidate of a new petition party, the People's party. Although he received over 10 percent of the total vote, thus qualifying the People's party to receive government support in the 1972 election, that party faded away with the abandonment of Sanchez Vilella's own political ambitions. Thus, although the Puerto Rican system allows third parties to emerge, it does not ensure their perpetuation.

GERMANY

The Federal Republic of Germany was the first major nation to develop public financing of politics. Two programs adopted in the post-Nazi era are important, although not decisive, in this development.

First, because of the post-war disenchantment with politics in general, the leaders of the infant republic initially found it very difficult to educate their citizens and encourage their participation in normal democratic political processes. One institutional response to this difficulty was the establishment in the early 1950s of publicly financed foundations for political education. Though nominally independent, these foundations correspond to the principal parties (one for each), receive government support in proportion to the parties' parliamentary strength, and are controlled by their leaders. They have become an important adjunct to the work of the parties. They do basic research on issues, publish material generally supportive of the philosophical or ideological dispositions of the parties, sponsor lectures and classes, and conduct exchange programs with comparable institutions in other countries. They are an important source of patronage for the parties, a training ground for party functionaries, and a launching pad for prospective candidates.

The second program was *Wiedergutmachung,* "making good again," providing compensation for deprivation and returning or paying for property lost under the Nazis. (This program is principally known in this country for providing restitution to surviving Jews.)

The Social Democratic party (SPD), alone among the legal postwar political parties in Germany, had survived and been reconstituted from pre-Nazi days. It received property and funds, mostly in newspapers and publishing, as compensation for assets seized during the 1930s, which grossed about $100 million yearly during the 1950s. The German labor movement, closely allied with the SPD, also received property and funds. In addition to these assets, a highly motivated dues-paying membership (twice that of the bourgeois parties combined) has given the SPD a much larger and more reliable source of funds than is available to any other party short of recourse to outside (usually industry) support.

During the early 1950s, while trying to build the economy and regularize the political life of his country, Konrad Adenauer also had to secure an adequate supply of funds for his Christian Democratic Union and its Bavarian partner, the Christian Social Union. Though the current virtual monopoly of the right by the CDU-CSU was clearly emerging, it was not yet established. A number of other bourgeois parties were competing for favor and for contributions from a business community that had not yet achieved its present financial capability or confidence.

In 1954, the Adenauer government amended the tax law to permit deductions for contributions to political parties. The limitation of deductibility for these gifts was 10 percent of income for individuals and 10 percent of gross for business firms. This limitation imposed no effective ceiling on the size of donations; as a result, expenditures in the 1957 federal election were twice those of the previous election in 1953.

A suit brought by the SPD government of the German *Land* (state) of Hesse resulted in a 1958 Supreme Court decision voiding the tax deduction law on the ground that, because it provided a greater public subsidy for the political participation of rich individuals than of poor individuals, it violated the equality-of-chances provision of the German Basic Law (constitution). In rendering this decision, the court went out of its way to state that the equality principle would not be violated by outright grants of public money for politics. The stage was set for the initiation of direct government financing.

In the same year, with considerable fanfare, the SPD abandoned its traditional socialist goal of nationalizing industry and adopted a reformist program more akin to that of the left wing of the Democratic party in the United States. This move was a clear bid to extend the SPD constituency beyond the working class, and it seemed likely to reduce industry's incentive to prevent SPD victories in future federal elections.

The CDU at the time was engaged in strengthening and increasing the number of its local organizations in order to undercut and absorb minor rival bourgeois parties and to improve its grassroots effectiveness relative to the well-organized SPD. Success in this effort required a substantial and permanent increase in the size of its operating budget. The party feared that the combination of the SPD's changed program and the elimination of the tax deduction would cause industry contributions to slacken. Chancellor Adenauer in particular wished to reduce dependence on industry contributions because he resented the increase in heavy-handed lobbying by a number of the business associations that had raised large sums for the 1957 campaign.

In 1959, Parliament passed legislation providing for the distribution of $1.7 million annually among the federal parties in proportion to their strength in the Bundestag. (The relative smallness of this amount—less than 10 percent of the estimated $18 million to $20 million total of federal election expenditures in 1957—reflects a deliberate effort by the CDU leadership to avoid provoking either public opinion or the opposition of an SPD indifferent to the CDU's concerns and well endowed with organizational funds.) The amount was increased to $6.6 million annually in 1962 (following the 1961 elections, in which the parties spent $25 million to $27 million) and to $13 million in 1964 (one year prior to federal elections that cost $31 million to $34 million).

In 1966, the Supreme Court ruled that the government's method of financing party activities implied control over the parties and threatened interference with the upward progression of political decision from the people to the state, as required by democratic theory. The court prohibited this approach but pointed out that, since elections are an indispensable part of that progression, the government could properly reimburse the parties for the costs of election campaigns.

Parliament thereupon devised the current system, which was enacted in the Party Law of 1967. Funds are allocated on the basis of a fixed amount (now $1) for every eligible voter and apportioned to the respective parties according to the votes they have received. Parties that have received 0.5 percent of the popular vote (the threshold was reduced from 2.5 percent by court decision in 1968) in the previous election are eligible for an advance allocation of the reimbursement for the next election. The money is disbursed in installments over the four-year election cycle—10 percent in the first pre-election year, 15 percent in the second, 35 percent in the third, and 40 percent following the election in the fourth year. The final 40 percent is adjusted upward or downward after the election so that the four-year total will conform to the vote in that election. The law also requires that money be repaid to the government after an election in which a party experiences a decline of more than 40 percent. (This provision was applied to the Free Democratic party following the election of 1969.)

The law states that these funds are to be used only in connection with the election to which they apply. But in practice, the absence of controls and the difficulty of distinguishing electoral activities from other activities of party organizations leave the parties free to use the funds much as they did under the earlier system—that is, as they wish.

Similar systems of party finance now operate at the state level in the German *Lander*. Allocations to the *Land* parties average fifty cents per voter, making the total of federal and *Land* subsidies to the parties about $1.50 per voter. With an electorate of more than 40 million people, the total election-to-election distribution to the parties is more than $60 million.

SWEDEN

Sweden today has developed a dynamic modern economy and a vigorously egalitarian distributive system which gives the small (8 million) population of this country the second-highest standard of living in the world, spread so evenly that even the poorest Swedes live better than one-quarter of the Americans who supposedly share the highest standard.

The Swedish polity has been described variously as democratic socialism, a new totalitarianism, a corporate state, and a democracy of organizations. It is in fact none of these. The state owns only 6 percent of the "means of production"—primarily railroads, broadcasting, telephone and some electric power generation (as in many other western nations). The electoral processes and formal organization of Sweden's government are comparable to those of other parliamentary systems, but there are palpable and important differences between public life in Sweden and that in other democratic countries.

The first key to these differences is a history and tradition of homogeneity and consensus common in isolated places with small populations, where eccentricity and even individuality may be perceived as threats to the social order.

Second is the socialist purpose of the Social Democratic party, which has dominated Swedish politics for the past forty years. Eminently practical about the need to compete successfully in world markets in order to achieve a high living standard, the Social Democratic government has worked in close harmony with Swedish capital, not hesitating to compromise both socialist ideology and trade union agendas. But without neglecting competitive production, the government has established the most elaborate and thoroughgoing welfare state now in existence. In the process, it has acquired and used increasing power over the educational and informational facilities of the country to influence the attitudes and life styles of its newly urbanized people—all with the aim of creating a society of equal and equally participating citizens.

The third distinctive feature of public life in Sweden is the means of political participation. Participation is unusually widespread but is channeled in a way that, according to some observers, limits the citizen's sense of personal efficacy (although it may provide more than most Swedes had earlier enjoyed).[2] Citizens participate in politics largely through labor, business, professional, and other organizations, primarily along lines of economic interest. The role of these groupings is responsible for the frequent descriptions of Sweden as a corporate state or a democracy of organizations. These organizations are not part of the formal government, but they are constantly consulted by government and have a substantial role in pre-legislative and administrative decision making.

Typically, the government appoints commissions on which all interested organizations are represented, or by which their views are conscientiously solicited. These commissions then make recommendations that become the basis for legislation, often without substantial modification and with little or no parliamentary resistance. The process is ponderous and slow-moving, but it serves to incorporate the views of all relevant power centers and it reinforces the highly prized Swedish consensus. Having participated in the decision-making process, the leaders of organizations are inclined to accept the recommendations of commissions and to justify them to their own constituencies.

This system reinforces the influence of the organizations both over their members, to whom they increasingly appear as the only vehicles by which political goals can be reached, and over the electoral process—in urging the nomination of particular individuals, approving candidates or parties, and generating financial assistance.

Public financing of politics in Sweden serves to dilute this organizational influence over the parties—or, as a Swede might observe, to strengthen one kind of organization, the parties, relative to other kinds of organizations so as to create a healthier balance among all of them.

In fact, public financing came about through a characteristic Swedish adjustment of differing interests: the desire of the Social Democrats to save their foundering press, and the need of the non-government parties for greater financial and organizational muscle.

Virtually all of Sweden's 400 daily newspapers (serving a population about equal to that of New York City) are owned by or have strong ties to the political parties. Rising costs, the competition of broadcast media, urbanization, and expanded circulation of success-ful metropolitan papers have driven an increasing number of lesser papers to the wall, as in other countries, and threaten still more.

Most of the already defunct or endangered papers have been Social Democratic. In the past, these papers were indispensable to the party as a means of disseminating information and propagating views. Even now, although their loss would not cripple the party's effectiveness in the same way, the party has been anxious to slow the attrition of its press, both for reasons of prestige and out of a sense of responsibility for the capital investment in, and the people employed by, its papers. Despite near-universal acknowledgment among newspapermen that the weaker papers cannot be kept afloat indefinitely, the Social Democrats have maintained, and public opinion generally agrees, that democracy is enhanced when each community has at least two competing newspapers.

In 1963, a government-appointed Commission on the Press recom-mended a $5 million subsidy to newspapers, to be distributed through the political parties and allocated according to the votes received by the parties. The recommendation was not unanimous, and its op-ponents resisted it bitterly. The papers supporting the bourgeois parties were doing relatively well and did not need or want a subsidy. Being privately owned for the most part, they also resented the suggestion that they be formally linked to the parties they supported.

But the Conservative, Liberal, Center (Farmers), and Communist parties did need operating funds to match those of the organiza-tionally and financially powerful Social Democrats. So the elements of a compromise were at hand. The other parties would receive the public financing they needed if they would consent to subsidization of the Social Democratic press. This financing would take the form of direct annual grants to the parties under a regulation prohibiting "state control . . . concerning the use of the grants" by the parties, so that the Social Democratic Party could pass its receipts on to its newspapers.

Though opposed in principle by Conservatives and Liberals, the proposal was enacted in 1965 with Center and Communist as well as Social Democratic support. All parties promptly accepted their share of the appropriated funds, and the modern Swedish, heavily public, system of political finance came into being.

To be eligible for support, a party must have at least one seat in the Riksdag and have received at least 2 percent of the total national vote in the preceding election. These grants are not earmarked under law, as they are in Germany, to finance election campaigns, but the parties generally set aside substantial amounts every year for expenditure in election years.

National grants to the parties began in 1966, at $12,000 per parliamentary seat per year. The total of $4.6 million increased the funds of the strongly industry-supported Conservative party by about 50 percent, those of the under-financed Center party by about 400 percent, those of the industry-supported Liberal party by about 150 percent, those of the union-supported Social Democratic party by about 140 percent, and those of the small Communist party by about 125 percent.

The Social Democratic party gave between 75 and 80 percent of its annual grant to its weaker papers (about $1.6 million, an amount previously supplied to these papers by the labor movement). The bourgeois parties expanded their staffs and strengthened their organizations.

Following the establishment of county and municipal support for local party organizations in 1969, and a 1971 increase to $14,000 in the grants per Riksdag seat, the Liberal party announced that it no longer would accept industry contributions, although it would continue to solicit donations from individuals. The Liberal leaders hoped that, in addition to generating favorable public opinion and perhaps spurring the Conservatives to emulate them, their move would ultimately create a climate in which the Social Democrats might be persuaded to refuse union contributions.

Bourgeois and Communist party leaders also pressed for further upward revision of party grants and of allowances for the legislative secretariats of non-government parties. The government, apparently in exchange for agreement on a system of separate and substantial direct support to weaker newspapers (which now permits the Social Democrats to use all their party support funds for the party itself), appointed a new Commission on Support of Political Parties. Comprising representatives of all the parties, this commission unanimously recommended raising party support to $17,000 per Riksdag seat in 1972.

With county and municipal support now amounting to $8 million per year and the new level of national support at $6.5 million, total support at all levels is over $14 million per year. With an estimated additional $11 million from dues, contributions, and other sources in non-election years (and much more in election years), the parties' total governmental and non-governmental income is in the neighborhood of $25,000,000, or $6.20 per voter, for each off year. Financing at the same rate per capita would amount to more than $650,000,000 in the United States—as much as we spend over a four-year period including a presidential election.

FINLAND AND NORWAY

Finland and Norway followed Sweden rather quickly in adopting public financing of politics. Although their respective political structures and practices differ from Sweden's in important ways, and although the question of press support was not a principal motivating factor in either country, Finland and Norway have close economic and cultural ties to their more populous neighbor and were well informed about the progress of this novel method of funding parties.

Sweden's new system impressed Finnish and Norwegian leaders as a sensible response to the problems of financing and integrity that afflict democratic politicians everywhere.

Finland began its program of national support for parties in 1969 and now pays $22,200 annually for each of its 200 parliamentary seats. Parties receive an estimated $1.5 million from other sources, and individual candidates perhaps another $1.25 million, for a total of $7 million—$7.5 million, or about $3.50 per voter, at the national level. Government support of parties is expected to spread to lower political levels as public acceptance grows and as parties adjust to the new system.

In 1971, the Finnish government began providing subsidies for the press to help pay for transportation and distribution costs. (The total press subsidy for 1972 was $2 million.) Although the government supposedly bases allocations on the economic condition of the newspapers, it in fact maintains a political balance in the disbursal of these funds.

Norway, which adopted national support for its politics in 1970, provides funds to all parties that run candidates in at least half the country's legislative constituencies, distributing them according to the percentage of votes received in the most recent parliamentary election. In 1972, public funding for parties totaled $1.5 million (up from an original $1.2 million). In addition, dues, contributions, and other non-government sources account for $1.5 million to $2.2 million in ordinary years and $2.2 million to $3.7 million in election years, making an election year total in the neighborhood of $4.5 million, or about $2.15 per voter, of which the government share is approximately one-third.

Norway prohibits grants to political parties other than at the national level, but this prohibition is expected to be lifted in the near future.

The Norwegian government made a special and unprecedented appropriation of $2.1 million for activity connected with the September, 1972, referendum on entrance into the Common Market. The nominally neutral information programs run by the Foreign Office received $1 million, $500,000 was divided equally between the People's Movement Against EEC and the Yes To EEC organizations, and $600,000 was divided among the parties according to the regular formula for party support. Opponents of the Common Market charged that this division stacked the deck against them by five to one, since all the largest parties supported entry and the Foreign Office, they claimed, was not neutral. The charge became an important issue in the referendum campaign and may have contributed to the victory of the anti-EEC coalition.

Since the beginning of 1973, Canada, Israel, and Italy have adopted national public financing systems, but they still are too new and untested for useful discussion in this context.

In each of the countries considered in this chapter, cloakroom discussion and public debate over the initiation of government financing covered many of the practical and theoretical questions that have been raised in the United States. The dominant party, and usually others as well, deemed private funds insufficient to maintain the desired level of political activity or perceived unrepresentative disparities in the financial resources available to the parties. The existing system of private financing was charged with either fostering outright corruption or, at a minimum, compromising the integrity of the political process. And the leadership demonstrated a sincere desire to perfect the operation of democracy.

In Puerto Rico, the principal impetus for public financing was the Popular Democratic party's discomfort with the system of levying contribution "quotas" on government employees, and the lack of alternative private resources. In Germany, it was the need of the Christian Democratic Union–Christian Social Union for a more assured supply of organizational funds between elections and the Chancellor's wish to be less dependent on big business. In Sweden, it was the Social Democrats' need to prop up their faltering press and to reduce their growing dependence on union contributions for this purpose. Yet each of the other elements was also present or emerged during the gestation and birth of the new system.

In each country, substantial and successful efforts were made to achieve consensus before the new system was enacted. Even in

Sweden, where the Conservative and Liberal parties initially opposed public financing, the two other non-government parties joined the Social Democrats in supporting it. All public financing systems provide funding to all parties that can demonstrate a minimal following. Whether calculated or not, this feature of the legislation has had the effect of seducing the original opponents of the plans—Conservatives and Liberals in Sweden, and Independentists in Puerto Rico.

Thirteen years after Germany adopted public financing, Dr. Fritz Burgbacher, who had been treasurer of Konrad Adenauer's CDU when the legislation was enacted, imparted his wisdom to an American visitor. "Start small," he said.[3] And all the governments that have enacted public funding did "start small," in part because too sudden an alteration of political practice (especially if it could be portrayed as a self-serving raid on the treasury) might have alarmed interest groups and the public, and in part because prudence justified a cautious approach to any change whose effects could not be clearly or fully anticipated and that might result in a major restructuring of political power.

Gradually, as parties and political interests have adjusted to the new system, the amounts of public funding have grown. Once a public financing system was adopted, its funding has expanded whenever rising costs, questions of integrity, ideological preference, or other considerations suggested the need for an increase.

Over time, theoretically, public funding could supplant private money altogether. But thus far, private funding has not even been reduced, let alone eliminated, in countries that have adopted public financing. The growth of private contributions appears to have been slowed and at times almost halted, but they remain important, even where the government now supplies most of the funds available for politics. Moreover, in none of these countries has a significant political movement developed to eliminate private money. On the contrary, party leaders, particularly in the left wing parties with large dues-paying memberships but also across the entire political spectrum, have steadfastly asserted the value of citizen participation and advocated fund raising as an indispensable method of reaching and activating their followers. The treasurer of the German Free Democratic party, which was deserted by business supporters and became 90 percent dependent on public funding after it formed a coalition with the Social Democrats in 1969, has expressed the view, widely shared in his country, that the most healthy division of political funds would be one-third from government, one-third from member dues, and one-third from contributions.[4]

But the growth of public financing has an inherent self-limiting effect. It diminishes the integrity problems and the unrepresentative effects of private funding by proportionately reducing their weight in the system. And these changes lessen the relative urgency of arguments for stronger regulation or elimination of private financing.

At the same time, what at first seemed radical becomes routine. The FDP in Germany learned to get along with very little private support. The Liberal party in Sweden has sought a moral advantage over the Conservative party by ceasing to accept industry contributions. Public financing gives rise to political habits and new forms of competition that may eventually make a transition to total public financing both logical and easy, if political leaders find a way to do without private contributions as a stimulus to public participation in the work of the party.

The question of whether to have public financing at all is relatively easily resolved. It is simply a matter of whether the supply of private money is sufficient, or whether the available private money is too tainted for comfortable use. Far more difficult and interesting is the question of how to distribute public funds.

A public treasury is, in theory, a neutral source of funds; in practice, it is likely to be biased in favor of the holders of government power. Perhaps ultimately no source of funds can be neutral. Democratic theory suggests, in fact, that the institutional arrangements for the choice of the people's representatives ought to be partisan in proportion as the people are partisan, so as to be representative of the electorate as a whole and to produce a representative result. Thus countries that have adopted public financing base the allocation of funds on an index of public support.

The Nordic systems, based on the number of parliamentary seats held by each party, provide resources for the next election according to what happened in the last. The German and Puerto Rican systems, geared in different ways to the number of votes cast in the current election, may be somewhat more flexible. However, no serious complaint of inflexibility has been heard from party leaders operating under either standard. Most maintain that an assured supply of equitably determined funds enhances competition. As in the United States, incumbency in these countries has certain natural advantages, but the non-incumbent parties believe that public funds help to give them "running room." Even the party secretary of the Swedish Conservative party, which had originally opposed public financing, speaks enthusiastically and in detail about how effectively public money enables his party to organize its staff and their activities.[5]

The greatest assurance that "out" parties need regarding any otherwise well-devised system of allocations is that its operation will be automatic, consistent, and not subject to legislative tampering for momentary partisan advantage. The Puerto Rican experience has not been entirely reassuring in this regard; but Germany and the Nordic countries have had stable allocation systems. The only significant structural cleavage has been that, in 1972, Sweden adopted modest flat grants as a base under the parties' proportional allocations; this base is intended to protect the lesser parties from large percentage effects of relatively small numerical losses in the Riksdag.

Although public financing has not caused any clear changes in the relative electoral strength of parties in any country, it has, of course, altered the relative financial strength of parties. Parties with limited private financial resources receive proportionately more public support than parties with extensive private resources.

Public financing may also affect the emergence of new parties and the demise of parties that have outlived their usefulness. In the United States, direct election of the president and the two-party system do not provide the flexibility of parliamentary systems, with their possibilities of shifting coalitions. Short-lived third parties, a recurring feature of our political landscape, provide the only mechanism by which elements of one coalition can detach themselves without joining the rival coalition and at least inferentially bargain with both. It might be harmful to place greater obstacles in the way of third party formation than now exist, or to structure the financing system so as to promote or ensure their continuation beyond their natural life.

In all public financing systems, a party must demonstrate some level of public support in order to qualify for funding. In Puerto Rico and Germany, the criterion is the number of votes in the current election, and the threshold is kept low. (In Puerto Rico, the collection of a reasonable number of pre-election petition signatures qualifies a party for some support.) In consequence, both countries have experienced the relatively easy emergence and natural disappearance of new parties—most notably the neo-Nazi National Democratic party in Germany, which had a brief flurry of strength in the late 1960s but whose receipt of proportionate public funds did not prevent it from dropping below the threshold in the 1970s. Sweden, Finland, and Norway, in contrast, have made the winning of parliamentary seats a condition of public support. This criterion represents a severe obstacle to the emergence of new parties, and none have appeared.

The most striking example of the politically liberating effect of public financing is the recent history of the Free Democratic party in Germany. This small party (usually receiving 8 to 12 percent of the vote) is an heir to nineteenth century liberalism, with a strong commitment to laissez-faire economics and an equally strong leaning toward civil libertarianism and educational and social (as distinguished from economic) reform. Although these two tendencies had a certain centrifugal effect, the FDP held together quite well as long as it was in coalition with the CDU-CSU, on which it exerted a moderating influence. It was well financed for a party of its size, receiving very substantial support from competition-oriented industry and small businesses that tended to oppose economic concentration.

Following the 1965 election, the CDU-CSU under Kurt-Georg Kiesinger and the almost as large SPD under Willy Brandt formed what was called the Grand Coalition in order to facilitate a rapprochement with Eastern Europe. Although the FDP was left out in the cold, it experienced a moderate growth in support because it was the only opposition party in the Bundestag. As the Social Democrats became more "respectable," sharing cabinet posts for the first time since pre-Hitler days, the FDP entered coalitions with them at the *Land* level in various parts of Germany. But in the 1969 election, the FDP was threatened with major defections whichever way it jumped—with the loss of its financial backers if it "put the Socialists in power" by forming a coalition with the SPD, and with loss of its many educated middle-class voters if it rejoined the CDU-CSU.

After much internal argument, the FDP committed itself to a coalition with the SPD and suffered a drastic loss of financial support in the 1969 election. Its share of the national vote fell below 6 percent, and it survived the following three years 90 percent dependent on its reduced allocation of public funds.

Having been forced to a choice, and having opted for the majority of its members rather than its sources of money, the FDP might well not have survived but for public financing, which saw it through the 1972 election with a doubling of its previous vote. Still in coalition with the SPD and in a stronger position than ever as the swing factor in German politics, the FDP is now freer of financial inhibition in determining its policies than any other important party in Western Europe or North America.

The essential principle of private funding for election campaigns is simplicity itself: let citizens support whatever candidates they favor to whatever extent they wish. The trouble is that citizens do not have equal means and that the disparity in their means has caused distortions throughout the system.

The essential principles of public financing are more complex. The government provides the money for politics because citizens cannot or will not do so. The inequality in citizen means and therefore in influence is ameliorated by public financing. The shortage of money to wage competitive campaigns, stemming from too little participation by citizens, is overcome by adequate government funding. And the misallocation of money to certain candidates, certain districts, or certain offices—to the detriment of other contests where adequately funded campaigns are also desirable—is overcome by a distribution formula for public funds that channels dollars somewhat more evenly throughout the political system.

The public financing schemes in other nations are relatively simple. But they could have been more complex if those nations had attempted to channel money to reflect the complicated interactions within and among their parties and at their many levels of government. Instead, they

 **10**

TOWARD PUBLIC FINANCING

put the responsibility for financing campaigns at each governmental level on the public authorities at that level. And they put the responsibility on each party to determine its own internal and inter-factional allocations of public money. Public financing has therefore remained a straightforward transaction between the government and the parties at each governmental level, based on fixed and universally applied indexes of public support for the parties—usually percentages of votes or parliamentary seats.

PROBLEMS IN THE AMERICAN POLITICAL CONTEXT

American politics presents serious obstacles to adoption of a straightforward public financing system modeled on those in effect elsewhere. An American public financing scheme must deal with complex problems posed by the separation of powers, the decentralization of American political parties, the variability of political constituencies, the political assets associated with incumbency, the use of primaries to nominate party candidates, the different roles of minor parties, several provisions of the American Constitution, and the orientation of American politics toward candidates rather than parties.

Separation of Powers. The separation of powers requires any public financing scheme to apply to both of the federal elective branches—legislative and executive. By law or practice, other nations allocate most public funds to those central party organizations whose leaders will form the executive if their party wins a mandate at the polls. But in parliamentary systems the executive and legislature are merged; their electoral fates and their programs are inextricably intertwined. In theory and practice, the United States enjoys a separation of powers. Legislative and executive candidates of the same party may run on different platforms, and funding must be separately provided them so they can propound their different views. Indeed, seeking separate mandates is essential if each branch is to check the power of the other.

Financing candidates for one branch and not the other would also jeopardize the esteem, visibility, and ultimately the power of the unfunded department. Publicly financed presidential campaigns would gradually raise public esteem for the executive because of its freedom from private money entanglements, while diminishing respect for a legislature still reliant on private and special interest sources. Similarly, generous public financing of presidential campaigns will gradually raise the visibility of the executive, increasing public reliance on and confidence in the president for policy leadership. If only presidential campaigns are publicly financed, a president could easily use his vast resources to raise private money for congressional races, extending his political influence over the legislative branch. Unless Congress too is publicly financed, its visibility as a policy maker and ultimately public support for its policy-making role fall into the shadow of the presidency.

Any American pattern of public financing must respect the separation of powers or risk unbalancing the carefully contrived system of checks and balances designed to limit government and protect liberty.

Party Decentralization. The resources of American political parties are scattered, albeit unequally, throughout the political parties' formal structure. Public money directed to one stratum within the party structure would greatly strengthen it relative to the others. Generous public grants to national party committees, for instance, would give them greater resources in dealing with local and state party committees. Public grants at the lower levels would also alter relationships within party strata—between county committees in the same state, for instance—by giving those formerly lacking in resources new means to conduct their affairs.[1]

It is also difficult to specify just where public grants might go in the party apparatus: to statutory groups, which in some places are merely fictions, or to voluntary groups that may be the real party organization; to established party groups or to the emerging, perhaps temporary outsider clubs that challenge the party establishment.

The activities, and hence the use of funds, of different elements within the party are somewhat specialized.[2] Local party units may emphasize registration, canvassing, and getting out the vote; state committees, by contrast, may emphasize publicity, candidate coordination, and campaign management. If all centers of activity within the party perform different useful activities, public grants to one segment of the party and not to others will support some significant activities at the expense of others of equal importance.

The relationship between the party organization and the "party in government"—that is, the party's officeholders and candidates—is also delicately balanced. Unlike the case in parliamentary systems, the officeholding partisans are not also in fact or by law the leaders of the party organization. Tension between party responsibility and official independence characterize the American system. Financing candidates but not parties strengthens the independence of the party in government and weakens the responsibility of officeholders to the party platform and the citizen activists who draft it. On the other hand, public financing of parties would greatly strengthen the party organization in its relationship with candidates and officeholders, imposing a kind of party discipline incompatible with the coalition nature of American parties and contrary to popular expectations about the independence of officeholders from party control.

Variability of Constituency. The size of the electorate, geographical size, density of population, strength of party organization, socio-economic composition, congruence of media and district lines, intensity of electoral competition, and other variables that social science may not yet have identified fully all bear on political finance reform.[3] Those who advocate public grants are often challenged to devise a formula that takes into account the different spending needs of candidates in various districts with vastly different characteristics. Yet the impact of these variables on the spending levels necessary to achieve vigorous competition is only imprecisely known, and factors as yet unidentified may well affect the amount of campaign spending that is necessary in any district.

Legislation can account for some variables; for example, it can meet the different spending needs of different-sized districts by tying public grants to the number of eligible voters. Some legislative proposals set special, higher minimum public grants for congressional candidates in statewide House districts, such as Nevada or Wyoming. These special floors recognize, in theory, that certain levels of spending must be achieved to run an effective campaign in states with small electorates, low population densities, and large geographical areas. The difficulty in developing such formulas to account for these variables can be seen when the same special grants for statewide House races are applied to Delaware and Vermont, with only a single congressman apiece but with few of the other characteristics of Nevada or Wyoming.

Incumbency. Any public financing scheme—indeed, any political finance regulation—will change the relationship between incumbents and challengers. At present, incumbents enjoy not only the visibility and perquisites of officeholding but also substantial advantages in political organization and money.[4] Public financing schemes that rest on citizen choice—such as vouchers, check-offs, or matching grants— are criticized as favoring the incumbent because his higher visibility and superior organization equip him better to woo citizen support. Also, given the one-party dominance of most American congressional districts, these citizen allocations will produce highly unequal financial resources for opposing candidates because greater majority-party registration and organization will combine to channel a lion's share of public money to the dominant party's candidate.

On the other hand, equal flat grants to candidates are strenuously criticized because they do not allow challengers extra money to offset the official and political advantages of incumbents. Any expenditure limit applied equally to incumbents and challengers, whether a separate regulation or in conjunction with public financing, is vulnerable to the same complaint.

The dilemma resists resolution. As a matter of legislative reality, regulations favoring challengers are unlikely to be adopted, since all who must enact them are incumbents. Further, there is the practical difficulty of identifying those entitled to preferred treatment in such schemes. If an incumbent senator is challenged by his home-state governor, should that powerful executive official be treated as a "challenger" entitled to an extra measure of public funding or permissible spending?

More to the point, however, is that the dilemma is primarily theoretical rather than real. In addition to enjoying the intangible advantages of officeholding, incumbents substantially outspend challengers in campaigns. In the nation's numerous one-party congressional districts, the challenger is typically so impoverished that his is a non-campaign. In competitive districts, spending on both sides is higher, but the incumbent still has a substantial funding edge.[5] Only in a few well-publicized races—usually involving special causes or wealthy candidates—do challengers muster enough money to outspend officeholders. Public financing of candidates, then, will tend to "level up" the challenger in virtually all districts, offsetting somewhat the financing advantage of the incumbent. In one-party districts, this leveling up will introduce vigorous and visible campaigning. In competitive districts, challengers will at least have financial equality at the outset—a condition likely to infuse their campaigns with the early resources and enthusiasm that heighten the prospects for success.

Nominations. No nation with publicly financed campaigns uses primaries to nominate candidates, and the widespread adoption of primary nominations in America poses a unique and thorny problem for public financing advocates. If public financing is available for general elections but not for primaries, the evils and misallocations of the present private financing system will simply be displaced from the former to the latter. Furthermore, campaign funds are probably more effective and more important in nomination than in general election campaigns. Nomination contests are intra-party feuds; because voters cannot rely on party labels to guide their ballot choice, they need vigorous and visible campaigns even more than in general elections to provide information about election choices. The well-financed candidate has a special edge in winning nomination, especially where saturation media campaigning is feasible. Finally, of course, most congressional districts are safe one-party bastions, and primary elections are the real arena of decision.

Against these arguments for public financing stands the problem of how to allocate such funds. The legal requirements for entering primaries are nominal in most states, and they should remain so to give effect to the democratic principle that voters should have a choice of candidates and programs representing all hues in the political spectrum. Nonetheless, public financing for all nomination contenders invites frivolous candidacies—those intended solely to generate publicity for a candidate's occupation, those malevolently intended to split the vote of another contender, those offering no additional choice to the electorate, and others. Virtually all advocates of public financing concede the need to distinguish serious from frivolous candidates for the purpose of allocating tax money to primary campaigns. The most common approach is to designate as serious candidates, eligible for public funding, those who demonstrate certain levels of popular support.

Public financing of primaries must also be sensitive to the varied balances struck across the country between party organization and popular participation in nominations. The party organization role has traditionally been strongest in making nominations, precisely because political activists have brought to these contests money and other resources that candidates cannot easily garner elsewhere. If political finance reform eliminates the party organization role in advancing candidates, the influence of party workers toward bringing policy cohesion to the party in government and the confidence of activists in the usefulness of party work will suffer still further blows. Any public financing system in primary contests must, therefore, respect the special role of political parties in making nominations.

Minor Parties. In the United States, most public funding proposals have distinguished between major parties and minor parties. A combination of equal funds for the major parties and proportionate grants for the minor parties affirms the predominant two-party pattern in America but allows for the various roles played by different minor parties and independent candidates in the nation's politics.[6]

Some minor parties affect the intellectual climate of politics or spawn ideas whose time will come later, without playing an effective part in electoral politics. The Socialist party illustrates the programmatic minor party's role. Other minor parties serve significant protest purposes, commanding enough votes to change the direction of major-party policy. Such parties may reflect divisions within a major party (the Bull Moosers); or they may serve as a bridge for vote blocs to abandon a major party on their way to affiliation with the opposition party (the La Follette Progressives and the Wallace movement); or they may be a force from outside the major parties, raising issues suppressed in the conflict between the dominant coalitions (the Populists). Occasionally a minor party rises to majority-party status, eclipsing one of the long-standing electoral leviathans—as the Republicans displaced the Whigs. The public financing experiences of countries with relatively fixed multi-party patterns are not relevant in a nation where minor parties play such varied roles, either transitory or permanent.

If minor parties are to receive public money, it must be with recognition that they may or may not be serious electoral contenders and that they may be more or less permanent or merely transient. Some qualifying test, perhaps vote performance, may be necessary to prevent every group with an idea from being treated as a party worthy of public financing. But tying financial support to past electoral performance may hinder some minor parties in fulfilling historically validated functions and may artificially preserve either major or minor parties when they no longer have an electoral role.

A past election qualifying test may deny a new minor party financial support in a year when its electoral strength is highest and its protest role most important. And then in the next election, when its cause may already be fading, it will receive handsome support based on conditions four years earlier. The Bull Moosers, La Follette Progressives, and Wallacites are cases in point. Further, both major and minor parties might be artificially sustained by financial subsidies in presidential elections following the effective demise of their electoral life. The Whigs and the three minor parties mentioned above would have found reasons to keep their party organizations together to receive government bounties based on prior vote performance. To avoid both denial of support to minor parties currently strong and continuation of support to parties no longer strong, a qualifying formula must base grants on current popular support.

Candidate Politics. Foreign nations solve most of the intricacies of public financing by making grants to political parties. Some provide funds to the party organizations for general activities; others make grants for campaigning. In America, public financing cannot be directed mainly to parties because our politics is candidate-oriented. The separation of powers and primary nominations focus attention on specific candidates rather than parties. So does the decentralized and coalition nature of American parties. The fascination of Americans with personalities, in sharp contrast to the ideological and partisan commitments in most other Western democracies, heightens the emphasis on candidates. And the unusual extent to which American politics is media politics has exaggerated this tendency.

Basing public financing on party categories therefore tends to distort the realities of American politics. Support must go mainly to candidates, although some aid to parties may be appropriate for certain activities and to maintain the balance between the party in government and the party organization. Indexes qualifying candidates for public grants and measuring the amounts of their grants must somehow bear directly on each aspirant and not on his party affiliation. A troublesome illustration involves United States Senate candidates who rotate seeking office in the same constituency. A landslide victory by a 1972 senatorial candidate should scarcely be the measure of support for a wholly different candidate, albeit of the same party, for the other senatorial seat to be filled in 1974 or 1976 in the same state. Nor should the rout of the opposition party candidate in 1972 bear on the finances available to the entirely different aspirant bearing that party's standard in 1974 or 1976.

Since support should center on candidates, the need for current indexes of eligibility and funding—already mentioned in connection with minor-party roles—is heightened in any American public financing scheme. Independent candidates, new-party candidates, or minor-party candidates as well as different major-party candidates should receive support that corresponds to the public's present measure of them, not the prior existence or success of their party or cause. The danger of using past performance as a financing index in a candidate-oriented system was apparent in the 1970 Senate contest in New York. The Conservative party candidate, James Buckley, who was elected with a plurality of the votes, would have been treated as a minor-party candidate or an ineligible candidate if past vote performance had been the test for public financing. And in 1974 the Republican party would have been treated as a minor party because its 1970 candidate, Senator Charles Goodell, received only 18 percent of the vote against the Democratic and Conservative candidates. Yet in 1974 the enormously popular Senator Jacob Javits was the Republican candidate, and his winning vote certainly reflected his "major-party" status as a contender. Similarly, Senator Harry F. Byrd's success as an independent candidate for the United States Senate in Virginia in 1970 suggests both that unaffiliated contenders are entitled to financing consistent with a measure of current public support and that financial support for candidates in subsequent elections should not turn on the poor showing of the major-party aspirants in 1970.

The schemes used elsewhere to fix financing to current indexes of public support are largely inapplicable to the United States. The

Puerto Rican system of making small advance grants prior to elections and major *pro rata* reimbursements following the voting leads to massive borrowing in campaigns and hence works against candidates without the support of wealthy lenders. Further, it discourages raising money in modest sums, since many small loans are difficult to negotiate, to account for, and to reimburse. The German method of paying 60 percent of the grants to parties in the years preceding the election and supplying the remainder after the election is also inapplicable. In the United States, the funds must run to candidates, not parties; and it is seldom known before the primary who will be entitled to grants. Also, the eligibility of independents, minor-party candidates, and even major-party contenders (such as the 1970 Republican senatorial hopefuls in New York and Virginia) for as much as 60 percent of grants cannot be known confidently in advance of election.

If the preceding election is too early to provide a fair measure of current public support for a candidate, and the voting in the present election is too late to provide a usable measure, how can a formula for publicly financing candidates be devised? No other country with candidate-oriented politics like that of the United States has confronted this question.

Constitutional Limitations. Opponents of financing have raised questions about the scope of governmental authority to regulate elections and, especially, money in campaigns. They maintain that the Constitution does not give the government authority to make public grants to political candidates. But Congress does have an imposing array of constitutional election powers under Article 1, the interstate commerce power, the Fourteenth and Fifteenth amendments, and the unwritten but oft-cited inherent power of a republican government to protect the integrity of its political process. It is not clear that Congress can regulate campaigns for state as well as federal office, although the interstate commerce clause and the Fourteenth and Fifteenth amendments do reach some state as well as national activities.[7]

Members of Congress from time to time have opposed public financing of campaigns on the ground that grants to candidates are expenditures for a private rather than a public purpose and are therefore beyond the taxing and spending powers of Congress. The United States Supreme Court has interpreted broadly the constitutional provision authorizing Congress to collect taxes to pay debts and to provide for the common defense and general welfare. The "general welfare" provision does not restrict the national government to spending for programs plainly within its constitutionally delegated powers, but rather allows spending for any purpose deemed within the general welfare.

Until recently, the Supreme Court had based its approval of projects of reclamation, irrigation, and other internal improvements on the expressly delegated constitutional power of Congress to regulate interstate commerce. But under the broader modern interpretation of the taxing and spending power, the justices have held that such projects advance the general welfare, and as long as they do so, may be justified under the taxing and spending power without resort to some other delegated power of Congress.[8] Providing enough money to assure competitive elections serves the general welfare by revitalizing the electoral system and strengthening the electorate's control over government officials. Public grants also eliminate the pressure, influence, and corruption that may accompany private contributions. These public purposes are undoubtedly sufficient under the Court's broad modern interpretation to sustain public financing of campaigns for federal office as an expenditure for the "general welfare."[9]

Proponents of public financing usually advocate limits on contributions and sometimes ceilings on expenditures.[10] Without contribution limits, they argue, a public financing scheme will not reduce the influence of big and special interest money. And without expenditure limits, the "fairness" or "equality" of opportunities for candidates to tell their story and the public to hear the alternatives is impaired. Further, without spending ceilings the corrosive pressures to raise unlimited campaign war chests will continue unabated. Both contribution and spending limits raise constitutional problems far more serious than does the congressional authority to make public grants for campaigning.

Contributing money is a form of expression, the constitutional argument goes, because it allows a candidate, committee, or individual to present views to the public and permits the public to hear such views. The most sweeping view of governmental power to limit contributions holds, on the other hand, that contributions are action, not speech, and that they are not encompassed within the First Amendment. A more limited view suggests that they are closely connected with free speech and that they are entitled to some measure of constitutional protection, but that the freedom of speech is not absolute or unlimited. Contributions can therefore be limited when they threaten the integrity of government or of elections by spawning corruption or even undue influence beneficial to contributors. If the only constitutional purpose of contribution limits is to protect the integrity of officials and voting, they cannot be applied to a candidate's spending on his own behalf, since his own funds presumably do not pose such dangers.

A second and complementary justification—arising, for instance, from the one-man, one-vote principle of the reapportionment cases —argues that all citizens are entitled to a roughly equal voice in the selection of officials. Low contribution limits on both candidates and other contributors are sustained by the need to maintain a rough parity between the potential influence that citizens of different means might attain by financial gifts.

The case for expenditure limits again turns on views that spending is action, not speech, that unlimited spending threatens the integrity of elections by spawning dangerous fund-raising practices, and that rough parity in spending must be attained between opposing candidates lest elections be bought by big spenders. A somewhat different case for spending ceilings acknowledges that they are related to free speech rights, insists that free speech is not absolute, finds that expression can be curbed for "compelling" governmental purposes, and holds that protecting elections against excessive spending or sordid contributions is a sufficiently compelling reason to warrant restrictions on free expression.

It is argued, on the other hand, that spending for expression of views about candidates or issues is so closely tied to speech that it falls within the First Amendment's ambit, that the integrity of elections can be protected by stringent contribution limits, that many variables other than money—both other political variables and situational circumstances—bear more on electoral victory than high spending, and that parity between candidates cannot be achieved by expenditure limits because so many inequalities in other resources exist.

Most important, however, is the argument that the means needed to assure effective spending limits cut deeply into the crossfire of comment about candidates and policies that is essential for public control of government. A spending limit solely on candidates is ineffective, as history has shown, because other committees then engage in unlimited spending. Effective spending limits therefore require the central treasurer system, with all spending on behalf of each candidate channeled through his treasurer and the total amount spent in that way limited by law.

This rule immediately raises questions about "negative" spending. Does it prevent citizens from expressing discontent with an office-holder or candidate by spending money to expose his public record? Must such money go through the opposition candidate's treasurer? Further, does a central treasurer have the authority to reject either negative spending or citizen spending to support his candidate? If so, the right of citizens to comment either negatively or positively about those seeking office may be cut off entirely. If not, the central treasurer may be required to take all citizen spending and therefore diminish the expenditures that his own candidate can make to shape his appeals in his own way. Theoretically, the treasurer might be the conduit for so much citizen spending that the candidate's expenditure limit would be reached before some interested citizens and the candidate himself had been able to make any expenditures to comment favorably on the aspirant's qualifications, record, or programs. In any law employing a central treasurer and expenditure limits, robust expression of views about candidates and issues from all concerned citizens and contenders is curtailed. If expenditure limits necessarily produce this result, their constitutionality is doubtful indeed.

ON THE BRINK OF POLICY

As Congress has come under increasing pressure to adopt a government funding scheme, the uneasiness of its members grows. Many are justifiably suspicious that some of the proposals have been partisan and self-serving. Their suspicions have been fed by sudden, surprise attempts to create *faits accomplis* by attaching irrelevant amendments to urgent bills at the last minute. And they have not been reassured by naive reformers who chant "private money bad, public money good," oblivious to the implications of the fact that the major financial sin of the Watergate year was coercion by government officials of private givers rather than the reverse.

Some ideologues oppose public financing of elections as another expansion of already bloated government and fear that governmental intrusions into the campaign process will eventually erode free elections themselves. It is unlikely that the ideological enemies of public funding can be won to it by any specific revisions in legislation. But there is a persuasive case for public financing of campaigns that turns on respectable conservative principles. The potential tyranny of government is checked not only by the institutional separation of powers but also by the checks and balances imposed by vigorous adversary campaigns. And increasingly, such campaigns are impossible without elements of public funding. Further, the traditional conservative concern, tracing its popular origins to Edmund Burke's Letter to the Electors of Bristol, for the independence of officials to act upon conscience, urgently requires that politicians be freed from the pervasive influence of private, special interest campaign money.

Some congressional opposition, on the other hand, must be attributed to self-interest rather than to ideology or to uneasiness about the merits of specific public financing proposals. The major stumbling block to public financing has been the House of Representatives; and it is there that constituency one-partyism and incumbency advantages are strongest and most likely to be upset by public financing of primary and general election opponents. Another significant bloc of self-interested opposition turns almost wholly on calculations of partisanship, with many Republicans seeking to preserve the existing private money system that has traditionally given them substantial campaign advantages. In a few cases, opposition to public financing has even baser motives: it will end the use of purported campaign gifts for personal uses.

The self-interested opposition cannot be won to reform by any discussion of the merits, and sound policy should not be warped to woo them. More enlightened opponents, however, search for a way through the tangled maze of competing considerations to find a public financing plan resting on acceptable principles, embodying sound policy goals, and respecting the institutional and political context of American democracy.

Reform, then, must serve a number of purposes: maintaining opportunities for more or less equal participation by citizens in the political process, including its financing; providing enough money to assure vigorous competitive campaigns that define alternatives for public choice at the polls; assuring a fair chance for all candidates to present their views; freeing candidates from disproportionate pressures and influences from campaign contributors; avoiding the use of campaign giving as a means to corrupt government; providing money for party activities desirable in a democracy; building public confidence in the electoral process; holding costs within a reasonable range; and devising regulations, administrative machinery, and enforcement apparatus that are easily understood and assessed by the people.

Reform must also be designed in such a way that the more or less fixed contours of the American political landscape will not be bulldozed away merely to smooth the regulation of political finance. It must acknowledge the delicate constitutional and political balances established by the separation of powers, the decentralization of American parties, the variability of characteristics among constituencies and districts, the troublesome advantage of incumbency in this country (as elsewhere), the primary election as a device for nominating candidates, the historically important roles of minor parties, the candidate orientation of American voters and electoral institutions, and the constitutional limits on governmental power and guarantees of individual liberty.

While none of the American proposals for public financing meet all these objectives, the legislative history of public financing in America may embody promising approaches. Although most of the patented public financing plans found in other nations will not sit well in the American political context, some home remedies may be more useful in curing our campaign finance ills.

Matching Grants. In 1962, the President's Commission on Campaign Costs suggested that as a last-resort solution to the campaign finance problem the government consider matching private contributions to candidates on a dollar-for-dollar basis up to $10.[11] Later advocates suggested matching from $50 to $250, and even at a two-for-one basis in some proposals. Safeguards to avoid fraudulent matchable gifts and the conversion of matched funds for personal benefit have typically been included in legislative proposals.

It is not at all clear whether the matching grants system would provide enough money to assure vigorous competitive campaigns, to allow candidates fair opportunities to present their views, to free candidates from disproportionate contributor influence, or to avoid the potential for corruption in political financing. Socio-economic factors and political attitudes seem the most important determinants of campaign giving. There is no evidence that a matching grant system would broaden participation. It would, however, double the candidates' take from present givers of sums up to the matchable limit. Hence some money, but probably not enough, would be added to existing campaign treasuries. Recognizing that small contributions and government matching funds would still not produce enough money to wage campaigns, sponsors of legislation have not banned larger, non-matchable gifts, thus leaving in place the disproportionate influence of big or special interest givers and the potential for corruption in financing campaigns.

Since matching grants provide public funds in mirror image of present giving patterns, campaign contributions would mainly be misallocated in the same way as private money now is—disproportionately to incumbents, to presidential candidates rather than congressional contenders, to conservatives, to competitive districts, and so forth. Although matching grants would not exaggerate the existing disparity between the visibility of the executive and legislative branches in campaigning, they would also not reduce that imbalance. Nor do matching grant proposals take account of the role of parties in American politics; most legislative recommendations permit matching only of contributions to candidates. (Legislation could, of course, be drafted to deal with this problem.) Further, because they follow existing giving patterns, matching grants are in no way tied to the variability in constituency characteristics and do nothing to check the existing financing advantages of incumbency.

The most important contribution of the matching grant proposals is that they emphasize more or less equal participation by citizens, since contributions eligible for matching are restricted to relatively small amounts and the disparity between the largest and smallest matchable amounts is far less than the difference between big and small gifts under present private financing arrangements. The second leading characteristic of matching grants is that they reflect current levels of support for candidates rather than relying on either past indexes of electoral enthusiasm or on measures of party strength. Minor-party and independent candidates therefore receive public support on the same eligibility formula as more prominent contenders representing the major parties. Third, matching grants can be readily adapted to primaries as well as general elections, as they have been in the Federal Election Campaign Act of 1974, resolving the controversy over who shall be eligible for nomination financing.

Although falling far short of most policy goals, matching grants have the particular appeal of allowing citizens to allocate public funds on a current support basis in both nomination and general election contests. Some comparable mechanism must be carried forward into any successful public financing program. Many object, however, to matching grants as this mechanism because they hinge eligibility on private funding support rather than on citizen or voter endorsement. Where private contributions are the trigger for public funds, the small, class-biased, and specially interested contributor corps retains its influence in American politics.

Vouchers. It is precisely in response to this criticism that the voucher plan, first urged by Senator Lee Metcalf in 1967, is most attractive.[12] Under the Metcalf plan each taxpayer who checked a box on his tax return would receive a voucher worth one dollar and could give that voucher to any presidential candidate of his choice. The candidate would then cash the voucher at the Treasury for public campaign funds.

The distribution of vouchers to each taxpayer and the unrestricted taxpayer allocation of vouchers to candidates not only ties public financing to a current index of support but also employs an index in which all taxpayers, not just campaign contributors, can participate. Further, the participation of taxpayers is exactly equal because each voucher bears the same value. The objection that taxpayers are the wrong body of participants has merit, of course; but simple changes in Senator Metcalf's original voucher plan could easily tie it to social security registrants who have reached eighteen years of age or even to registered voters if Congress were to enact universal voter registration.

Some reservations about the voucher plan arise from the potential for well-organized groups or powerful institutions to collect certificates from members, employees, and other affiliated persons and then to pass along blocs of vouchers to favored candidates. The leaders of these organizations—especially those with mass member-ships—become political power brokers as influential as those who now exercise clout because they manage or possess concentrated wealth. A voucher plan might, therefore, include some limits on the collec-tion and bloc allocation of vouchers, especially where economic or other sanctions could be used directly or indirectly to gather them. The need to protect individual choice does not, however, offset the usefulness of vouchers as a current index of popular support for allocating public funds to candidates.

On other policy criteria the original voucher plan is a less attrac-tive alternative. Citizen participation would be highly unpredictable, creating serious uncertainties in financing campaigns. Even if citizen participation reached relatively high levels, the one-dollar vouchers originally proposed by Senator Metcalf would probably not supply enough money for the conduct of vigorous, adversary campaigns. Some proponents have recommended that the value of vouchers be raised to two dollars or more so that at reasonable participation rates very substantial sums would flow into campaign treasuries. Again, the strength of the voucher plan is also one of its weaknesses: by tying public financing to citizen participant support, the voucher plan creates the possibility of vast disparities in candidate funding.

Here the conflict is most apparent between the principle of citizen participation in allocating public financing and the principle that candidates should have fair opportunities to present their views so that interested citizens will have a full opportunity to weigh the alternatives before going to the polls. If voucher response in 1964 and 1972 had followed voting patterns, Lyndon Johnson would have received 50 percent more public funding than Barry Goldwater, and Richard Nixon would have held an even greater public money edge over George McGovern. From a policy perspective, the losers here are not Senators Goldwater and McGovern—for the public has little stake in their personal ambitions—but the voters who are deprived of a full and fair presentation of alternatives.

The original voucher plan would not have curbed disproportionate contributor influence or the potential for corruption; recognizing that one-dollar vouchers and modest participation would not raise sufficient campaign funds, the plan did not significantly restrict private contributors. Such limitations could, however, easily be at-tached to a modified voucher plan, especially if the value of vouchers was raised to channel more public money to campaign treasuries. Elaborate administrative machinery is needed to distribute, collect, and redeem vouchers, and these activities have a high unit cost rela-tive to the value of each voucher. But all systems of mass collection, including the direct mail techniques traditionally favored by reformers, involve high unit costs. It is less expensive to raise large sums from a few millionaires gathered in a room.

Like the matching grant proposal of the President's Commission, Senator Metcalf's voucher plan provided public financing only for presidential campaigns, ignoring the delicate balances involved in the American separation of powers. Congressional as well as presidential vouchers are, of course, easily imaginable, though they would increase somewhat the administrative burden of public financing. But the Metcalf plan also ignored the legitimate role of political parties.

The voucher plan also does not take into account the variability in constituency characteristics or the advantages of incumbency. A number of factors—one-party electoral domination, the unequal strength of the majority and minority party organizations, and the high visibility of the majority party incumbent—are likely to combine, especially in House districts, to produce substantial inequalities in the numbers of vouchers collected by incumbents and challengers. In many congressional districts, these factors would undermine the public financing policy objectives of providing enough money for vigorous adversary campaigns and assuring the candidates a fair opportunity to present their views.

Although the original voucher plan also did not encompass primary elections, it could easily be adapted to primaries. The danger would arise, however, that in a large field of candidates and with moderate citizen participation in the voucher plan (paralleling low voter turnout in primaries), vouchers would be so scattered that serious and non-serious candidates alike would be dramatically underfunded. The policy goals of assuring enough public money for vigorous competition and for candidates to present their views adequately would be defeated. And as aspirants were therefore necessarily thrown back on traditional private funding sources, disproportionate big giver and special interest influence and the potential for corruption in campaign financing would reassert themselves. Like matching grants, vouchers do not raise serious constitutional problems.

The voucher plan's most attractive element is its extension of the matching funds principle that public financing should turn on a current index of support. It expands the index from campaign contributors, a traditionally small and unrepresentative segment of the population, to all participating taxpayers (or social security registrants or voters). Further, it promotes broad citizen participation, and it makes financial participation roughly equal on a "one-man, one-voucher" basis. But other policy objectives are potentially forfeited by the successful promotion of current support indexes, citizen participation, and equal voter weight in campaign financing. Sometimes the amount of money will be insufficient for vigorous adversary campaigns, and disparities in citizen participation in particular circumstances or constituencies will deny to candidates the opportunity for a fair hearing.

The Tax Check-Off. Like vouchers, the tax check-off promotes roughly equal citizen participation in campaign funding: each taxpayer earmarks one dollar of public money for politics. To a greater extent than either matching grants or vouchers, the check-off fosters the illusion that only those who choose to participate pay for public financing. But, as in all public financing plans, those who do not participate must still pay additional taxes to make up for the dollars others have withdrawn from the treasury to subsidize campaigns.

And unlike either matching grants and vouchers, the tax check-off participant has no influence over who receives his dollar. Under both the 1971 Revenue Act and the 1974 Federal Election Campaign Act, check-off dollars are distributed to general election candidates for president according to past or current party electoral performance.[13] And the 1974 act allocates check-off dollars in presidential primaries on a matching grant basis, which means that the contributor of a matchable grant rather than the check-off participant determines which candidate will receive public funds.

These defects are not easily cured in the context of a tax check-off system. Senator Charles Mathias, for instance, successfully sponsored an amendment to the 1971 check-off plan that allowed taxpayers to earmark their dollars to a specific party and that provided formula allocations only for those dollars not earmarked. (This amendment was repealed in the Debt Ceiling Act of 1973.) But the Mathias amendment required taxpayers to earmark dollars to parties long before their presidential candidates were chosen. This arrangement, like the allocation formula based on party vote performance in the prior presidential election, ignores completely the candidate orientation of American voters and electoral institutions.[14] Finally, participation through the tax check-off is open only to those who pay taxes and thus excludes at least 18 million voting age persons from the public financing system. Yet it is difficult to conceive a check-off alternative that does not hinge at least on the filing of tax returns.

Unlike the voucher and matching grant plans, the tax check-off can predictably accumulate enough money for vigorous competitive campaigns. The 1971 act calculated support for major-party presidential candidates at fifteen cents multiplied by the voting age population, or roughly $20.5 million in 1972 and a projected $22 million in 1976; these sums would be readily available if the 15 percent check-off participation rate remains constant. The 1974 act provides a flat grant of $20 million for major-party presidential candidates. Minor-

and new-party candidates receive proportional support. The general election grants under both check-off plans are substantially on the low side of the amount needed to wage a vigorous presidential campaign. And this weakness is exaggerated by the acts' prohibitions of expenditures beyond the public grants.

The check-off formula could easily be adjusted to provide increased grants so that major-party candidates would be able to air their views amply. Minor- and new-party candidates would have less opportunity, but their funding would be proportional to past or current voting and would permit a higher level of expenditure than is available to them under the existing private money system. The fairness issues raised by the check-off formula turn on the index of support used to allocate grants. Basing major-party and minor-party designations on vote performance in the previous presidential election may artificially preserve parties after their support has waned, or it may deny funding to a party whose support has swelled since the last balloting. Public funding of major, minor, and new parties may be alternatively calculated on the basis of current electoral support and take the form of post-election reimbursement to pay debts. For those who cannot borrow during the campaign, this *post hoc* allocation of funds effectively denies an opportunity to appeal for voter support.

Neither the 1971 nor the 1974 check-off plan showed enough sensitivity to the main landmarks of American politics. By financing presidential but not congressional campaigns, they heighten the power imbalance between the executive and legislative branches. The 1971 law entirely ignored the role of political parties, and the 1974 law recognized only a limited role for them by publicly financing presidential nominating conventions and by allowing party committees to aid federal candidates with nominal separate expenditures beyond those that the nominees' own campaign organizations can make.[15]

Changing campaign costs won only limited recognition. The 1971 check-off plan acknowledged changes in constituency size by fixing public grants to the number of eligible voters, but the 1974 plan eliminates this proviso and substitutes a fixed dollar amount. Both plans provided a cost-of-living increase in public grants by tying them to the Consumer Price Index. Other constituency variables bearing on campaign costs were not considered because these check-off plans fund only the nationwide presidential race. Both check-off plans diminish the fund-raising advantages of incumbency by supplying equal grants to major-party candidates, thereby giving the challenger as much money as the incumbent. The 1974 act recognizes the importance of the nominating process by publicly financing presidential nomination races through a matching grant system, but the formula creates serious problems of assuring adequate check-off dollars to fully match private contributions in the nomination process. Finally, to the extent that the act involves expenditure limitations and a ban on contributions to publicly funded general election candidates, it spawns almost insurmountable constitutional objections. The proviso that only those receiving 5 percent of the vote in the past or current presidential balloting are eligible even for proportional grants might well survive a constitutional test, but it ignores the historic role of minor parties.

More than any other plan, the check-off falls short of essential policy objectives and fails to accommodate significant contours of the American political landscape. Its impressive advantage is the flat and proportional grant system which, if not tied to low spending limits, would assure enough money for vigorous campaigning and allow candidates fair opportunities to present their views.

TOWARD PUBLIC FINANCING

The main barrier to public financing becomes clear from this review of American legislative proposals. Flat and proportional public grants best provide enough money for vigorous adversary campaigning and for candidates to fairly air their views. Such a system supplies enough public money to limit sharply the need for private contributions that potentially influence or corrupt government. Flat grants are administratively simpler. They can also more easily curb the financial advantage of incumbents by providing challengers with equal or proportional funding in districts where officeholder visibility, powerful majority party organization, and lopsided voter allegiances have previously thwarted effective challenge.

On the other hand, a current index for calculating public grants—such as those used by the matching and voucher plans—best assures meaningful and roughly equal public participation, is most adaptable to the unique American system of primary nominations, respects the role of both major and minor parties, and reflects the candidate orientation of American politics.

Both approaches can presumably be fashioned to aid political parties as well as candidates, to give whatever limited recognition is possible to constituency variables, to respect the separation of powers by financing both congressional and presidential campaigns, and to avoid infringing on the constitutional safeguards of speech and association.

Public funding requires a creative merger of current indexes of eligibility based on equally weighted citizen participation with flat and proportional grants to provide adequate financing for campaigns. These eligibility and allocation principles have been the Capulets and Montagues of public financing legislation. Effective reform awaits their wedding.

To meet the policy objectives for political finance reform and to respect the main landmarks of American politics, we propose basic public financing of campaigns for federal office through a voucher-based system of flat and proportionate grants in general elections and matching grants in primaries, public funding of party conventions, modest public grants to political parties, and stringent limits on contributions to campaigns. In addition, we advocate the repeal of tax incentives for political gifts. We oppose both comprehensive spending limits of the kind enacted in the Federal Election Campaign Act of 1974 and segmental limits such as those on communications media formerly in the Campaign Communications Reform Act of 1971. We believe that expenditure limits trench on the constitutionally guaranteed freedom of speech and curb the vigorous political competition essential for self-government. Other measures provide for nationwide universal voter registration, full disclosure of campaign expenditures and receipts, and vigorous independent administration of election laws.

NATIONWIDE, UNIVERSAL VOTER REGISTRATION IN FEDERAL ELECTIONS

1. We recommend a federally sponsored universal voter registration for federal elections. Admin-

11

PROPOSALS FOR REFORM

istered by the states under federal guidelines, this program would employ both postcard and door-to-door registration techniques to put all eligible citizens on the voting rolls.

Comment. The United States has lagged far behind other nations in taking governmental responsibility for voter registration. As many as 25 percent of non-voters report in public opinion polls that they did not vote because they were not registered. Existing registration methods discriminate against transient or migrant elements of the population—such as traveling workers, students, and minority groups seeking better living conditions—and against those whose jobs make it difficult to travel to registration offices during daytime working hours. As an incidental benefit, universal voter registration makes possible a public financing plan in which virtually all eligible voters can participate. It also substantially reduces the need for campaign funds by parties and candidates because it lifts from them the expensive task of searching out and registering their supporters.

A VOUCHER-BASED PLAN
FOR FLAT AND PROPORTIONATE
GRANTS IN GENERAL ELECTIONS

2. On the tenth Tuesday before each general election for the respective offices, the Federal Elections Commission shall distribute one Presidential Election Voucher, one Senate Election Voucher, and one House of Representatives Election Voucher to each registered person eligible to vote in such elections.[1] In states that regularly nominate candidates for senator or representative at a later time, the commission shall promptly distribute vouchers for those offices as soon as possible after the nominations are complete.

3. On the seventh, fifth, and second Tuesdays before the general election, the commission shall distribute funds to candidates based on the number of vouchers deposited with the commission by the candidate on the eighth, sixth, and third Tuesdays preceding election. In states nominating candidates for senator and representative less than eleven weeks before general elections, the latter two distribution dates will be used.

4. Presidential candidates depositing 38 percent or more of the vouchers submitted on each of the submission dates would receive grants of six cents times the voting age population of the nation. In 1972, each candidate submitting this proportion of collected vouchers would have received $8.4 million on each distribution date, or slightly more than $25 million during the full campaign if he qualified at each of the three dates. This sum is two-thirds or more of the funds now needed to mount an effective general election

campaign for the presidency. Candidates presenting less than 38 percent of the vouchers at each submission date would receive a proportional grant equivalent to the same percentage of the highest grant (six cents times the number of persons of voting age) as their submitted vouchers were of 38 percent. Respecting the right of independent and minor-party candidates to be treated proportionally, no minimum percentage of vouchers would be required of any candidate qualified for a place on the ballot. Write-in candidates would be required to submit a minimum of 2 percent of the cumulative number of vouchers at each presentation date for entitlement to a *pro rata* distribution of funds.[2] This provision acknowledges that a write-in candidate has not met even the minimum requirements of bona fide candidacy involved in filing petitions, fees, or declarations under state law.

5. Senate candidates depositing 38 percent or more of the vouchers submitted on each of the submission dates would receive grants of six cents times the voting age population or $50,000, whichever was greater. The largest grants under this formula would occur in California, where a Senate candidate in 1972 would have received about $837,000 on each distribution date or slightly more than $2.5 million during the full general election campaign if he qualified at each of the three dates. (California did not have a Senate contest in 1972, and it is used for illustration only because it suggests the top limit of public grants for United States Senate candidates.)

In states nominating candidates for senator less than eleven weeks before the general election, vouchers would be deposited only on the sixth and third Tuesdays and grants made only on the fifth and second Tuesdays preceding election. Grants on these two dates would be nine cents times the number of voting age persons in the state or $75,000, whichever was greater.

The provision for minimum grants of $50,000 at the three distribution dates ($75,000 in states with two distribution dates) is intended to provide a floor of $150,000 in public grants for major contenders. This floor recognizes that statewide campaigns require certain basic outlays and that in states with small populations public grants based on the number of voting age persons would not provide this minimum financing.

Candidates presenting less than 38 percent of the Senate vouchers at each submission date would receive a proportional grant calculated in the same manner as in presidential contests. Qualified candidates and write-in candidates would be treated somewhat differently, under the same rules as provided in presidential campaigns.

6. Candidates for the House of Representatives depositing 38 percent or more of the vouchers submitted from their districts on

each of the submission dates would receive grants of eight cents times the voting age population. In states with only a single House seat, the grants would be $50,000 on each occasion. The national voting age population in 1972 (excluding the District of Columbia) was 139,124,000, and the average congressional district therefore included 319,800 persons of voting age. (In fact, most districts were somewhat larger, because states with less than the average voting age population were nonetheless entitled to a House seat and other states therefore had a higher ratio of population to seats.) The average grant on each distribution date would therefore be roughly $25,600, or about $77,000 for the entire general election campaign.

In states nominating candidates for representative less than eleven weeks before the general election, vouchers would be deposited only on the sixth and third Tuesdays and grants made only on the fifth and second Tuesdays preceding election. Grants on these two dates would be twelve cents times the number of voting age persons in the district. In states with only a single House seat, the grant would be $75,000 on each occasion.

The provision for minimum grants acknowledges that it costs as much to run for representative as for senator in statewide districts, that there are certain minimum costs for effective campaigns in state-wide districts, and that we have previously recommended a floor of $150,000 in statewide Senate campaigns.

Candidates presenting less than 38 percent of the House vouchers at each submission date would receive a proportional grant calculated in the same manner as in presidential contests. Qualified candidates and write-in candidates would be treated somewhat differently, under the same rules as provided in presidential campaigns.

7. The per capita payment and the minimum payment would be increased in each election year by the percentage increase in the Consumer Price Index over the base year of 1972.

8. Each voucher would be imprinted with the name and address of the registered voter to whom it is sent. The voter would have to sign the voucher before it could become negotiable by a candidate. All vouchers distributed to voters should be accompanied by literature explaining their use; by a postage-paid envelope for mailing to candidates; by a listing of the name, party identification, and address of each candidate whose name appears on the ballot for the respective office; and by a brief statement by each such candidate.

9. The Federal Elections Commission would hold all vouchered funds in the name of the respective candidates and disburse them in payment only of billed and certified expenditures for such verifiable items as metered postage, printing, advertising, broadcasting, rent,

telephone, air tickets, and equipment purchases. No portion of salaries in excess of $1,000, fees for services, or personal expenses could be paid from vouchered funds. All unexpended or unobligated funds would revert to the commission after the election for which they were distributed.

Comment. This modified voucher system does not replace all private giving; rather it is intended to provide a substantial proportion of the money needed for campaigns, making it possible for candidates to meet the remainder of campaign expenses from small private contributions. Public participation is therefore encouraged on a nearly equal basis, because each citizen receives vouchers of the same value and each citizen's opportunity to contribute privately is restricted to small amounts within the reach of most Americans.

This proposal does not tie the amount of public funding to the number of vouchers collected, which initially may be quite small. Rather, it uses the vouchers as a current index of popular support to trigger flat and proportional grants to candidates. The flat and proportional grants are designed to provide substantial money for vigorous campaigning and to allow candidates a fair opportunity to present their views. "Fair" in this arrangement means in proportion to their current support reflected in voucher collections.

The voting age population, rather than the number of registered voters, is used for calculating public grants to recognize that the cost of many campaign appeals, especially mass media advertising and travel, hinges on the whole population rather than the segment registered to vote.

The voucher system provides powerful incentives for all candidates to go to the grassroots to maximize voucher collections and therefore campaign finances. Further, it invites party organizations and interest groups to collaborate with candidates in these efforts. Voucher collection by candidates and organizations turns on their support among the electorate, not on the wealth or other resources of special constituencies. It is this "one man, one voucher" principle that distinguishes this proposal from existing candidate and organization solicitations aimed at small constituencies with concentrated wealth.

The 38 percent threshold for maximum entitlement, rather than a distribution of funds completely proportionate to the percentage of vouchers presented, represents a bow to the importance of the two-party system in American political life. In most situations it will guarantee equal funds for the two leading candidates, as would a flat grant system for major parties, without arbitrarily imposing this equality in all situations. The figure itself is not quite arbitrary; it represents the apparent outer limit of presidential election landslides.

Neither Barry Goldwater in 1964 nor George McGovern in 1972 fell below 38 percent of the vote, and if voucher collections are proportional to voter support this formula would have provided equal funding in both those situations.[3]

While acknowledging the historic role of the major parties, the voucher trigger for public grants would not discriminate against independents or minor-party candidates.[4] It would award them public financing in proportion to their current support, measured by the flow of vouchers from their supporters. It would not have denied funding to parties without established track records, such as the Bull Moose party in 1912, the Progressive party in 1948, or the American Independent party in 1968. But it would have allowed them and, for example, the Whig party to die a natural death in the following elections when they lost their following. The voucher plan would have treated proportionally both James Buckley and Charles Goodell in the 1970 New York Senate election, and it would have recognized that independent office seeker Harry F. Byrd, Jr., was a major candidate in Virginia's 1970 Senate contest.

The funding levels recommended here are generous, particularly when supplemented by the limited private giving we endorse below. The $25 million general election grants in presidential races are about two-thirds of the funding needed for vigorous campaigning in 1972. If voucher collections had followed voter support, the public grants recommended for Senate races would have provided about half the money spent by the highest spender in several of the 1972 contests won by 52 percent or less of the vote, and a far larger proportion in most of them. The lowest proportions were in Delaware, where Democrat Joseph Biden spent $262,700 and would have received a grant of $150,000, and in Montana, where Republican Henry Hibbard spent $286,800 and would have been eligible for public financing of $150,000. At the other extreme were Colorado and Virginia, where more than 90 percent of campaign costs would have been covered by public financing. Colorado Republican Gordon Allott spent $308,300 and would have been eligible for public grants of $285,800; Virginia Republican William Scott's $619,900 campaign would have been supported by public funding of $575,000.

In sixty-six House contests won by less than 55 percent of the vote, winners spent an average of $107,000 and losers $101,000. The public funding proposed here would provide more than 75 percent of the money needed to wage vigorous campaigns in such closely competitive circumstances. Similar grants in the less narrowly contested districts would dramatically invigorate competition and improve voter control over officials.

At the same time, the formula does not produce an artificial equality of funding. In one-party districts where voters, and therefore presumably vouchers, favor the dominant party by more than 62 to 38 percent, the challenger will receive a proportional rather than a full grant. In such districts, however, even proportional financing will greatly reduce the disparity that now exists between entrenched majority party incumbents and minority party challengers. Further, the sanction for small private gifts will produce some inequalities in all districts, with those supported by traditional contributing constituencies winning funding advantages. But again, the imbalance will be much smaller than at present.

The most serious objections to this modified voucher system center on its administration and costs. Mailing vouchers to all registered voters, redeeming the vouchers and validating them, providing postage for return mailing to candidates, printing explanatory materials and candidate statements, managing the campaign accounts of candidates, and other similar expenses far exceed the cost of simply calculating grants according to the past voting record of each party's candidates. It is possible that a voucher system's administration might run as high as sixty cents for each voter who mailed his vouchers to a presidential, senatorial, and House candidate and thirty cents for those who returned them in another way or did not use them at all. If participation by mail approximated the 15 percent who took the trouble to check off a dollar on their 1973 tax returns, administrative costs for those citizens and the remaining 85 percent making some alternative disposition of their vouchers would run nearly $50 million. This relatively high administrative cost may be justified as the price of a fair public financing system and as necessary for curbing the misallocations and abuses in the existing private financing system.

A SYSTEM OF MATCHING GRANTS FOR CANDIDATES FOR NOMINATION FOR FEDERAL OFFICE

10. The Federal Elections Commission would establish separate special contribution and matching accounts for each candidate seeking nomination in any state for election to any federal office. The commission would deposit in the matching account an amount equal to twice the amount of each individual contribution by a natural person up to an aggregate of $100 per individual contributor, which the candidate would deposit in the special contributions account.

A candidate would become eligible for matching grants only after he had deposited a threshold amount in matchable contributions. In the case of candidates for nomination to the House of Representatives, the minimum could be $5,000. In the case of candidates for nomination to the Senate, the minimum could be $5,000 multiplied by the number of congressional districts in the state in which nomination is sought, but in no case more than $50,000. In the case of candidates for nomination for president, the minimum could be $100,000.

The commission would disburse funds from the matching accounts under the same regulations provided for the disbursement of voucher accounts. All unexpended funds in the matching and special contributions accounts would revert to the commission after the nomination. In the case of candidates for nomination for president, accounts might be opened for each state in which they were running, and funds could be transferred from one comparable account to another at the direction of the candidate.

The ceiling on matching grants for candidates for nomination for the House of Representatives would be sixteen cents times the total number of eligible voters in the district. The ceiling on matching grants for candidates for nomination for senator or president would be twelve cents times the total number of eligible voters in the constituency.

Comment. Nominations are made in diverse ways—by primaries, conventions, caucuses, and other procedures—under state laws or party rules. To accommodate this diversity, the regulation of nomination financing is often considered a state responsibility. But, in the words of Justice Stone, "we cannot close our eyes to the fact . . . that the practical influence of the choice of candidates at the primary may be so great as to affect profoundly the choice at the general election."[5] Nominations bear so directly on the public's stake in general elections that the federal government may provide an adequate supply of clean money to assure the integrity and competitiveness of the whole process. Any other result would simply push all of the inadequacies and abuses of private financing from the general election into the nomination stage, where money may even more effectively influence electoral decisions.

Voucher-based grants are given to candidates, whether or not they can demonstrate financial support, as long as they can demonstrate *voter* support. Matching grants are given to candidates in proportion to their ability to demonstrate a broad base of *financial* support. A matching system is not as reflective of the electorate, and therefore not as democratic, as a voucher system. But public interest in primaries is not nearly as broad or intense as it is in general elections, and the percentage of voters who returned vouchers would almost certainly be far too low to provide a meaningful index of entitlement to government funds.

Moreover, there are greater difficulties in adapting a voucher system to nomination races than to general elections. What percentage of submitted vouchers should trigger a full financial entitlement? If the threshold is a high percentage, it is likely that in a large field no candidate will even approach the requirement. All will win small proportional grants, and even the serious contenders will not receive enough money for adequately competitive campaigning. If the percentage is set at a low level, all candidates in small fields—including some who enter only to take advantage of public financing—will easily reach the mark and win full grants.

There is also the problem of identifying who shall receive vouchers. In closed primary states, do only registered members of each party receive vouchers for the respective party nomination contests? Or do all receive vouchers to be used in any contest, thus allowing financial raiding of opposition party primaries? Must separate systems be devised for closed and open primary states? And are vouchers appropriate at all in states that make nominations by caucus or convention, where the public is involved only indirectly and nomination costs are ordinarily low? Finally, frivolous candidates are far more common in primaries than in general elections, and a public financing scheme must set a reasonable threshold, rather than relying on strict proportionality, to safeguard against the wanton squandering of public funds.

The matching grant proposal advanced here requires that nomination candidates for the House obtain at least fifty $100 contributions (or the equivalent in smaller sums) and aspirants for the presidential nomination at least a thousand such gifts to qualify for federal funds. The prospect of public funding might offer a somewhat greater temptation to frivolous candidates than the present system, but the matching fund thresholds are a somewhat greater barrier than the present requirements for ballot eligibility. On the whole, few frivolous candidates will be able to obtain public funds under this scheme.[6]

The converse problem is whether there will be enough money for serious candidates. Even significant nomination candidates frequently draw very few small contributions. Appeals to party loyalty are futile because nomination contests are feuds within the party family. Nomination contests usually occur early in the political season, before most citizens are paying attention. And the visibility of nomination contenders is often low because media coverage is slight and candidates have not had the opportunity to make an impact on voters. To provide enough money for vigorous campaigning in these circumstances we provide a two-for-one public matching of gifts up to $100.[7]

On the other hand, unlimited two-for-one matching could support spending far in excess of that needed to inform voters. We have imposed limits on public grants that, when taken together with the one-third private money they matched, would be equal to the total public funding allowed for the same offices in general elections. This limit may be high, and in most nomination contests it would not be approached. But the limit recognizes that in reality the nomination in many one-party districts is tantamount to election, and there is no justification for holding spending in such critical contests below that allowed in general elections.

A two-for-one matching grant system greatly increases the prospect that adequate funds will be available to nomination candidates with a broad base of citizen support, and it reduces the recent tendency for nominations to become the playground of wealthy individuals, interests, or institutions and of incumbents. Frivolous candidates are deterred by reasonable financial thresholds, and excessive spending is discouraged by limiting total matching grants to two-thirds the public financing allowed for the same office in general elections.

A SYSTEM OF DIRECT PROPORTIONAL GRANTS TO POLITICAL PARTIES

11. At the beginning of each calendar year, the central committee of each party that ran a candidate in the last presidential election would receive from the Federal Elections Commission a cash grant equal to two cents for each vote cast for its presidential candidate. At the same time, the central committee of each party that ran one or more candidates for the United States Senate and/or House of Representatives during the last general election would also receive from the Federal Elections Commission a cash grant equal to two cents for each vote cast for its candidate(s) in such election(s). There would be no restriction on the use of these funds.

12. In each presidential election year, each party qualifying for cash grants in that year would have a special national nominating convention account opened in its name by the Federal Elections Commission, into which the commission would deposit an amount equal to double the party's grants for that year. The commission would disburse funds from the convention accounts at the direction of the parties for national nominating convention expenses only, according to regulations prescribed by the commission. Unexpended and unobligated funds would revert to the commission following each convention.

Comment. The failure of parties to dominate the stage of American politics does not mean that they have no role. Party activists do influence nominations by organization endorsement, by their personal and collective campaign efforts, and by selection of candidates or delegates where conventions and caucuses still do that work. The

Republican party also plays a major role in financing its candidates, especially where it has a working "United Fund" apparatus. Both parties sponsor national and state conventions where platforms are written and candidates sometimes named or endorsed. Both parties recruit candidates, especially in districts dominated by the opposition. They also recruit and train the activists who do campaign work, man the polls, and conduct party affairs between elections.

Public financing of parties runs the risk of artificially preserving their roles, which have been declining steadily, and of upsetting delicate balances between elected officials and party organizations. On the other hand, financing candidates but not parties may tip the scales farther in the opposite direction. Financing parties may also strengthen their influence over public officials. Limited public financing of national parties seems appropriate as recognition of the limited role they play and perhaps as support for their activities in some areas where there is no adequate alternative. Because parties, unlike candidates, are and should be more or less permanent institutions, it is appropriate to use past rather than prospective performance to measure their entitlement.

A financing formula based on congressional as well as presidential votes can cushion parties against exaggerated drops due to catastrophic individual candidacies such as those of Goldwater in 1964 and McGovern in 1972. Temporary parties, which normally will have entitlement only for presidential voting, will have some access to funds, but not enough to keep them alive if they do not develop a broad electoral following.

This system would treat all parties proportionally, including temporary parties, small doctrinal parties, and parties that operate only in limited areas, such as the Conservative and Liberal parties in New York State. The public funds provided for all parties, added to the funds supplied by private sources, would permit expansion of party activities. The proposed grants to the national committees of the two major parties would be upwards of $1.6 million each per year, increasing as the electorate enlarges. Despite the Nixon-Agnew landslide of 1972, grants to the major parties following that election would be roughly equal based on congressional and presidential voting: $1.7 million annually for the Democrats and $2 million for the Republicans. Party funds could be used to assist candidates in fund raising and voucher collection. If changes in the role of parties justified increased grants to sustain their larger responsibilities, Congress could adjust the total by appropriate increments.

National nominating conventions are entitled to financing because they are as much a part of the nominating process as the nationwide candidate canvass or state presidential primary contests. Although run by political parties and serving campaign purposes, they are important to the national election machinery. Public financing of the conventions may be justified as part of the cost of election administration, as is the counting of primary ballots. We have set public grants for conventions at a level substantially higher than the $2 million maximum needed for convention operations because we intend a reasonable allowance for delegates' expenses in attending the conventions. Otherwise delegates must be drawn from wealthy classes or must be financed by party leaders, interest groups, or others who might exert influence over delegate decisions.

Some local parties, such as the Liberal party in New York, may hook on to major-party nominations but hold their conventions primarily to gain attention for their local tickets. Giving such parties access to federal funds for their conventions or their ongoing activities might simply encourage others to form such parties. But denying them funds would result in discrimination against genuine doctrinal or temporary parties that run candidates in earnest, or would require establishing a motives test rather than a performance test as a basis for public financing. The Liberal party's entitlement would not derive from the strategic calculations of its leaders who arranged its nomination of the presidential candidate already named by the Democrats, but from the individual choices of the 200,000 citizens who voted for that candidate on the Liberal line. The $4,000 per year that would consequently go to the Liberal party is presumably a cost to the Democrats, who might otherwise have gotten it, not to the government that would have to pay it out either way.

The national parties would merit greater support if most of the more desirable party activities such as recruitment, getting out the vote, voter registration, and inter-election opposition were not conducted by local and state party committees. Grants to national party committees might well be used in a cooperative effort with local and state party groups for the collection of vouchers. If national party committees expended funds for useful purposes, especially for cooperative activities with local and state units, Congress might find both the justification and the incentive for increasing party grants.

Public financing for local and state party organizations is also theoretically desirable, to recognize their significant political activities and to maintain delicate intra-party balances. But given the patchwork of statutory and party rules as well as the profusion of voluntary and regular party committees in a host of overlapping constituencies, it would be almost impossible to decide which organizations should receive federal grants. The interweaving of party activity furthering federal, state, and local office campaigns means also that federal grants to state and local party groups in advancing a policy of public financing of federal campaigns would inevitably impinge upon state and local policies about financing campaigns within those jurisdictions. Finally, of course, states and localities can easily take responsibility for financing party units at those levels if that is a desirable policy. This would imitate experiments abroad, where state parties in federal systems receive the money from the state rather than the national governments.

STRINGENT LIMITS ON POLITICAL CONTRIBUTIONS

13. No individual should be permitted to influence elections by making contributions to political committees or candidates or expenditures to support or oppose candidates that aggregate more than $1,000 in any calendar year.

14. No candidate or political committee, except a multi-district committee, should receive transfers exceeding 20 percent of its public plus in-district private contributions from multi-district committees. Multi-district committees are those receiving less than 80 percent of their funds from natural persons residing in any constituency where they support candidates or transfer funds. Communications to voters by such committees should acknowledge that more than 20 percent of their funds originated outside the constituency. Contributions to candidates or committees from outside their headquarters district should be separately aggregated in their financial reports.

15. In nomination contests, individual contributions from outside the district would not count toward the threshold for matching grant eligibility and would not be eligible for public matching grants.

Comment. Campaign contributions are an activity related to expression, and they therefore probably enjoy some First Amendment protection. This protection is not unlimited, however. Campaign contributions may work undue influence in governmental decision making or may spawn direct corruption of officials. They may therefore be limited to sums that minimize such threats. Furthermore, Congress may have authority under the Fourteenth Amendment to preserve for citizens the equal protection of the laws by reducing the disparity between the size of campaign contributions, and hence the amount of political influence, of different citizens of varying financial means. The goal is to maintain the one-man, one-vote principle against the vastly unequal electoral influence that some can attain through large campaign contributions.[8]

Campaign contributions by individuals and groups are consistent not only with constitutional values but with the policy objective of encouraging citizen participation in public affairs and with the matching grant system for financing nomination contests. The limit on contributions minimizes the dangers arising from these desirable ends—the vastly disproportionate political influence of owners and managers of wealth and the potential for corruption of public officials. Aggregate individual contribution limits of $1,000 per calendar year are consistent with these goals; they allow participation, but they hold the amount to levels which are not menacing and they substantially reduce the disparity between the financial influence of citizens of different means. The limit allows direct expenditures as an alternative to campaign contributions so that citizens can participate by expressing their views directly in support of or opposition to a candidate. This becomes especially important where a citizen wants to raise issues that neither candidate is willing to sponsor or to censure rather than support an office seeker's record or program.

Aggregate limits also eliminate the need for ceilings on gifts to individual candidates and political committees. And by fixing a ceiling on each individual's total financial activity, we foreclose the traditional evasion of contribution limits by channeling maximum gifts to many different committees supporting the same candidate. Aggregate limits allow an individual to multiply his influence in a single race by concentrating his permitted giving there or to make a smaller impact on several contests and programs by spreading his $1,000 to various campaigns and committees. The latter strategy will usually make more sense in primaries because the matching grant system is an incentive for contributors to spread their gifts in sums of $100 to various candidates seeking nomination to federal office.

The influence any contributor amasses under this limitation is therefore severely limited. The recommended contribution ceiling is, furthermore, very low by current political standards. But it is high relative to the resources of typical American voters. The combined total of $2,000 available to a married couple for expenditures and contributions is almost 20 percent of median family income in the United States in the last presidential election year.

Since the limitation applies to gifts to all candidates and committees, it embraces state and local as well as federal politics. The aggregate limitation would probably be useful even if it were raised to $3,000 or $5,000, and at that level it might give state and local jurisdictions time to adjust and provide some form of public financing for campaigns for state and local office. The higher figure might permit wealthy interests to acquire overbearing influence in some Senate and House elections, but the relative weight of such contributions would be much reduced by the availability of public financing.

The limit on contributions to candidates by multi-district political committees is intended to limit non-constituency pressures on office-holders and to reduce spending disparities that arise when one candidate wins massive financial support from interest groups. Organizations have a legitimate place in American politics, and they may well be a necessary vehicle for functional representation of citizens. Their contributions are therefore protected by the First Amendment freedoms of speech and association. But organizations even more than individuals are a source of pressure on public officials; and this pressure is particularly dangerous when it originates outside an official's district, creating a financial constituency whose members are not drawn from his electoral constituency. Because the leaders of organizations frequently dominate group policy and allocate group resources, such pressure from out-of-district organizations may not reflect membership views within the constituency. And because interest group money may be raised in one locale and allocated to politics elsewhere, contributions from out-of-district organizations cannot be justified as proportionate to a group's membership within a candidate's constituency. Nor can massive infusions of out-of-district money be justified as a necessary means of supporting vigorously competitive campaigning in the face of adequate public financing based on citizen choices within the district. Where political committee funds are raised and spent in the same constituency, we would impose no limits on their contributions.

Limiting out-of-district organizational contributions tends, secondarily, to curb vast spending disparities between candidates. Multidistrict organizations typically raise money in many locales and redistribute it to a few, giving their favored candidates in those target districts a long spending lead over their opponents. Usually funds are redistributed to marginal districts and to those with a high-seniority incumbent eligible for a ranking position on a congressional committee affecting the group's interests. Where out-of-district groups channel large sums to such races, the favored candidates so far outspend their challengers that office seekers cannot present and voters cannot hear the competing views in a balance roughly proportionate to citizen support for them.

The seniority system's uneven allocation of congressional power, the high visibility of certain officials on crucial national issues, and the equal vote of legislators from many districts on issues that transcend their bailiwicks are legitimate reasons for citizens in one district or state to be concerned about elections elsewhere. We allow some contributions by multi-district committees to give play to those concerns. But we limit such contributions to strike a balance between those legitimate concerns and the dual dangers of undue influence on officials by out-of-district financial contributions and massive spending disparities between candidates resulting from those contributions.

Organization contributions are difficult to limit, since setting a ceiling on them simply invites the group to make the maximum outlays through its branches and affiliates. We therefore limit to 20 percent of its funds the amount a candidate or committee can receive from all multi-district groups. This limit does not raise a constitutional question by precluding expression: if a candidate or committee cannot or will not take a group's money, the group can spend its money directly to express its views.

Direct spending might, of course, produce vast disparities in expenditures on behalf of competing candidates or might implicitly obligate the advantaged candidate to out-of-district interests. We therefore require that, in communications to voters, multi-district committees report that their appeals are substantially funded from outside the constituency. Fearing that voters will rebuff candidates supported by outsiders, both out-of-district committees and their favored candidates may conclude that large contributions and direct expenditures from outside the constituency are politically unwise.

Moreover, we require a separate aggregation of out-of-district contributions in the financial reports of candidates and committees. This measure has the same purpose as the 20 percent out-of-district contribution limit and the out-of-district spending disclosures, namely, to discourage out-of-district financing that could cause massive spending disparities between candidates or create undue non-constituency pressures on officeholders.

Finally, our recommendations will tend to reduce the financial influence of both multi-district and local political organizations on nominations and elections. Since each individual can contribute only $1,000 annually to political causes, groups and candidates must compete for those limited dollars. In a candidate-oriented political system, most givers will direct their limited contributions to office seekers they favor rather than to political organizations. The matching of contributions in nomination contests will be a further incentive for givers to channel their money to candidates rather than organizations.

Our recommendation that out-of-district individual contributions count neither toward the eligibility threshold for matching grants nor as matchable gifts is bottomed on the same premises as our regulation of contributions from multi-district committees. Elections in any constituency have an impact on citizens elsewhere, and they may wish therefore to contribute as an expression of their concern. On the other hand, out-of-district contributions may create a financial constituency which is not drawn from the electorate, thereby diluting the responsiveness of elected officials to those who vote for them. We balance these competing considerations by allowing out-of-district individuals to make contributions but by diminishing the importance of those contributions for matching grant purposes.[9]

PROTECTION AGAINST COERCION
IN THE SOLICITATION OF
PRIVATE CONTRIBUTIONS

16. No person should be permitted to solicit or receive contributions for or on behalf of any party, candidate, or political committee from any individual at his place of business or employment unless that place is also his residence or unless the individual is self-employed, except as might occur inadvertently through mail, advertising, or other appeals addressed to a general public. This regulation should not limit the collection of funds by any organization for any account that does not transfer or contribute money to support or oppose any party, candidate, or political committee and does not spend money directly for such purposes except among its own members or its own shareholders.

Comment. Many reformers have decried the power that labor, business, professional, conservative, liberal, conservationist, sports, and other groups derive from their ability to deploy large political sums based on many small contributions. Yet citizens should be free to allocate their political funds through instruments of their own choosing. It may make perfect sense for a black man to contribute his money through an NAACP affiliate (if one existed), or for a union member to do it through COPE, or a doctor through the AMA. Moreover, constitutional questions would arise if the government allowed its citizens to act through some organizations, such as candidate or party committees, but not through economic or other interest organizations.

But the activities of certain organizations may result in donations that are not of the donor's free choosing. Congress long ago prohibited the solicitation of government employees on government property or by government officials.[10] If this protection is extended to other citizens, it may help to eradicate the substantial abuses that now occur in certain unions and businesses without curbing their members' freedom to associate voluntarily for electoral purposes or abridging their organizations' ability to operate on business premises for non-electoral purposes.[11]

The collection of money by associations for political action and education among their members is excluded from these regulations. The Supreme Court has broadly hinted that groups have a constitutional right to spend money to communicate about politics with their own members and shareholders.[12] In addition, it is sound policy in a democracy to encourage political education and action among citizens, whether individually or through associations. At the same time, money solicited or collected at the work site to further the constitutional mandate and democratic values should be limited to these internal activities and should not be spent to address the general public about candidates and issues.

Membership control over internal political activities is usually greater than its influence over general campaign appeals. At the very least, members may ignore or reject the political programs directed to them. Usually they have a hand in selecting those who manage these programs. It is the leaders, on the other hand, who allocate money to candidates or for general appeals to the citizenry; and frequently there is little consultation with the members about what candidates or causes are endorsed, how much money and effort will be devoted to promoting them among the citizenry, or how this advocacy will be undertaken. An effective check on these activities is a requirement that they be financed from voluntary contributions collected away from the work site, where the coercive elements of fund raising are reduced to a minimum. Few voluntary contributions will be available on this basis if political leaders stray far from the political preferences of the members.

LIMITS ON EXPENDITURES

17. Segmental expenditure limits, such as the communications and broadcast media limits of the Campaign Communications Reform Act (now repealed by the Federal Election Campaign Act of 1974), should not be enacted as part of a national political finance policy.

18. The general campaign spending limits in the Federal Election Campaign Act of 1974 and similar comprehensive limits on expenditures should not be part of a national political finance policy.

19. The lowest-unit-charge rule for broadcast media and the comparable space-charge rule for print media, as well as the reasonable access rule, all enacted in the Campaign Communications Reform Act, should be retained.

Comment. Segmental communications media limits for political campaigns did not work (see Chapter 5). They were set so high that they did not limit spending. Further, they ignored the substantial differences between media spending in metropolitan and nonmetropolitan areas. They also ignored the merit of allowing candidates to choose their own campaign strategies. Some must use media advertising extensively because they do not have the support of party organizations, interest groups, editorial writers, and other alternate centers of opinion leadership. Some may use it because they communicate effectively through television and radio; others may shy away because their personal mannerisms or political style are not well suited to broadcasting. Finally, if effective, media spending limits would merely displace spending to other campaign methods.

The more challenging question is whether general spending limits, such as those in the Federal Election Campaign Act of 1974, should be enacted. They are almost impossible to enforce. Do spending limits apply to negative spending to oppose a candidate, or to issue spending that mentions no candidate but implies a position about an aspirant whose posture is well known? Further, spending limits are easily avoided by a profusion of political committees spending up to the legal maximum.

Effective ceilings require that all funds promoting a candidate (and opposing his opponent) flow through a central treasurer. But this raises constitutional issues if the treasurer refuses money from some contributors, denying them freedom to express themselves; if the treasurer refuses to allow individuals or groups directly to spend money under his imprimatur to make their own comments on his candidate or on the opposition; if the treasurer accepts and spends funds from citizens and groups to the point where his candidate has little or no opportunity to shape his own appeals by spending adequate sums; or if the treasurer accepts and spends money from citizens and groups up to the spending limit and then must turn away others who wish to express their views by making outlays.[13]

A more practical objection is that expenditure limits cannot take into account variable and changing campaign circumstances. A formula can be devised to keep spending ceilings abreast of inflation and larger electorates, but it cannot anticipate or make provision for technological changes that add new, and perhaps thoroughly desirable, costs to campaigning. Further, the wide variations in America in constituency size and composition, media arrangements, party organization strength, and the like generate varying campaign costs; no legislative expenditure ceiling can adequately account for these differences. Most important, while a spending limit might conform quite reasonably to the routine costs of doing political business, it cannot anticipate or provide for those extraordinary elections in which public interest is inflamed, debate rages hot and heavy, and additional expenditure is appropriate to satisfy the public demand for information and argument.

Excessive political expenditures can be absolute or relative. On the rare occasions when a candidate's spending is out of all proportion to the requirements of an effective campaign, it saturates the media, annoys the voters, and degrades the political system. But it is not very harmful except to those who do it. More often, campaign spending is excessive primarily in relation to the paucity of resources available to an opposing candidate. Then it distorts election results and is destructive of democratic values.

The best protection against absolute excess is to limit the large private contributions that breed it, and the best defense against relative excess is to level up the resources of underfinanced candidates through public funding. Limitations on private contributions and the provision of public funding would limit political expenditures within reasonable margins. These limits on political expenditure could be adjusted upward or downward by simply changing the level of public funding and/or altering the limits on individual giving. Such measures are preferable to a directly prescribed limitation.

Retention of the lowest-unit-charge rule for broadcast media and the comparable space-charge rule for print media would allow publicly funded candidates to make substantial media appeals with the limited money available to them, perhaps reducing the urgency of higher spending. And political speech may well be entitled to treatment no worse than that of commercial speech. Indeed, most students of the First Amendment regard political speech as preferred over commercial expressions in the hierarchy of values underlying that constitutional provision.

Reasonable access rules also are desirable to assure that political candidates can reach the voters with their arguments. The mass media are the most widely attended communications channels in our society, and they are therefore essential for effective presentations by many political candidates. They should not be closed to those appeals by the fiat of private owners holding valuable public licenses to use the airwaves.

REPEAL OF TAX INCENTIVES

20. The tax deduction-or-credit option for campaign contributions enacted as part of the Revenue Act of 1971 should be repealed.

Comment. Our evidence suggests that few people take advantage of tax incentives for campaign contributions and that those who do are even more disproportionately from upper socio-economic classes than is the highly unrepresentative contributor class as a whole. Tax incentives serve mainly to provide a tax windfall for the wealthy who are already givers. Elimination of tax incentives would generate an estimated $30 million in revenues that could be applied toward the cost of public financing and administration of campaigns.

EFFECTIVE ENFORCEMENT
UNDER INDEPENDENT
ADMINISTRATION

21. An independent Federal Elections Commission should be established. Its members should be designated respectively by the president, the leader of each party in each house of Congress that has

more than 5 percent of membership of that house, and the central committee of any party to which none of these belong whose candidate for the presidency received more than 5 percent of the vote in the preceding election. The commission would be responsible for the administration and enforcement of all political finance regulations, with special authority to prosecute violators rather than referring cases for prosecution to the Department of Justice.[14]

22. Any committee contributing or spending and any individual spending more than $1,000 of public and private funds to influence any nomination or election for federal office should maintain financial accounts with the commission or in depository banks named by it. Receipts would be deposited with the commission or those named depository banks, and every deposit would be accompanied by the information presently required by law plus the social security number of each contributor of a sum to be matched or of any sum greater than $100. Except for small sums, which could be drawn in cash for petty cash expenditures as defined by the commission, expenditures could be made only by checks issued after submission of a bill or draft signed by the provider of goods or services and certified by the holder of the account.

23. Every candidate should be required to report all political debts to the commission prior to receiving matching or vouchered funds. No candidate or his agent might incur any political debt, except for goods and services, after receiving matching or vouchered funds, until after the election for which the funds were supplied. Every contribution would be deposited within five days of receipt by the candidate or his designated agent. Every obligation would be registered within five days of being incurred. No new contributions would be permitted after the eighth day preceding an election.

24. The commission should monitor political accounts, making periodic disclosure of the contributions and expenditures of each candidate and committee and of each person who spends money to influence elections. It should itemize all contributions and expenditure aggregates greater than $100.

25. The commission should be authorized to make rules and regulations necessary to fulfill its various responsibilities, including administering public financing of campaigns, overseeing the receipt and expenditure of funds, and enforcing disclosure provisions and contributor ceilings. It should investigate all apparent violations discovered by itself and brought to it by private complainants; and it should prosecute violations confirmed by its investigators.

Comment. Although American schemes for regulating political finance have often been flawed in other ways, weak enforcement has been their most consistent and notable defect. The politicians who passed the laws often feared strong enforcement. Expenditure limitations low enough to please the people and the press were acknowledged by all professionals as too restrictive to allow effective campaigning. Hence the people and the press were given expenditure limits that were then not enforced. Contribution limits often met the same fate. But with public financing to replace the private funds lost through low contribution limits, vigorous enforcement would not starve the political process.

Another barrier to enforcement has been the proliferation of groups receiving and spending money. This has blocked full disclosure and hindered effective auditing. Public financing would encourage each candidate to centralize his major accounts. Further, candidate, committee, and independent financing would be channeled through accounts at the Federal Elections Commission and designated depository banks. Like the Kentucky central registry, the commission would be in a position to compile information about receipts and expenditures, to disclose its compilations, and to audit for enforcement purposes.

PUBLIC FINANCING AND
PUBLIC POLICY

Vouchers, matching grants up to $100, and individual contributions or expenditures not exceeding $1,000 allow substantial citizen participation on a basis far more equal than the present private financing system. The use of vouchers to trigger flat and proportional grants and the two-for-one matching of contributions up to $100 will provide a high percentage of the funds needed for vigorous competitive campaigns and in many cases all of the money necessary for that purpose. These flat and proportional grants will in most cases allow a fair presentation by candidates and a fair opportunity for citizens to hear from office seekers. The permissible private giving—matchable contributions up to $100 and total individual gifts up to $1,000—is small enough to ameliorate disproportionate influence by contributors and to diminish the prospect of ostensible campaign contributions serving in fact to corrupt officials.

Small per-vote grants to political parties and public financing of national conventions are an initial recognition of the role of parties in American politics. Further, parties may be vehicles for voucher drives and perhaps for broadly based appeals for matchable contributions. This activity will require new collaboration among party units at every level and between the party organization and the party in government. The impetus for intensified party activity and heightened intra-party collaboration does not, however, provide party organizations with campaign funds that might be the instrument for imposing discipline on officials. Other associations and even candidate organizations could collect vouchers and matchable grants. But parties are already in the field, and they can play this role with relative ease. The small direct grants to national parties may provide the seed money for this effort.

The public-plus-private financing scheme we recommend respects the separation of powers by financing races for both the executive and legislative departments. It acknowledges the decentralization between the party organization and the party in government by financing them separately. The public grants to party organizations may be too small, but modest support does not unbalance traditional relationships between local, state, and national party units. If small grants to parties revitalize the party organization, the principle might be extended to local and state party units and the level of support increased. Successful grants to national party committees will also encourage states and localities to finance parties at their levels, just as they do in federal systems elsewhere.

Candidate grants based on the number of eligible voters respect the difference in size of American constituencies. Other constituency variables cannot be recognized by formula. But the absence of expenditure limits and the sanction of modest private contributions allow spending in excess of public funding where circumstances require it.

Public financing cannot eliminate all the advantages of incumbency; indeed, we know of no formula to do so. But one of the most important advantages of incumbency is greater campaign funding. Often the challenger's cause seems so hopeless that the effect of incumbency is to deny him even nominal private financing to launch his campaign. Public funding provides a substantial base for the challenger, and stringent limits on contributions will usually prevent the incumbent from far outdistancing his opponent by adding hefty private financing to his public grant. Well-financed opposition may also offset other incumbency advantages; when a challenger can afford to publicize his own program and his opponent's record, voters may give less weight on election day to the incumbent's visibility, his past constituent services, and similar advantages of officeholding. A substantial opposition campaign sponsored with public funds and a significant reduction in the financial advantage of officeholders greatly diminish, but do not eliminate, the long lead incumbents have.

The matching grant system is a suitable means for financing nomination contests. The two-for-one matching formula should provide a substantial public funding base to spur competition. And the private money threshold for eligibility for matching grants prevents wholly frivolous candidates from misusing public funds. The use of matching grants bases public financing on money support rather than voter support, but we are unable to adapt the voucher scheme to primaries or devise an alternative that turns equally on citizen participation. By limiting public matching grants to small private contributions, we hinge public funding on the *breadth* of a candidate's financial support among the electorate.

By making both nomination and general election grants directly to candidates and allowing them to use these funds to shape their own campaign appeals, we acknowledge the candidate orientation of American politics. Public financing that turns on current indexes of popular support—that is, vouchers and matching grants—again recognizes that candidates, not parties, are the main focus of American voters. Finally, of course, vouchers and matching grants involve direct citizen support for candidates.

Minor parties are respected by both vouchers and matching grants. They are eligible for nomination and general election funds proportional to their public support. No threshold for general election eligibility is established, except for write-in candidates, and the threshold in nomination contests is the same for all parties. There is no discrimination against minor parties in securing flat grants because they may do so by gaining 38 percent of the vouchers. Nor are the two traditional major parties assured flat grants; in some districts a major-party candidate may secure less than 38 percent of the vouchers, and his public financing will be proportional to the vouchers he collects. The use of current eligibility indexes guarantees new minor parties and independent candidates proportional public funding immediately; they need not wait two, four, or six years after establishing an electoral track record to receive public grants.

Finally, we have attempted to respect the constitutional framework of the American polity. Individual contribution and expenditure limits are set to allow substantial expression and to effectuate rough equality of citizens in the electoral process. No expenditure limits are set for candidates and associations because the means necessary for enforcement would deny some citizens any opportunity to express their views. Associations are prohibited from raising money in circumstances that are implicitly coercive. We are confident that public grants promote the general welfare and are therefore within the constitutional spending power of Congress. Funding vigorous competition that informs citizens of their alternatives and reduces the disproportionate influence of big givers serves public purposes.

All aspects of the system we propose may stir opposition, but two invite the most intense reaction. Many will object that we have not imposed expenditure limits. They hold the Jacksonian view that every man should be able to run for office and that Everyman's opportunity depends on keeping campaign spending within his means. But the Jacksonian view puts the emphasis on individual ambitions rather than on the democratic system's requirements. In democracies, election campaigns serve public purposes—competition, choice, checks. The individuals that must be enabled to run for office are those who present a significant alternative that a substantial portion of the public supports and wants voted on in elections. Any candidate of that kind should be able to raise the modest sums needed to enter the primaries and to collect enough vouchers to be competitive in general elections. Unless people understand the public function of campaigns, they will not recognize the importance of adequate spending. And beyond the need for adequate candidate spending, the absence of expenditure limits is justified by a policy preference for vigorous public discussion by all who are interested and by insurmountable First Amendment barriers to any effective ceiling on outlays.

Despite polls showing wide majority support for public financing of campaigns, some will see it as an abuse or waste of taxpayers' money. They will protest that their tax dollars should not fuel the campaigns of candidates and parties they detest. Campaigns, many believe, are a struggle by individual politicians to get comfortable jobs; and they hold that candidates ought to find their own money for this self-promotion.

Public financing has public purposes, however, that override both these objections. It sustains vigorous competition in campaigns, which allows the people a choice of governors and policy, and it imposes checks on those in power. Public financing also ameliorates disproportionate influence and corruption by contributors and extortion by politicians. These public purposes exist side by side with the private ambitions of politicians in campaigns. Citizens can no more refuse to pay taxes to support such public purposes than they can refuse support for public schools or the fluoridation of water, although the private ambitions of educators and chemical companies may also be advanced by such policies. Finally, however, citizens are most likely to be persuaded that public financing is not a misallocation of their tax dollars because a voucher and matching grant system gives them more equal opportunity to participate in and direct the nation's politics.

From a national perspective, the cost of public financing is not very great. Taxpayers who take this broad view will be less antagonized by public financing of campaigns. There is no precise way to assess the dollar cost of our proposals since they turn on the number of matchable gifts in nomination campaigns, the number of votes on which party grants will be based, and the number of candidates collecting vouchers.

Most presidential and congressional campaigns involve only two candidates with significant citizen support. To understand the financial implications of public financing, however, we calculate its maximum cost. Assume that two major contenders in all races for president, senator, and representative in 1972 each submitted no more than 38 percent of vouchers and that lesser candidates received proportional grants accounting for the remaining 24 percent of vouchers. The cost of public financing of the general election would then have been $177.6 million. Major- and minor-party support would have been $4.4 million and convention grants an additional $8.8 million.

It is difficult to predict the cost of matching grants because public opinion polls do not tell us how many contributors give in nomination contests or how much they give. Also, we cannot predict whether a larger number of givers or larger contributions might be stimulated by the incentive of two-for-one matching. We think an outside cost figure would be $100 million. As much as $50 million might be required to administer the voucher system and another $10 million to manage the matching grant scheme and to enforce the law. These generous estimates would put total public costs at $350 million in each presidential year. They would be at least $100 million less in off-year elections.

If non-federal office expenditures had stayed the same—about $225 million—in 1972 and if we assume total private spending in federal office campaigns of $100 million (including $50 million in private matching money), total 1972 campaign expenditures would have reached $675 million, or about 160 percent of actual outlays. In a comparable non-presidential year, total campaign costs might be estimated between $525 million and $550 million, still $100 million higher than estimated spending in presidential year 1972. These estimates can be regarded as a scandalous escalation of campaign spending or as a measure of how badly underfinanced many candidates are, especially in nomination contests and in general election campaigns for the Senate and House. We hold the second view, believing that the additional public funding will support more vigorous competition for public office and will present alternatives more fully to voters.

Even at higher spending levels American campaign costs would still not be "high" by most measures. The share of the nation's personal income devoted to political campaigns in 1972 was 0.05 percent, about the same as in 1968. Under this public financing system, it would rise only slightly, to 0.07 percent.

In more personal terms, the whole public-plus-private expenditure for all contests for all offices in 1972 would have been $4.83 per eligible voter, up from the $3.11 actually spent. The public financing component would have been $2.50 per eligible voter, and the remaining $2.33 would have been raised from private contributions. Since public funding would be collected annually through taxes, it would cost about $1.25 per eligible voter per year. The whole public-plus-private cost would be a few pennies over $2.40 per eligible voter annually.

The approximate average hourly wage for production workers in 1972 was $3.77. Campaigning, with a generously funded public financing component, would have required the allocation of one hour and fifteen minutes' labor in an election year, or thirty-eight minutes annually—a small effort to pay for costs of democratic elections. The wages allocated to politics by the average American would still be less than the comparable cost of politics in such other democracies as West Germany, Japan, Italy, and Israel.

What the average American will get for committing seventy-five minutes' wages, $2.50 of it through the tax system, to pay the cost of campaigns is a more competitive and thus more responsive government, public officials who are not beholden for campaign funds to special interests, and a more stable political system strengthened by greater confidence in government. As Senator Hart observed in introducing his Congressional Election Finance Act of 1973, with a price tag of $500 million:

> Many will regard this as a new raid on the Treasury by greedy officeholders. But I think many people, upon reflection, will realize that this will be as wise an investment as a democracy can make. When a politician's success depends on a combination of dollars and votes, the Nation is clearly less democratic than it would be if victory depended on votes alone. Congress annually disposes of a Federal budget in the hundreds of billions of dollars and takes actions with tremendous impact on a trillion-dollar economy, not to mention their impact on the incalculable values of our health, safety, and liberty. Surely in that context public campaign subsidies would be a growth stock for everyone.

CHAPTER 1

1. E. E. Schattschneider, *Party Government* (New York: Holt, Rinehart and Winston, 1942), p. 52.
2. U.S., Congress, Senate, Subcommittee on Privileges and Elections of the Committee on Rules and Administration, *Hearings on S. 1103, S. 1954 and S. 2417*, 93d Congress, 1st Sess., 1973, p. 30, press release of George A. Spater.
3. The 1964 figures are from a national survey taken by the Survey Research Center of the University of Michigan. The 1973 and 1974 results were found in George Gallup, "U.S. Financing of Campaigns," *San Francisco Chronicle*, September 19, 1974, p. 6.
4. The Federal Election Campaign Act of 1974 is discussed more fully in later chapters. Its limits on contributions and spending are covered in Chapter 4, its disclosure provisions in 6, and its public financing and other provisions in 9.
5. U.S., Congress, Senate, Committee on Commerce, *Hearings on Federal Election Campaign Act of 1973*, 93d Congress, 1st Sess., 1973, pp. 129–30.
6. U.S., *Congressional Record*, 93d Congress, 1st Sess., 1973, Vol. 119, S. 14807.
7. *Ibid.*, S. 14809.
8. Joseph R. Biden, Jr., "Public Financing of Elections: Legislative Proposals and Constitutional Questions," *Northwestern University Law Review*, Vol. 69 (March–April, 1974), pp. 1–2.
9. The literature on the weakness of American parties is endless. For almost three decades modern political scientists and commentators have been urging a revival of the party system to provide more disciplined and coherent policy making and to assure clearer, more responsible choices at the polls. Statements of this view appear in Schattschneider, *op. cit.*; Committee on Political Parties of the American Political Science Association, *Toward a More Responsible Two-Party System* (New York: Holt, Rinehart and Winston, 1950); and David Broder, *The Party's Over* (New York: Harper & Row, 1972).
10. Gerald M. Pomper, "From Confusion to Clarity: Issues and American Voters, 1956–1968," *American Political Science Review*, Vol. 66 (June 1972), pp. 415–28; Richard W. Boyd, "Popular Control of Public Policy: A Normal Vote Analysis of the 1968 Election," *ibid.*, pp. 429–49.
11. Clinton Rossiter, *Parties and Politics in America* (Ithaca, N.Y.: Cornell University Press, 1960), p. 1.
12. See Chapter 7 below.
13. Estimates of total political expenditures in presidential election years from

NOTES

1952 to 1968 are reported in Herbert E. Alexander, *Financing the 1968 Election* (Lexington, Mass.: Heath Lexington Books, 1971), p. 1. Dr. Alexander's preliminary estimates for 1972 were $400 million, but studies of presidential and congressional campaign spending suggest that a somewhat higher figure would be closer to reality. The authors have tentatively put this at $425 million.

CHAPTER 2

1. Alexander Heard, *The Costs of Democracy* (Chapel Hill: University of North Carolina Press, 1960), p. 20.
2. Herbert E. Alexander, *Money in Politics* (Washington: Public Affairs Press, 1972), p. 79.
3. Herbert E. Alexander, *Financing the 1960 Election* (Princeton, N.J.: Citizens' Research Foundation, 1962), p. 10.
4. Herbert E. Alexander, *Financing the 1964 Election* (Princeton, N.J.: Citizens' Research Foundation, 1966), p. 8.
5. Herbert E. Alexander, *Financing the 1968 Election* (Lexington, Mass.: Heath Lexington Books, 1971), p. 2.
6. *Ibid.*, p. 4.
7. These estimates by the authors are based on official reports filed under the Federal Election Campaign Act of 1971. See U.S., Office of Federal Elections, *Report of 1972 Presidential Campaign Receipts and Expenditures* (Washington, 1974).
8. Alexander, *Financing the 1968 Election*, p. 3.
9. Alexander, *Money in Politics*, pp. 24–25.
10. The authors are grateful to Common Cause for making available to us the sweeping thirteen-volume "Common Cause Study of 1972 Congressional Campaign Finances." Portions of the study have been published in U.S., Congress, Senate, Committee on Rules and Administration, Subcommittee on Privileges and Elections, *Hearings on S. 1103, S. 1954, S. 2417*, 93d Congress. 1st Sess., 1973, pp. 96–111; *Congressional Quarterly Weekly Report*, Vol. 31, No. 38, September 22, 1973, pp. 2515–17; and *ibid*, Vol. 31, No. 48, December 1, 1973, pp. 3130–37. These data are referred to in the remainder of the text as the Common Cause Study.
11. The figures on Nelson's campaigns are based on the first author's research on campaign finances in Wisconsin. Other figures for years prior to 1972 are taken from David W. Adamany, *Campaign Finance in America* (North Scituate, Mass.: Duxbury Press, 1972), pp. 36–38. Expenditure statements for 1972 are from the Common Cause Study.
12. Heard, *op. cit.*, p. 425; Common Cause Study.
13. Figures for years prior to 1972 are taken from Adamany, *op. cit.*, p. 39; those for 1972 are based on the Common Cause Study.
14. Adamany, *op. cit.*, pp. 43–44.
15. The leading analyses of variables affecting campaign spending are Heard, *op. cit.*, pp. 380–87; Adamany, *op. cit.*, pp. 51–78; and David W. Adamany, *Financing Politics: Recent Wisconsin Elections* (Madison: University of Wisconsin Press, 1969), pp. 61–107. The most precise analysis, using sophisticated statistical techniques, is John R. Owens, *Trends in Campaign Spending in California, 1958–70: Tests of Factors Influencing Costs* (Princeton, N.J.: Citizens' Research Foundation, 1973), pp. 70–80.
16. Derived from the Common Cause Study.
17. *Hearings on S. 1103, op. cit.*, p. 97.
18. Reported in the Common Cause Study.
19. Howard R. Penniman, "Financing Campaigns in the Public Interest," *Campaign Finances: Two Views of the Political and Constitutional Implications* (Washington: American Enterprise Institute, 1971), p. 16. Penniman also details the substantial budgets and perquisites received by members of Congress.

20. David L. Rosenbloom, "Background Paper," in Twentieth Century Fund Task Force on Financing Congressional Campaigns, *Electing Congress* (New York: Twentieth Century Fund, 1970), pp. 35–36.
21. Arnold J. Heidenheimer, "Comparative Party Finances: Notes on Practices and Toward a Theory," *Journal of Politics*, Vol. 25 (November, 1963), pp. 796–801. Subsequent refinements and extensions of these comparative campaign cost statements are found in Adamany, *Financing Politics*, pp. 53–56; Adamany, *Campaign Finance in America*, pp. 33, 48, n. 10; and Owens, *op. cit.*, pp. 34–35.

CHAPTER 3

1. All survey data on the 1972 election are drawn from the Twentieth Century Fund Survey of Political Finance, commissioned for this study and conducted by the National Opinion Research Center of the University of Chicago. A nationwide random sample yielded 1,481 usable responses. The survey was taken in November and December 1972. These data are referred to in the remainder of the text as the Twentieth Century Fund Survey.
    Unless otherwise noted, all survey data on prior elections are found in Herbert E. Alexander, *Money in Politics* (Washington: Public Affairs Press, 1972), pp. 335–36, n. 2.
2. Twentieth Century Fund Survey.
3. E. E. Schattschneider, *The Semisovereign People: A Realist's View of Democracy in America* (New York: Holt, Rinehart and Winston 1960), p. 35.
4. Herbert E. Alexander, *Financing the 1968 Election* (Lexington, Mass.: Heath Lexington Books, 1971), pp. 44 (McCarthy) and 160 (Wallace).
5. Herbert E. Alexander, *Financing the 1964 Election* (Princeton, N.J.: Citizens' Research Foundation, 1966), pp. 18, 71.
6. These estimates are based on official reports filed under the Federal Election Campaign Act of 1971. See U.S., Office of Federal Elections, *Alphabetical Listing of 1972 Presidential Campaign Receipts* (Washington, 1973); idem, *Report of 1972 Presidential Campaign Receipts and Expenditures* (Washington, 1974).
7. Alexander, *Financing the 1968 Elections*, p. 163.
8. *Ibid.*, pp. 167–68.
9. *Congressional Quarterly Weekly Report*, Vol. 31, No. 40, October 6, 1973, pp. 2655–60.
10. *Ibid.*, p. 2656.
11. All data in this paragraph are from the Common Cause Study. See Chapter 2, n. 10.
12. On the advantages of wealthy candidates, see Alexander Heard, *The Costs of Democracy* (Chapel Hill: University of North Carolina Press, 1960), pp. 219–24; Herbert E. Alexander, *Money in Politics* (Washington: Public Affairs Press, 1972), pp. 37–50.
13. Quoted in Joseph R. Biden, Jr., "Public Financing of Elections: Legislative Proposals and Constitutional Questions," *Northwestern University Law Review*, Vol. 69 (March–April, 1974), p. 6.
14. The Common Cause Study.
15. Heard, *op. cit.*, pp. 105–29, 154–68, 178–89; Alexander, *Money in Politics*, Chap. 10.
16. Heard, *op. cit.*, pp. 123–25; George Thayer, *Who Shakes the Money Tree?* (New York: Simon and Schuster, 1973), pp. 215–19.
17. Heard, *op. cit.*, pp. 155–68; Thayer, *op. cit.*, pp. 241–45; National Advisory Commission on Criminal Justice Standards and Goals, *Community Crime Prevention* (Washington, 1973), pp. 225–27.
18. Thayer, *op. cit.*, pp. 211–12.
19. Alexander, *Money in Politics*, p. 329, n. 24.
20. Alexander, *Financing the 1968 Election*, pp. 181–85.

21. For the years 1956 through 1968, see *ibid.*, pp. 182–83; for 1972, Herbert E. Alexander, "G.O.P.'s Big Bankrollers of 1972," *New York Times,* September 3, 1974, sec. 3, p. 1.

22. Alexander, *Financing the 1968 Election,* pp. 185–87; "G.O.P.'s Big Bankrollers of 1972."

23. "Oil Companies: $5-Million in Donations to Nixon," *Congressional Quarterly Weekly Report,* Vol. 32, No. 3, January 19, 1974, pp. 113–15; "Study Shows Defense Contractors Gave $5.4 Million to Nixon Campaign" (Washington: Office of Congressman Les Aspin, 1973).

24. Data in this and the succeeding four paragraphs are drawn from the Common Cause Study.

25. On labor's political role generally, see Heard, *op. cit.,* Chap. 7; Alexander, *Money in Politics,* pp. 169–77.

26. Theodore H. White, *The Making of the President 1968* (New York: Atheneum, 1969), p. 365.

27. Alexander, *Financing the 1968 Election,* pp. 194–95.

28. Based on the authors' analysis of data in U.S., Office of Federal Elections, *Report of 1972 Presidential Campaign Receipts and Expenditures.*

29. Alexander, *Financing the 1968 Election,* p. 127.

30. This study of seventeen labor committees is reported in *Congressional Quarterly Weekly Report,* Vol. 31, No. 11, March 17, 1973, pp. 568–88.

31. "Letter Reveals Dairy Offer to Aid Nixon's Campaign," *Wisconsin State Journal,* October 24, 1973, p. 12.

32. "AMPI Defends Gifts to Nixon," *Wisconsin State Journal,* November 11, 1973, sec. 2, p. 4.

33. Center for Public Financing of Elections, "Corporate Abuses of Campaign Spending Laws Underscore Need for Change in System," *Progress Report* #9 (Washington, May 17, 1974); "Nixon's Money Hustlers Employed 'Quota' System to Raise Donations," *Madison Capital Times,* July 7, 1973, p. 1; Jack Anderson, "How LBJ and Bobby Baker Made Peace," *Madison Capital Times,* August 8, 1973, editorial page.

34. Philip M. Stern, "Politics and Public Financing: A Great Bargain," *Washington Post,* October 7, 1973, Sec. C, p. 1.

35. "Milk Group Gave $462,000 Just Before Election," *Congressional Quarterly Weekly Report,* Vol. 31, No. 11, March 17, 1973, p. 570.

36. *Ibid.*

37. *Ibid.*

38. "Nixon's Fund-Raisers Pushed Secret Deals," *Wisconsin State Journal,* September 30, 1973, p. 1.

39. Jerry Landauer, "Another View of Election Financing," *Wall Street Journal,* May 14, 1973, p. 3.

40. "Milk Group Gave $462,000 Just Before Election," *op. cit.,* pp. 571–73.

41. Monroe W. Karmin, "Throughout the U.S., Public Contractors Tied to 'Campaign Gifts,'" *Wall Street Journal,* October 17, 1973, p. 1.

42. *Ibid.*

43. *Ibid.*

44. "Illinois Governor Seeks Funds Data," *New York Times,* August 26, 1973, p. 43.

45. "Ambassadorships for Sale: Congress Considers Action," *Congressional Quarterly Weekly Report,* Vol. 31, No. 24, June 16, 1973, pp. 1516–18.

46. Frank J. Sorauf, *Party Politics in America,* 2d ed. (Boston: Little, Brown and Co., 1972), pp. 87–89; Robert J. McNeill, *Democratic Campaign Financing in Indiana, 1964* (Bloomington, Ind.: Institute of Public Administration, and Princeton, N.J.: Citizens' Research Foundation, 1966), pp. 15–19.

47. On the mix of contributor motives, with special emphasis on incentives not involving personal gain for givers, see Heard, *op. cit.,* Chap. 4, esp. pp. 69–74; Alexander, *Money in Politics,* pp. 141–48; William Buchanan and Agnes Bird, *Money as a Campaign Resource: Tennessee Democratic Senatorial Primaries, 1948–1964* (Princeton, N.J.: Citizens' Research Foundation,

1966), pp. 77–81; David W. Adamany, *Campaign Finance in America* (North Scituate, Mass.: Duxbury Press, 1972), pp. 136–52.

CHAPTER 4

1. *A Survey of State Statutes Regulating Political Finance* (Princeton, N.J.: Citizens' Research Foundation, 1971), p. 10.
2. The Twentieth Century Fund Task Force on Financing Congressional Campaigns, *Electing Congress* (New York: Twentieth Century Fund, 1971), p. 19 (hereafter cited as *Electing Congress*).
3. U.S., Congress, Senate, Committee on Commerce, Subcommittee on Communications, *Hearings on the Federal Elections Campaign Act of 1971*, 92d Congress, 1st Sess., 1971, p. 518.
4. Sanford Watzman, *Conflict of Interest* (Chicago: Cowles Book Co., 1971), p. 117.
5. Herbert E. Alexander, *Financing the 1968 Election* (Lexington, Mass.: Heath Lexington Books, 1971), p. 180.
6. Herbert E. Alexander, *Money in Politics* (Washington: Public Affairs Press, 1972), p. 143.
7. Quoted in Watzman, *op. cit.*, p. 114.
8. Alexander, *Money in Politics*, p. 147; Max McCarthy, *Elections for Sale* (Boston: Houghton Mifflin Co., 1972), p. 58.
9. George Thayer, *Who Shakes the Money Tree?* (New York: Simon and Schuster, 1973), pp. 15–18.
10. Alexander, *Money in Politics*, pp. 43–47.
11. Thayer, *op. cit.*, p. 155.
12. *A Survey of State Statutes Regulating Political Finance, op. cit.*, p. 10; U.S., Office of Federal Elections, *Analysis of Federal and State Campaign Finance Law* (Washington, 1974), pp. 41–53.
13. The Supreme Court has held that union members in a union shop under the Railway Labor Act are entitled to withhold or obtain refunds of portions of dues money that would otherwise be committed to political purposes. *International Ass'n of Machinists v. Street*, 367 U.S. 740 (1961).
14. U.S., Office of Federal Elections, *op. cit.*, pp. 28–40.
15. Alexander, *Money in Politics*, p. 191.
16. Herbert E. Alexander, with the assistance of Laura Denny, *Regulation of Political Finance* (Berkeley, Calif.: Institute of Governmental Affairs, and Princeton, N.J.: Citizens' Research Foundation, 1966), pp. 10, 59–60.
17. Committee for Economic Development, *Financing a Better Election System* (New York, 1968), pp. 25–26; *Electing Congress*, pp. 17–18; President's Commission on Campaign Costs, *Financing Presidential Campaigns* (Washington, 1962), pp. 17–18; National Municipal League, *Model State Campaign Contributions and Expenditures Reporting Law*, 4th draft (New York: National Municipal League, 1960), p. 19. See also Delmer D. Dunn, *Financing Presidential Campaigns* (Washington: Brookings Institution, 1972), pp. 150–52, 155.
18. Alexander, *Money in Politics*, p. 230.
19. *Ibid.*, pp. 190–91; *A Survey of State Statutes Regulating Political Finance, op. cit.*, pp. 7–9.
20. Reported expenditures are far below actual spending. Presidential campaign costs probably rose above the $3 million mark earlier than these reports reveal and persisted at higher levels for a longer period. Congressional Quarterly, *Politics in America 1945–1966*, 2d ed. (Washington, 1967), p. 88.
21. *Electing Congress*, p. 18.
22. *State Statutes Regulating Political Finance* (Princeton, N.J.: Citizens' Research Foundation, 1974).
23. 37 *Fed. Reg.* 6158 (1972).
24. *American Civil Liberties Union v. Jennings*, 336 F. Supp. 1041 (1973) (three-judge court).

25. Alexander, *Money in Politics*, p. 233.
26. *Ex parte Siebold*, 100 U.S. 371 (1880). On sources of national power to regulate elections generally, see Albert J. Rosenthal, *Federal Regulation of Campaign Finance: Some Constitutional Questions* (Princeton, N.J.: Citizens' Research Foundation, 1972), pp. 12–20. Also see Joel L. Fleishman, "Freedom of Speech and Equality of Political Opportunity: The Constitutionality of the Federal Election Campaign Act of 1971," *North Carolina Law Review*, Vol. 51 (January, 1973), pp. 399–404.
27. *Smiley v. Holm*, 285, U.S. 355, 366 (1932).
28. Article 2, section 1, clauses 2, 3.
29. *Burroughs and Cannon v. United States*, 290 U.S. 534, 545 (1934).
30. *Ex parte Yarborough*, 110 U.S. 651, 657 (1884).
31. *Newberry v. United States*, 256 U.S. 232 (1921).
32. *United States v. Classic*, 313 U.S. 299 (1941).
33. *Smith v. Allwright*, 321 U.S. 649 (1944); *Terry v. Adams*, 345 U.S. 461 (1953).
34. A provocative commentary setting out this argument is Marlene Arnold Nicholson, "Campaign Financing and Equal Protection," *Stanford Law Review*, Vol. 26 (April, 1974), pp. 815–54.
35. Article 1, Section 8, clause 18; Rosenthal, *op. cit.*, p. 14.
36. Article 1, section 8, clause 3.
37. *Perez v. United States*, 402 U.S. 146 (1971). Commentators tend to discard this approach: Rosenthal, *op. cit.*, pp. 13–14; Nicholson, *op. cit.*, pp. 824–25.
38. *West Virginia Board of Education v. Barnette*, 319 U.S. 624 (1943); *Stromberg v. California*, 283 U.S. 359 (1931); *NAACP v. Button*, 371 U.S. 415 (1963); *Tinker v. Des Moines School District*, 393 U.S. 503; *Thornhill v. Alabama*, 310 U.S. 88 (1940).
39. Ralph K. Winter, Jr., "Money, Politics and the First Amendment," *Campaign Finances: Two Views on the Political and Constitutional Implications* (Washington: American Enterprise Institute, 1971), pp. 60–61.
40. *NAACP v. Button*, 371 U.S. 415, 438 (1968) ("compelling"); *NAACP v. Alabama*, 357, U.S. 449, 464 (1958) ("substantial"); *Bates v. City of Little Rock*, 361 U.S. 516, 524 (1960) ("subordinating"); and *Gibson v. Florida State Investigating Comm.*, 372 U.S. 539, 546 (1963) ("overriding and compelling"). For a sophisticated analysis of the manner in which the Supreme Court could proceed in ascertaining when and how campaign financing might be regulated consistent with the First Amendment, see Fleishman, *op. cit.*, pp. 404–10. Also see Rosenthal, *op. cit.*, pp. 20–25. The strongest statement of congressional power to regulate campaign financing despite First Amendment guarantees is "Common Cause Memorandum on the Constitutionality of Contribution and Expenditure Limits" (Washington, 1973).
41. *United States v. O'Brien*, 391 U.S. 367 (1968).
42. *Cox v. Louisiana*, 379 U.S. 559 (1965); *Adderly v. Florida*, 385 U.S. 39 (1966); *Cameron v. Johnson*, 390 U.S. 611 (1968); *Grayned v. Rockford*, 408 U.S. 104 (1972). On the right to regulate picketing generally, see *International Brotherhood of Teamsters v. Vogt*, 354 U.S. 284 (1957).
43. *United States v. Harriss*, 347 U.S. 612, 625 (1954); *Burroughs and Cannon v. United States*, *supra*, at pp. 547–48.
44. Quoted in *New York Times*, November 3, 1974, Sec. 4, p. 1.
45. Rosenthal, *op. cit.*, pp. 20–25; Fleishman, *op. cit.*, pp. 442–45.
46. Fleishman, *op. cit.*, p. 443.
47. The equal protection argument is persuasively stated in Nicholson, *op. cit.*
48. *Reynolds v. Sims*, 377 U.S. 533, 565 (1964).
49. *Bullock v. Carter*, 405 U.S. 134, 144 (1972).
50. The broadest statement of congressional power to assure equal protection against actions not judicially recognized as violating Fourteenth Amendment guarantees is *Katzenbach v. Morgan*, 384 U.S. 641 (1966). It is not clear whether the full scope of congressional authority set forth there remains intact

after *Oregon v. Mitchell*, 400 U.S. 112 (1970), which struck down a federal law extending the vote to eighteen-year-olds in state elections as a guarantee of equality. For an analysis suggesting that the broad view of congressional authority can survive *Mitchell*, see Nicholson, *op. cit.*, pp. 836–42. And on the special weight judges should give a congressional determination on campaign finance under the rationale of *Morgan*, see *ibid.*, pp. 839–40.

51. *State ex rel. La Follette v. Kohler*, 200 Wis. 518, 228 N.W. 895 (1930).
52. *Abercrombie v. Burns*, 377 F. Supp. 1400 (1974).
53. *Bare v. Gorton*, —Wash. 2d —, 526 P. 2d 379, 382 (1974).
54. Fleishman, *op. cit.*, p. 451; Rosenthal, *op. cit.*, pp. 34–38. But an optimistic view about the constitutionality of the central treasurer is Theodore Mitau, "Selected Aspects of Centralized and Decentralized Control over Campaign Finance: A Commentary on S. 636," *University of Chicago Law Review*, Vol. 23 (Winter, 1956), pp. 630–35. Also see "Common Cause Memorandum on The Constitutionality of Limitations on Independent Expenditures Advocating the Election or Defeat of Candidates for Federal Office" (Washington, 1974).
55. *State v. Pierce*, 163 Wis. 615, 158 N.W. 696 (1916).
56. *American Civil Liberties Union v. Jennings, supra*, at p. 1053.
57. *Smith v. Ervin*, 26 So. 2d 166 (Fla., 1953).
58. Forceful arguments that any limit on campaign spending is unconstitutional are advanced by Winter, *op. cit.*, pp. 58–62; Fleishman, *op. cit.*, pp. 434–79 (asserting that expenditures are constitutionally protected speech, that there is no counterbalancing governmental interest sufficient to sustain limitations, that appropriate means for narrowly curbing evils without broadly encroaching on speech are not available, and that the means presently employed are so inadequate as to jeopardize the validity of the legislative proscription); Martin H. Redish, "Campaign Spending Laws and the First Amendment," *New York University Law Review*, Vol. 46 (November 1971), pp. 907–24.

Rosenthal, *op. cit.*, pp. 32–39, suggests that limits might be acceptable as advancing equality of opportunity for candidates to be heard, especially if set at levels that permit ample speech. He warns, however, that while limits on candidate spending might survive on this rationale, other measures needed to make limitations effective—such as curbing the activities of independent committees—probably would not.

Common Cause has argued that expenditure limits can be sustained because unlimited spending endangers democracy, thwarts equality, and therefore justifies some limitation upon free speech. "Common Cause Memorandum on the Constitutionality of Contribution and Expenditure Limitations," pp. 15–21. Further, it argues (pp. 3–7) that expenditures are more action than speech and thus are not so fully protected by the Constitution as "pure speech."

CHAPTER 5

1. The leading story of the Political Broadcast Act's passage is Robert J. Peabody, Jeffrey M. Berry, William G. Frasure, and Jerry Goldman, *To Enact a Law* (New York: Praeger Publishers, 1972).
2. A useful review of the act's passage and provisions is Jeffrey M. Berry and Jerry Goldman, "Congress and Public Policy: A Study of the Federal Election Campaign Act of 1971," *Harvard Journal on Legislation*, Vol. 10 (February, 1973), pp. 331–65.
3. The act does not address the problem of how media expenditures that oppose a candidate for a federal office without favoring anyone else might be limited. Should his opponent be given a veto over such expenses? Should they be counted against the opponent's spending limit? These problems are, of course, simply an extension of the same difficulties faced by an overall spending limit. Recognizing the intractability of this problem, the Comptroller General provided by regulation that expenditures opposing a candidate

would not be deemed an outlay on behalf of any other candidate and would not be charged to any candidate's spending limits. 37 *Fed. Reg.* 6158 (1972).

There is, of course, the more general issue of whether any central treasurer system would be an unconstitutional abridgment of free speech, press, and association. The requirement that the candidate give his authorization for media advertising and the imposition on the media of "first line" responsibility to enforce this arrangement caused a federal court to strike down this portion of the act and its accompanying regulations. *American Civil Liberties Union v. Jennings,* 366 F. Supp. 1041 (1973) (three-judge court).

For a more complete discussion of these constitutional problems as they relate to spending limits generally, see Chapter 4 above.

4. Broadcast Spending figures here and elsewhere in this chapter are based on *Survey of Political Broadcasting* issued by U.S., Federal Communications Commission, for 1966, 1968, and 1970, and U.S., Congress, Senate, Subcommittee on Communications of the Committee on Commerce, *Hearings on Federal Election Campaign Act of 1973,* S. 372, Appendix A, 93d Congress, 1st Sess., 1973.

5. Alexander Heard, *The Costs of Democracy* (Chapel Hill: University of North Carolina Press, 1960), pp. 403–5.

6. Other commentators differ over the impact of the act's broadcast limits. One concluded that "the typical candidate must decrease his spending for broadcast advertising in order to comply with the new law, in direct contrast to the upward spiral of campaign spending that currently exists." Note, "Campaign Finance Reform: Pollution Control for the Smoke-Filled Rooms?" *Case Western Reserve Law Review,* Vol. 23 (1972), pp. 658–59. An analysis of the FCC data similar to the narrative in the following text agreed that only a small number of races would be affected. Comment, "Campaign Spending Controls under the Federal Election Campaign Act of 1971," *Columbia Journal of Law and Social Problems,* Vol. 8 (1972), pp. 309–12, 317–19.

7. This thesis is the direct opposite of the views expressed by President Nixon in his veto message of the Political Broadcast Act of 1970, as described above. We assume that, even if the law permitted high-cost media campaigns in metropolitan districts, candidates would not spend for this purpose because it is inefficient, reaching far too many persons living outside the district. Table 5-1 confirms this hunch by showing that broadcast spending was lower in metropolitan districts than in non-metropolitan districts in 1970 when there were no broadcast spending limits.

On the other hand, if candidates in metropolitan areas were inclined to spend money for broadcast media notwithstanding the inefficiency of this practice in their districts, the broadcast limits would discriminate against them because rates are much higher in their locales. The cost of a "minimum marketing package" in metropolitan areas is much higher than elsewhere. See Comment, "Campaign Spending Controls under the Federal Election Campaign Act of 1971," *op. cit.,* pp. 313–20.

CHAPTER 6

1. Louise Overacker, *Money in Elections* (New York: Macmillan Co., 1932), p. 202.

2. Herbert E. Alexander, *Money, Politics and Public Reporting* (Princeton, N.J.: Citizens' Research Foundation, 1960), p. 7.

3. President's Commission on Campaign Costs, *Financing Presidential Campaigns* (Washington, 1962), pp. 17, 18.

4. Twentieth Century Fund Task Force on Financing Congressional Campaigns, *Electing Congress* (New York: Twentieth Century Fund, 1970), p. 15.

5. *Ibid.*

6. *A Survey of State Statutes Regulating Political Finance* (Princeton, N.J.: Citizens' Research Foundation, 1971), pp. 3–4.

7. *Ibid.*

8. Herbert E. Alexander, *Money in Politics* (Washington: Public Affairs Press, 1972), p. 25.
9. Elston E. Roady, "Florida's New Campaign Expense Law and the 1952 Democratic Gubernatorial Primaries," *American Political Science Review*, Vol. 48 (June, 1954), pp. 465–76. A more comprehensive and current survey of the law's operation is idem, "Ten Years of Florida's 'Who Gave It–Who Got It' Law," *Law and Contemporary Problems*, Vol. 27 (Summer, 1962), pp. 434–54.
10. Roady, "Ten Years of Florida's 'Who Gave It–Who Got It' Law," *op. cit.*, p. 434.
11. Quoted in Murray B. Levin, *Kennedy Campaigning: The System and the Style as Practiced by Senator Edward Kennedy* (Boston: Beacon Press, 1966), p. 250.
12. *Ibid.*, Chap. 5.
13. Alexander, *Money in Politics*, p. 189.
14. A useful brief description of the passage of this act is Jeffrey M. Berry and Jerry Goldman, "Congress and Public Policy: A Study of the Federal Election Campaign Act of 1971," *Harvard Journal of Legislation*, Vol. 10 (February, 1973), pp. 331–65.
15. The Federal Election Campaign Act of 1971, Public Law No. 92-225, 86 Stat. 3 (codified in scattered sections of 2, 18 and 47 United States Code Annotated). For administrative regulations under the act, see 37 Federal Register 6156–68 (1972).
16. *State Statutes Regulating Political Finance* (Princeton, N.J.: Citizens' Research Foundation, 1974); U.S., Office of Federal Elections, *Analysis of Federal and State Campaign Finance Law* (Washington, 1974), pp. 11–27.
17. Federal Election Campaign Act of 1974, Public Law 93-443, 93d Congress, 2d Sess., 1974. For a comparison of the original Senate and House Bills and a useful commentary on the law, see the Conference Committee text: U.S., Congress, House of Representatives, *Report of the Committee on Conference*, Report No. 93-1438, 93d Congress, 2d Sess., 1974.
18. For a discussion of the bases for congressional power to regulate elections and campaigns, see Chapter 4 above. Also see, for a general survey, Albert J. Rosenthal, *Federal Regulation of Campaign Finance: Some Constitutional Questions* (Princeton, N.J.: Citizens' Research Foundation, 1972), esp. pp. 12–25.
19. *NAACP v. Alabama*, 357 U.S. 449 (1958); *Louisiana v. NAACP*, 366 U.S. 293 (1961); *Bates v. City of Little Rock*, 361 U.S. 516 (1960).
20. *Talley v. California*, 262 U.S. 60 (1960).
21. *Braden v. United States*, 365 U.S. 431 (1961); *Wilkinson v. United States*, 365 U.S. 399 (1961) (both relating to subversion). Other cases warn, however, that there must be a legitimate governmental purpose for the investigations, that they should not go beyond measures necessary to protect against subversion, and that the government must show its need and basis to make such inquiries about a citizen before doing so. *Sweezy v. New Hampshire*, 354 U.S. 234 (1956); *Watkins v. United States*, 354 U.S. 178 (1956); and *Gibson v. Florida Legislative Investigation Comm.*, 372 U.S. 539 (1963). Compelled disclosure has also been sustained in circumstances not related to subversion. *In re Anastaplo*, 366 U.S. 82 (1961); *Konigsberg v. State Bar*, 366 U.S. 36 (1961); *Adler v. Board of Education*, 342 U.S. 485 (1952) (the first two requiring disclosure by attorneys and the third by teachers); *Branzburg v. Hayes*, 408 U.S. 665 (1972) (pertaining to reporters' news sources); *Lewis Publishing Co. v. Morgan*, 229 U.S. 288 (1913) (concerning the ownership of newspapers).
22. The most persuasive critics are Joel L. Fleishman, "Freedom of Speech and Equality of Political Opportunity: The Constitutionality of the Federal Election Campaign Act of 1971," *North Carolina Law Review*, Vol. 51 (January, 1973, esp. pp. 410–33; and Ralph K. Winter, Jr., "Money, Politics and the First Amendment," *Campaign Finance: Two Views of the Political and*

Constitutional Implications (Washington: American Enterprise Institute, 1971), esp. pp. 62–66.

23. Fleishman, *op. cit.*, p. 423.

24. Ralph K. Winter, Jr., in association with John R. Bolton, *Campaign Financing and Political Freedom* (Washington: American Enterprise Institute, 1973), p. 21; Fleishman, *op. cit.*, pp. 431–32.

25. The constitutional arguments to sustain disclosure of campaign finances are best set forth in Note, "The Constitutionality of Financial Disclosure Laws," *Cornell Law Review*, Vol. 59 (January, 1974), esp. pp. 354–70; and "Common Cause Memorandum on the Constitutionality of Contribution and Expenditure Limits," pp. 3–8 (relating solely to the argument that contributions are actions which, though related to speech, may be regulated without incurring a First Amendment violation). See also Joseph R. Biden, Jr., "Public Financing of Elections: Legislative Proposals and Constitutional Questions," *Northwestern University Law Review*, Vol. 69 (March–April, 1974), pp. 66–69.

26. *Burroughs and Cannon v. United States*, 290 U.S. 534 (1934); *United States v. Harriss*, 347 U.S. 612 (1954).

27. *Stoner v. Fortson*, 379 F. Supp. 704 (1974) (three-judge court).

28. Bob Woodward and Carl Bernstein, "$100,000 Gift to Nixon Campaign Traced to Texas Corporation," *Washington Post*, October 6, 1972, p. 1.

29. Morton Mintz, "Political Donors Used Committees to Hide Direct Campaign Gifts," *Washington Post*, November 12, 1973, p. 1; "Loopholes: A Persistent Problem," *Congressional Quarterly Weekly Report*, Vol. 30, No. 14 (April 1, 1972), p. 713.

30. Morton Mintz, "700 Violations of Election Law Reported," *Washington Post*, September 7, 1972, p. 5.

31. Lou Cannon, "GOP Hits M'Govern On Funds," *Washington Post*, August 31, 1972, p. 1.

32. United Press International, "GAO Says Sinatra's $50,000 Donation to Nixon Unit Not Reported Legally," *Madison Capital Times*, February 14, 1973, p. 6.

33. U.S., Congress, Senate, Committee on Commerce, *Minority Report, Federal Elections Campaign Act of 1971*, Report No. 92-96, 92d Congress, 1st Sess., 1971, p. 90.

34. Berry and Goldman, *op. cit.*, p. 361.

35. *Ibid.*, pp. 360–62; "House Discord Over New Law," *Congressional Quarterly Weekly Report*, Vol. 30, No. 14, April 1, 1972, p. 712.

36. Morton Mintz, "Politics, Gifts and Taxes," *Washington Post*, December 25, 1972, sec. C, p. 10.

37. "Campaign Finance Reporting: More Than Meets The Eye," *Congressional Quarterly Weekly Report*, Vol. 31, No. 2, January 13, 1973, p. 48.

38. Ben H. Bagdikian, "The Fruits of Agnewism," *Columbia Journalism Review*, Vol. 11 (January–February, 1973), pp. 15–16.

39. Morton Mintz, *Washington Post*, November 5, 1972, p. 10.

40. "283 More Donors of $1,000 or More to Nixon Campaign," *New York Times*, November 4, 1972, p. 26.

41. Louis Harris, "Bugging, Fund Charges Leave Public Apathetic," *Washington Post*, October 19, 1972, p. 12.

42. Jack Rosenthal, "Poll Finds Issues Not at Issue in '72," *New York Times*, October 8, 1972, p. 1.

43. Harris, *op. cit.*

44. See Chapter 3, note 1, above.

45. A good summary of some of these facts is found in Fred I. Greenstein, *The American Party System and the American People*, 2d ed. (Englewood Cliffs, N.J.: Prentice-Hall, 1970), pp. 9–16.

46. E. E. Schattschneider, *The Semisovereign People: A Realist's View of Democracy in America* (New York: Holt, Rinehart and Winston, 1960), pp. 136–37.

47. V. O. Key, Jr., *The Responsible Electorate* (New York: Random House,

Vintage Books, 1968), p. 7, Chaps. 1–4. Studies showing that voters supported 1968 presidential candidates whose views coincided with their own are Richard W. Boyd, "Popular Control of Public Policy: A Normal Vote Analysis of the 1968 Election," *American Political Science Review*, Vol. 66 (June, 1972), pp. 429–49; and Philip E. Converse *et al.*, "Continuity and Change in American Politics: Parties and Issues in the 1968 Election," *American Political Science Review*, Vol. 63 (December, 1969), pp. 1095–1101.

48.   Gerald M. Pomper, "From Confusion to Clarity: Issues and American Voters, 1956–1968," *American Political Science Review*, Vol. 66 (June, 1972), pp. 415–28.

CHAPTER 7

1.   Donald G. Balmer, *State Election Services in Oregon* (Princeton, N.J.: Citizens' Research Foundation, 1972), pp. 15–19.

2.   *Ibid.*, p. 19.

3.   Committee for Economic Development, *Financing a Better Election System* (New York: Committee for Economic Development, 1968), p. 22 (subsequently referred to as *Financing a Better Election System*). A similar argument for universal voter registration is found in the Twentieth Century Fund Task Force on Financing Congressional Campaigns, *Electing Congress* (New York: Twentieth Century Fund, 1970), p. 23 (subsequently referred to as *Electing Congress*).

4.   Irwin N. Gertzog, "The Electoral Consequences of a Local Party Organization's Registration Campaign: The San Diego Experiment," *Polity*, Vol. 3 (Winter, 1970), pp. 247–64.

5.   Balmer, *op. cit.*, p. 21.

6.   The following description of the Oregon Voters' Pamphlet is drawn from *ibid.*, pp. 19–31.

7.   David W. Adamany, *Campaign Finance in the United States* (North Scituate, Mass.: Duxbury Press, 1972), pp. 36–38.

8.   Burns W. Roper, *An Extended View of Public Attitudes Toward Television and Other Mass Media 1959–1971* (New York: Television Information Office, 1971), pp. 1–9.

9.   Twentieth Century Fund Commission on Campaign Costs in the Electronic Era, *Voters' Time* (New York: Twentieth Century Fund, 1969) (subsequently referred to as *Voters' Time*).

10.   Delmer D. Dunn, *Financing Presidential Campaigns* (Washington: Brookings Institution, 1972), pp. 36–40.

11.   *Electing Congress*, pp. 23–27.

12.   *Voters' Time*, pp. 36–37; President's Commission on Campaign Costs, *Financing Presidential Campaigns* (Washington, 1962), pp. 13–16 (subsequently referred to as President's Commission on Campaign Costs); *Electing Congress*, pp. 68–71; Dunn, *op. cit.*, pp. 148–49.

13.   Herbert E. Alexander, with the assistance of Laura Denny, *Regulation of Political Finance* (Berkeley, Calif.; Institute of Governmental Studies, and Princeton, N.J.: Citizens' Research Foundation, 1966), pp. 24–25.

14.   The Revenue Act of 1971, Title VII, Public Law 92-178, 92d Congress, 1st Sess., 1971; U.S., Office of Federal Elections, *Analysis of Federal and State Campaign Finance Law* (Washington, 1974), pp. 62–69.

15.   A summary of poll data on campaign giving is found in Herbert E. Alexander, *Money in Politics* (Washington: Public Affairs Press, 1972), pp. 335–36. The 1972 figure was obtained from the Twentieth Century Fund Survey (see Chap. 3, n. 1).

16.   Rev. Rul. 72-355. Also see Morton Mintz, "Politics, Gifts, and Taxes," *Washington Post*, December 25, 1972, sec. C, p. 10.

17.   *Tax Analysts and Advocates v. Schultz et al.*, 74-2 U.S. Tax Cases, para. 13,006 (D.C.D.C., 1974).

18. Mintz, *op. cit.*
19. "Two 'Secret' Donors Gave Nixon Drive $250,000," *New York Times,* January 23, 1973, p. 1.
20. Associated Press, "Executive Reports 150 Secret Groups for Gifts to Nixon," *New York Times,* December 17, 1972, p. 9.
21. Morton Mintz, "Leasco, Oil Executives Gave to Nixon," *Washington Post,* January 23, 1973, p. 4.
22. Morton Mintz, "Reports Show Second Wave of Election's Big Donors," *Washington Post,* October 29, 1972, p. 3.
23. Mintz, "Politics, Gifts, and Taxes."
24. Mintz, "Reports Show Second Wave of Election's Big Donors."
25. *Ibid.*
26. Mintz, "Leasco, Oil Executives Gave to Nixon."
27. This unfavorable appraisal is found in Alexander, *Money in Politics,* pp. 220–23.
28. "Campaign Fund Tax Check-Off Gains in Users," *Congressional Quarterly Weekly Report,* Vol. 32, No. 27 (July, 1974), p. 1743.
29. *Ibid.,* p. 1742.
30. *Ibid.,* pp. 1743–44.

CHAPTER 8

1. The Federal Election Campaign Act of 1974, Public Law 93-443, 93d Congress, 2d Sess., 1974.
2. *Ibid.,* Title IV.
3. The Revenue Act of 1971, Title VIII, "The Presidential Election Campaign Fund Act," Public Law 92-178, 92d Congress, 1st Sess., 1971.
4. This description of state experiments is based on comments and explanations received directly from state officials in those states as well as on the statutory provisions themselves. We are grateful for the assistance of Gerald D. Blair, acting director, Iowa Department of Revenue; Ernest H. Johnson, state tax assessor, Maine; Charles H. Furst, legal officer, Maryland Comptroller of the Treasury; Arthur C. Roemer, commissioner of revenue, Minnesota; Howard O. Vralsted, administrator, Income and Inheritance Tax Division, Montana Department of Revenue; Robert S. Raymar, assistant counsel to the Governor, New Jersey; John H. Norberg, tax administrator, Division of Taxation, Rhode Island Department of Administration; Elvin E. Todd, auditing division, Utah State Tax Commission. See also U.S., Office of Federal Elections, *Analysis of Federal and State Campaign Finance Law* (Washington, 1974), pp. 62–69.

CHAPTER 9

1. Luis Muñoz Marin, "Plight of Puerto Rico," *New Republic,* January 11, 1943, pp. 51–52.
2. Roland Huntford, *The New Totalitarians* (New York: Stein and Day, 1972).
3. Agree interview, Bonn, Germany, May 16, 1972.
4. Agree interview with Hans Wolfgang Rubin, Gelsenkirchen, Germany, May 17, 1972.
5. Agree interview with Bertil af Ugglas, Stockholm, Sweden, May 25, 1972.

CHAPTER 10

1. For a discussion of financing patterns within a state's party organizations, see David Adamany, *Campaign Funds as an Intraparty Political Resource: Connecticut, 1966–1968* (Princeton, N.J.: Citizens' Research Foundation, 1972), pp. 7–38. Also see Alexander Heard, *The Costs of Democracy* (Chapel Hill: University of North Carolina Press, 1960), Chap. 11, esp. pp. 309–10.
2. On specialization in campaign spending, see Heard, *op. cit.,* pp. 394–99; Adamany, *op. cit.,* esp. pp. 33–38, 48–51.

3.   The main descriptions of variables affecting political spending are Heard, *op. cit.*, pp. 380–87; David W. Adamany, *Campaign Finance in America* (North Scituate, Mass.: Duxbury Press, 1972), Chap. 3; John R. Owens, *Trends in Campaign Spending in California, 1958–70: Tests of Factors Influencing Costs* (Princeton, N.J.: Citizens' Research Foundation, 1973), pp. 70–80.

4.   Incumbents' advantages are described in Howard R. Penniman, "Financing Campaigns in the Public Interest," *Campaign Finances: Two Views of the Political and Constitutional Implications* (Washington: American Enterprise Institute, 1971), pp. 16–18; and Twentieth Century Fund Task Force on Financing Congressional Campaigns, *Electing Congress* (New York: Twentieth Century Fund, 1970), pp. 35–36.

5.   Common Cause has reported the low level of spending in non-competitive districts and the large advantage of incumbents in all districts. These data are reported in Chapter 3.

6.   This analysis of minor party roles depends heavily on V. O. Key, Jr., *Politics, Parties and Pressure Groups*, 5th ed. (New York: Thomas Y. Crowell, 1964), Chap. 10.

7.   A useful summary of the constitutional bases for congressional regulation of elections is Albert J. Rosenthal, *Federal Regulations of Campaign Finance: Some Constitutional Questions* (Princeton, N.J.: Citizens' Research Foundation, 1972), pp. 12–20.

8.   Compare the traditional constitutional doctrine set forth in *Arizona v. California*, 283, U.S. 423 (1931) and *Oklahoma v. Atkinson Co.*, 313 U.S. 508 (1941) with the modern view of the spending power expounded in *United States v. Gerlach Live Stock Co.*, 339 U.S. 725 (1950).

9.   At least one state supreme court has advised that campaign subsidies do not serve a public purpose. *Opinion of the Justices*, 347 Mass. 797, 197 N.E. 2d 691 (1964). But special circumstances, including a wide disparity in the funding of the two major parties, may have influenced the decision. See Note, *Harvard Law Review*, Vol. 78 (1965), p. 1260.

10.   A more complete discussion of constitutional issues surrounding expenditure and contribution limits is found in Chapter 4 above.

11.   President's Commission on Campaign Costs, *Financing Presidential Campaigns* (Washington, 1962), pp. 31–32.

12.   Herbert E. Alexander, *Money in Politics* (Washington: Public Affairs Press, 1972), p. 241.

13.   The 1971 act is described above in Chapter 7, and the 1974 act is reviewed in Chapter 8.

14.   Provision could be made for taxpayers who want to waive judgment on checking off until after the candidates are chosen by the simple device for an "ask me later" box on tax return forms. Persons who checked that box could be given an opportunity to indicate the party whose candidate they preferred via a special form mailed to them in late August of an election year.

15.   Although limiting the role of parties in direct support of candidates, the 1974 law indirectly foreshadows a major increase in party funding and activity. It is likely that much of the money barred from candidate support by the limitations on individual and aggregate contributions and by the full public funding of major party presidential candidates will find its way to party organizations and will be used for activities such as registration, getting out the vote, and public opinion polling, which will benefit all the candidates of a party.

CHAPTER 11

1.   We also intend these recommendations to apply to special elections, to elections for delegate from the District of Columbia or from any of the territories, and to elections for resident commissioner. We do not include these elections in the text for reasons of simplicity in explanation and format.

2.   This 2 percent minimum might be subject to constitutional challenge. The proposals we make would work without it, and it is therefore severable. We

include the 2 percent threshold to respect the provisions of state law for ballot eligibility.

The Supreme Court has sustained a distinction between political parties that received 20 percent or more of the vote at the last gubernatorial or presidential election and "political bodies" whose candidates received a smaller vote. Candidates other than those nominated by political parties were required to file signatures of at least 5 percent of the registered voters at the last general election for the office sought. The Court justified this requirement because "there is surely an important state interest in requiring some preliminary showing of a significant modicum of support before printing the name of a political organization's candidate on the ballot—the interest, if no other, in avoiding confusion, deception and even frustration of the democratic process at the general election." *Jenness v. Fortson*, 403 U.S. 431, 442 (1971).

The 2 percent voucher collection threshold we recommend for participation in public financing of candidates is well within the 5 percent rule announced by the Court and serves similar governmental interests.

3.   The device of a percent threshold for maximum entitlement tends to equalize the funding of all candidates, including those who do not pass the threshold. This effect is not significant where candidates are relatively evenly matched, since disparities in funding will be slight. Even with a 50 percent threshold, for example, a candidate with 45 percent of the vouchers, although he would have nearly 20 percent fewer vouchers than a candidate with 55 percent, would receive only 10 percent less funding.

A threshold thus tends to prevent runaway situations in which a candidate with 70 percent or 80 percent support would receive massive and quite unnecessary funding in a non-competitive election. By the same token, however, a threshold of this kind tends to "level up" weaker candidates and to make them somewhat more competitive. Thresholds also would benefit third-party and independent candidates, with the degree of benefit varying inversely with the level of the threshold.

4.   The 38 percent threshold for full flat grants does, however, inherently deny the possibility of a multi-party system with several fully funded parties. The development of more than two parties with roughly equal support would reduce all parties below the 38 percent level and would result in funding for all candidates on a proportional basis. We assume that the parties would then agree to reduce the threshold to accommodate the major parties in a developing multi-party system.

Historically, significant parties outside the two-party framework have been regional and have become the "second party" in their region. In these cases, full funding would go to the regional "second party" in preference to the weaker of the national major parties in that region. The United States has no prolonged experience with a multi-party system at the national level, and our recommendations recognize the enduring two-party pattern of American politics. (The multi-party pattern of 1860 resulted from the fragmentation of a major party and did not persist.)

5.   *United States v. Classic*, 313 U.S. 299, 319 (1941).

6.   We doubt that such low thresholds, although based on money rather than votes, would be unconstitutional. The case for upholding them is strengthened by the low $100 limit on contributions counting toward the threshold; the sum is small enough so that most citizens could contribute all or a significant part of it if they felt strongly about a candidate. This near equality ameliorates the objection to money rather than votes as a qualifying factor.

But see *Lubin v. Panish*, 415 U.S. 709 (1974), where the Supreme Court held unconstitutional a California law establishing a filing fee as the sole means for a candidate to get on the ballot. Although the filing fee there was $701, substantially larger than the $100 matchable threshold gifts proposed here, the Court apparently applies its decision to any filing fee no matter how small. *Ibid.*, at 714–719.

It might be argued that qualifying for public funds is different from qualifying for the ballot. No candidate should be denied ballot listing because of a financial threshold, but the additional qualification for public funds may be based on a small number of modest contributions as an indication of a modicum of public support.

If the teaching of *Lubin v. Panish* is that a financial threshold cannot be the sole means of eligibility for public financing as well as ballot listing, then we believe that the threshold for matching grants should be petitions signed by residents of the district. These petitions should be somewhat more carefully regulated than the nominating petitions in many states, where little effort to verify signatures is made.

Several members of Congress have recommended petitions rather than or as an alternative to financial thresholds as qualifying mechanisms. Senator Richard Clark of Iowa suggested petitions bearing the signatures of more than 2 percent of the voting age population of the district. See S. 3943, 93d Congress, 2d Sess., 1974. Senator Biden recommended that full primary funding be granted to those obtaining signatures of 10 percent of the registered voters in a district, that 90 percent of the funding be awarded for 9 percent of the voters, and so on down to 10 percent for 1 percent. See Joseph R. Biden, Jr., "Public Financing of Elections: Legislative Proposals and Constitutional Questions," *Northwestern University Law Review*, Vol. 69 (March–April, 1974), p. 35.

7.   It might be argued that the $100 matchable contribution is too large, denying citizens of varying financial means even rough equality in the electoral process. We believe that all citizens can make some modest matchable contribution and that many could make a gift of $100 if they felt very strongly about a candidate. Further, the disparity between the poorest and richest citizens would be less with a $100 limit on matchable gifts than it now is. If there is a constitutional problem with the $100 level, however, we would recommend that the amount of the matchable gift be reduced to $50 or even $25 and that the matching formula be increased to five to one or even ten to one to maintain the flow of money to support vigorous campaigning.

8.   See Chapter 4 for a more complete discussion of the constitutional issues surrounding contribution limits.

9.   We would not advocate any limitation on inter-district transfers of money in the absence of a system, such as is recommended in this chapter, that would give substantial assurance of adequate funding resources within a district.

10.   The Supreme Court has recently affirmed these Hatch Act provisions against First Amendment challenge, citing as one justification for restrictions on the political participation of public employees the need to protect government workers from coercion in political activity or voting. *Civil Service Comm. v. Nat'l Ass'n of Letter Carriers*, 413 U.S. 548, 566–67 (1973).

11.   The Supreme Court has held that there would be an invasion of First Amendment rights of dissenting union members whose dues, mandatorily collected under a union shop agreement, were used for political purposes. *International Ass'n of Machinists v. Street*, 367 U.S. 740 (1961). The kind of coercion implicit in fund raising at the job is less direct than in the mandatory collection of union dues but may nonetheless be dangerous enough to First Amendment rights of individuals to justify some curbing of the rights of organizations under this amendment to solicit, collect, contribute, or expend political funds.

12.   See *United States v. Congress of Industrial Organizations*, 335 U.S. 106, 121 (1948).

13.   See Chapter 4 for a more complete discussion of the constitutional issues surrounding expenditure limits.

14.   This commission is similar to one provided in the Federal Election Campaign Act of 1974. It goes a step further, however, with its minor-party provisions.

INDEX